CONFRONTING GLOBAL NEOLIBERALISM

CONFRONTING GLOBAL NEOLIBERALISM

THIRD WORLD RESISTANCE AND DEVELOPMENT STRATEGIES

EDITED BY

RICHARD WESTRA

CLARITY PRESS, INC.

© 2010 Richard Westra
ISBN: 0-932863-61-2
     978-0-932863-61-4

In-house editor: Diana G. Collier

Library of Congress Cataloging-in-Publication Data

Confronting global neoliberalism : third world resistance and development strategies / edited by Richard Westra.
    p. cm.
  Includes bibliographical references and index.
  ISBN-13: 978-0-932863-61-4
  ISBN-10: 0-932863-61-2
  1. Developing countries--Economic policy. 2. Neoliberalism--Developing countries. 3. Globalization--Economic aspects--Developing countries. 4. Globalization--Social aspects--Developing countries. I. Westra, Richard, 1954-
  HC59.7.C6282 2010
  338.9009172'4--dc22

                              2009045326

Clarity Press, Inc.
Ste. 469, 3277 Roswell Rd. NE
Atlanta, GA. 30305, USA
http://www.claritypress.com

TABLE OF CONTENTS

Part III Miracles or Mirages under Global Neoliberalism

Notes on the Contributors

Patrick Bond, a political economist, is research professor at the University of KwaZulu-Natal School of Development Studies where he directs the Centre for Civil Society (http://www.ukzn.ac.za/ccs). His training was in economic geography at Johns Hopkins University, finance at the University of Pennsylvania, and economics at Swarthmore College. Patrick's recent authored and edited books include *Climate Change, Carbon Trading and Civil Society* (UKZN Press and Rozenberg Publishers, 2008); *The Accumulation of Capital in Southern Africa* (Rosa Luxemburg Foundation, 2007); *Looting Africa: The Economics of Exploitation* (Zed Books and UKZN Press, 2006), *Talk Left, Walk Right: South Africa's Frustrated Global Reforms* (UKZN Press, 2006); *Elite Transition: From Apartheid to Neoliberalism in South Africa* (UKZN Press, 2005); *Fanon's Warning: A Civil Society Reader on the New Partnership for Africa's Development* (Africa World Press, 2005); and *Against Global Apartheid: South Africa meets the World Bank, IMF and International Finance* (Zed Books and University of Cape Town Press, 2003). Patrick was the drafter of 15 policy papers for the South African government from 1994-2001, and before that worked in the NGO sector in Johannesburg for several years. He was born in Belfast, Northern Ireland in 1961; grew up in Alabama and Maryland; and moved permanently to Southern Africa in 1989 following work in the media (Marketplace Radio and Pacifica Radio) and at the Institute for Policy Studies in Washington, DC.

Al Campbell is a professor of economics at the University of Utah in the United States. His research interests are focused on theoretical and empirical issues concerning the political economy of contemporary capitalism and its transcendence. His work has appeared in numerous international peer reviewed journals including *Review of Radical Political Economics*, *Science and Society* and *Critique*.

Paul Cooney Seisdedos received his doctorate in Economics from the New School for Social Research in 1990. He has worked at the United Nations and at several universities, including the University of Buenos Aires in the early 1990s, Queens College in New York and currently at the Universidade Federal do Pará in the Brazilian Amazon since 2006. He has conducted research and published in the areas of economics and environmental science. His research includes the following topics: NAFTA and the issues of labor and the environment in *maquiladoras*, analysis of the neoliberal experiences in Argentina, Brazil and Mexico, the general law of capitalist accumulation in Latin America, international transfers of value and unequal exchange, competition and monopoly, and air transport of pesticides and dioxin. His current areas of research include globalization and accumulation in the Brazilian Amazon, deforestation and ecology, the free trade zone of Manaus, as well the current crisis and the role of fictitious capital. He has publications in several scholarly refereed journals, such as: *Latin American Perspectives, Revista de Economia Contemporânea* and the *Revista de Economia, UFPR*. He is also a member of the editorial board of the international journal *Capitalism, Nature, Socialism* and has served on the steering committee and as treasurer for the Union for Radical Political Economics.

Cliff DuRand is a founder and Research Associate at the Center for Global Justice located in San Miguel de Allende, GTO Mexico. He holds a Ph.D. in Social Philosophy from Florida State University and taught Philosophy at Morgan State University in Baltimore for 40 years.

Seongjin Jeong is a professor of economics and the Director of Graduate Program of Political Economy at Gyeongsang National University, South Korea. He is also the Editor of *MARXISM 21*, a representative Marxist journal in South Korea. He received his PhD from Seoul National University, and has written widely on Marxism and the Korean economy, including articles in *Review of Radical Political Economics* and *Rethinking Marxism*. Some of his works, especially *Marx and the Korean Economy* (2005), *Marx and Trotsky* (2006), and *Marxist Perspectives on South Korea in the Global Economy* (Ashgate 2007), a volume he co-edited and contributed to, are received as major contributions to the development of classical Marxism in Korea. He has also translated some Marxist works into Korean, including books by Robert Brenner, Alex Callinicos, Tony Cliff and Roman Rosdolsky.

Angela Joya is a PhD candidate in the department of Political Science at York University. She is currently completing her dissertation titled "Building Capitalism in Egypt: A Study of the Construction and Housing Sectors, 1991-2004". She has recently published an article titled "Syria's Transition, 1970-2005: From Centralization of the State to Market Economy" in the journal *Research in Political Economy*. She has also written and published on US imperialism in the Middle East. Her future research project will examine the internationalization of the State in Afghanistan.

Minqi Li received his PhD in economics from University of Massachusetts Amherst in 2002. He taught political science at York University, Canada, from 2003 to 2006. Since 2006, he has been teaching economics in University of Utah. His recent book: *The Rise of China and the Demise of the Capitalist World Economy* was published by Pluto Press and Monthly Review Press in 2009.

Ananya Mukherjee Reed is Associate Professor in the Department of Political Science at York University, Toronto, Canada. She is also director of the International Secretariat for Human Development (ISHD) at York. Her most recent book is, *Human Development and Social Power: Perspectives from South Asia* (London: Routledge, 2008). The book attempts to develop a critical conceptualization of human development by focusing on the three dimensions of political-economy, difference and agency. Her earlier publications include an edited volume *Corporate Capitalism in Contemporary South Asia: Conventional Wisdoms and South Asian Realities* (Basingstoke: Palgrave 2003); *Perspectives on India's Corporate Economy: Exploring the Paradox of Profits* (Basingstoke: Macmillan, 2001); and numerous articles in international refereed journals.

Ake Tangsupvattana is Associate Professor at the Faculty of Political Science, Chulalongkorn University, Bangkok. He is also Associate Dean for Academic and International Affairs and was a University Council Member. He obtained his BA in Political Science from Chulalongkorn University, Thailand, and MA in Political Theory and Ph.D. in Sociology from the University of Essex, England. His major research interests are in globalization, governance, the relations between politics and business, the role of transnational corporations, especially in the context of corporate social responsibility. His recent international publications are as follows: "Driving the Juggernaut: From Economic Crisis to Global Governance in Pacific Asia" in *Pacific Asia 2022: Sketching Futures of a Region*, Japan Center for International Exchange (2005); 'Thailand Election 2005: Towards Authoritarian Populism or Participatory Democratic Governance' in *Elections in Asia: Making Democracy Work?*, Marshall Cavendish International (Singapore) Private Limited (2006); Co-principle researcher "National Integrity Systems: Transparency International Country Study Report – Thailand 2006", Transparency International.

John Weeks is Professor Emeritus of Development Economics, School of Oriental and African Studies, University of London. He is author of numerous books on development, political economy and economic theory. His research in Southeast Asia has been on Indonesia and Vietnam. In addition to his academic work he is the principle author of macroeconomic studies for the United Nations on Vietnam, Zambia and Moldova.

Richard Westra has taught at universities around the world including Queen's University and Royal Military College, Canada; International Study Center, East Sussex UK; and the College of The Bahamas, Nassau. He has been a Visiting Research Fellow at Focus on the Global South/Chulalongkorn University Social Research Institute, Chulalongkorn University, Bangkok Thailand and is currently Associate Professor in the Division of International and Area Studies, Pukyong National University, Pusan, South Korea. His work has been published in numerous international scholarly refereed journals including *Journal of Contemporary Asia*, *Review of International Political Economy*, *Review of Radical Political Economics* and *Historical Materialism*. He is author of *Political Economy and Globalization*, Routledge 2009 and co-edited and contributed to *Political Economy and Global Capitalism: The 21st Century, Present and Future*, Anthem 2007 and *Marxist Perspectives on South Korea in the Global Economy*, Ashgate 2007.

Gregory Wilpert is adjunct professor in political science at Brooklyn College's Graduate Center for Worker Education and is founder and editor of the website Venezuelanalysis.com. He received his Ph.D. in sociology from Brandies University in 1994 and in 2000 received a Fulbright grant to teach and do research at the Central University of Venezuela. He ended up living in Venezuela for eight years, where he wrote articles on Venezuelan politics for publications such as the *New Left Review*, *Le Monde Diplomatique*, *Z Magazine*, NACLA Report on the Americas, among many others. He is the author of *Changing Venezuela by Taking Power: The History and Policies of the Chávez Government*, Verso 2007.

PREFACE AND ACKNOWLEDGMENTS

With the world's attention transfixed on the travails of the leading global economies in an unfolding financial crisis of gigantic proportions, there has been a rather disturbing silence on the fate of the third world—those states referred to over the past several decades as the "developing world", "emerging markets", "global south", and so forth—as the malaise increasingly impacts them. I say disturbing because questions of potential pitfalls in the neoliberal policy package, adopted with little choice by the third world (unlike Western Europe and Japan), were never countenanced: third world state after third world state discovered international institutions effectively hostile to their existence if they chose alternative models of economy.

As the governments of the United States, Britain, Germany, France and others scurry with fistfuls of cash—trillions of dollars for that matter—to essentially purchase private businesses ranging from the world's major automobile companies to insurance companies, to "save" them, there is little recall of the fact that for decades, third world states' governments found themselves excoriated in international economic intercourse for seeking to protect what were often clearly viable public companies or striving to publicly fund key national industrial projects or even social projects such as health care.

The new-fangled financial instruments captured under the rubric "securitization" which are front and center in the current economic meltdown were initially experimented with in the third world. Following the first global "debt crisis" of the post-World War II period, that of the early 1980s, a way of transferring "risk" in international lending from lenders to borrowers was instituted by eliminating the exposure of particular banks to third world indebted states through the repackaging of "loans" as marketable securities. Not only were the risks associated with financing zero sum neoliberal experiments in the third world spread around a phalanx of private financial intermediaries but, at the first sign of economic trouble in a given third world state or region, securitization enabled global lenders to rapidly desert such economies with most of their "investments" in hand and retreat to the safe havens of the powerful economies of their roots leaving a scorched earth of misery, destitution and economic collapse in their wake. As the major economies like the US face a potentially similar scenario, however, their political leaders' jet set across the globe beseeching investors not to abandon them and continue to hold the virtually worthless "assets".

The chapters in this collection constitute a veritable tour de force of countering not only the neoliberal ideology of development as a whole but the collective amnesia over past neoliberal exhortations to the third world and the marginalizing within mainstream crisis discourse of today any discussion of the suffering of third world peoples and the monstrous misallocation of global resources to the detriment of third world societies wrought by the so-called "Washington Consensus".

From the introductory chapter which traces the ebbs and flows in development thinking over the past two centuries through the chapters on specific development cases and regions, this book also points to the grim future portended by the neoliberal course; a situation only exacerbated by the current economic malaise. This edited volume is intended as both a textbook for introductory classes in global development or area studies and as a conduit for advanced students, policymakers, NGO activists and an educated readership to gaining knowledge about the socio-economic conditions existing across much of the world we live in and the neoliberal policies at the root of these. It also provides inspiring examples of ways in which third world states have resisted neoliberal policy and the struggles and international condemnations they have faced, and continue to face it may be added, even as the bankruptcy of neoliberal policy has been so vividly exposed in the current world economic meltdown.

The present volume is unique in both the breadth and depth of its analysis. The specially commissioned and peer reviewed chapters are written by experts in the fields of economics, politics, sociology and international studies. Chapter authors hail from around the world including: Brazil, Canada, United States, United Kingdom, South Africa, South Korea, Mexico and Thailand. Each chapter also draws upon the authors contributions to critical development theory as well as their mastery of empirical questions. The countries/regions neoliberal experiences and potential futures covered in this book are: Brazil, China, Cuba, Egypt, Mexico, Southeast Asia (Indonesia, Malaysia and Vietnam), South Africa, South Korea, Syria, Thailand and Venezuela.

As this book's editor I would like to thank all the chapter contributors for their efforts in producing excellent work. Editorial assistance was provided by Alan Campbell. The editing of the book was completed during my 2008-9 sabbatical at Focus on the Global South, Chulalongkorn University, Thailand. Finally, I wish to thank the Editorial Director at Clarity Press, Diana G. Collier, for her patience in seeing this book through.

INTRODUCTION

DEVELOPMENT THEORY AND GLOBAL NEOLIBERALISM

Richard Westra

Whether explicitly problematized or secreted tacitly into the analysis at the root of all theories of development is a particular conceptualization of capitalism and concomitant view of the impact capitalism has had in shaping modern history. This, of course, is not to suggest that societies antedating capitalism had absolutely no notion of development, only that in the largely agricultural milieu of the pre-capitalist feudal era in Europe (and like societies in Asia) the tortuously slow processes of economic change mitigated against any sustained need for elaboration of such a concept. In other words, though development studies commences as an academic field only in the period following World War II (WWII), interest in development broadly conceived (development itself was initially conceptualized in terms of a universal notion of human progress[1]), emerges in tandem with the rise and spread of capitalism.

The originators of the major traditions of economic thought on capitalism—Adam Smith and Karl Marx—while holding radically divergent understandings of the fundamental modus operandi of capitalism, both saw capitalism as a positive transformatory force and the capitalist marketizing of economic life as a process tending to diffuse across the globe. Smith, seeking to explain the novel upsurge in production of material wealth under capitalism, offered a teleological argument for development. He maintained that capitalist wealth creation springs from an innate human propensity to "truck and barter" which increasingly bears fruit to the extent the division of labor in society becomes more complex through the growth of markets and trade. Though Smith and the "classical" political economists following him were largely interested in capitalist development of Britain and Western Europe, they nevertheless uncritically assumed the world beyond this zone to be in a state of so-called "backwardness".[2] Given the ideological affinity of Smith and influential followers such as David Ricardo with the rising bourgeois class, development was proffered as a matter of simply eliminating barriers to expanding markets and trade. The economic writings of Smith and Ricardo then largely turned on technical questions of application of their theories in support of capitalist laissez faire state policies.

Marx's approach to questions of the geospatial diffusing of capitalism built on a complex argument over the historical and ontological peculiarity of capitalism. For Marx, the genesis of capitalism resided not in purported transhistorical human psychological propensities but in the crisis and dissolution of the pre-capitalist feudal economy and political ascendency of the bourgeois class. Marx discerned the ontological uniqueness of capitalism in the way in which marketization broke down the face-to-face, interpersonal economic relations of domination and subordination characteristic of the pre-capitalist economy, replacing these with what he famously described as impersonal "relations between things". Examined from another angle, the conversion of use values or goods that sustained human life, including even the wellspring of social wealth itself—human labor power—into commodities, elevated the commodity and abstract, quantitative logic of market operations to the center of human material intercourse; this in effect *reifying* human economic life. Decades after Marx had passed away, the economic historian Karl Polanyi approached the peculiarity of the capitalist market in terms of what has become a more readily apprehended notion of the economic "disembedding" from the politics, religion, culture, and so forth in which it had been enmeshed since the dawn of human society. Yet, Polanyi's analysis never answered questions of what precisely "caused" the economy as such to suddenly levitate from the social or why, if the economy had always been present, have we have only just become aware of the fact and attempted disciplined study of it.[3] So often overlooked, however, are answers Marx had provided to these questions over a century ago. For Marx, though every human society in history necessarily requires at its core a governing economic principle or set of these ensuring its material reproducibility, the very condition of possibility for economic theory resides in the ontological tendency of capitalism to reify human material life. Hence, in the commodity economic chrematistic of the capitalist market, the material economic relations of use value production without which human society would be impossible are rendered transparent, amenable to being theorized for the first time in human history. Approached from another angle, in market subsuming of human economic intercourse it is not just a question of the economy disembedding or levitating from the social a-la-Polanyi. Rather, it is a peculiar incidence of an historically constituted object in the social world—the human material relations of the capitalist commodity economy—"taking on a life of its own"; where capital then wields the social (the politics, religion, ideology, and so forth with which the economic had historically been enmeshed) as an "extra-human force" for its own self-aggrandizement—the augmenting of value or profit-making.[4] Thus, it is precisely because the modus operandi of capitalism is impersonal, self-abstracting and self-synthesizing that we are able to analyze its fundamental operations or inner logic in abstract theory.

In Marx's lifetime it did appear that the commodity economic force of marketization was in fact purging economic life in Britain of all pre-capitalist non-economic encumbrances and Marx expected the capitalist synthesizing of human material life to proceed as such across the globe: Though Marx also believed the working class in the capitalist heartlands of Britain and Western Europe would organize to challenge capitalism, leading to its dismantling long before a "pure" global capitalist economy ever materialized, and that a socialist kingdom of freedom would be emplaced as the human future. Marx, hence, did initially concur with classical political economists' characterization of the world beyond Britain and Western Europe as backward. And numerous quotations may be culled from his writings in which he speaks somewhat disparagingly of peoples living in societies outside Britain and Western Europe (and British "white settler" colonies). However in his later empirical work on the "colonial question", Marx demonstrated a greater degree of sensitivity to the plight of dominated peoples under the thrust of colonial expansion and arguably countenanced the possibility that colonization could obstruct development of capitalism.[5] Nevertheless, in his primary economic writing—*Capital*—Marx never problematized the relation between the logical self-synthesizing tendencies of capitalism which informed his economic theory construction and the actual course of capitalist history; this leading to gross misapprehensions of his work (we will deal with these below).

Considerations on development by both major traditions of economic thought remained largely frozen in this vein through the first half of the twentieth century. Bourgeois economics turned "inwards", shifting the course of economic theory away from the classical economists' concern with production of wealth toward the narrow "neoclassical" fixation upon the distribution of resources among competing ends—a move which dogmatically accepts capitalist development as a fait accompli. Neoclassical proponents devoted their attention to mathematizing their field and refining a theory of relative prices to explain how market forces of supply and demand purportedly realize an "optimal" allocation of resources in a "static" equilibrium.[6] Leon Walras' *Elements of Pure Economics* is a forerunner here. Followers of Marx, such as Rudolf Hilferding and V. I. Lenin, turned "outwards", away from examining the fundamental modus operandi of capitalism toward theorizing of "imperialism" as a way of explaining both the persistence of capitalism into the twentieth century and absence of socialist revolution. To the extent theories of imperialism touched on the fact that by the time of World War I (WWI) virtually all of the globe was in the colonial embrace of the dominant imperialist powers—the formative Western European capitalist developers plus the United States (US) and Japan—this effort was driven by interest in the aforementioned points of capitalism's perduring, not in questions relating to the development future (capitalist or otherwise) of the dominated states. Indeed, during the inter war years, as the Soviet Union (SU) consolidated what was hailed as the world's first socialist revolution, the prescription it offered to states yoked by colonialism and seeking a revolutionary path to liberation and socialist development, as in the case of nascent socialist aspirations of China under Mao Zedong, was simply to foster capitalist development as a precondition for socialism, with little attention devoted to the issue of whether capitalist development could proceed in such an environment.

Development Theory and International Decolonization

Development theory as a field of study arises within the twin contexts of wholesale processes of formal decolonization that swept across the globe in the aftermath of WWII and that of the Cold War waged between the US and SU, around which international politics was configured from the 1950s to the unceremonious fall of the SU in 1989. The formative approach to the field and that which arguably shaped its evolution was "modernization theory". Modernization theory follows classical bourgeois economics in proffering a teleological view of development; such purportedly commencing in an original state of so-called backwardness a-la-Adam Smith and culminating in the attainment of "modernization" in the image of dominant capitalist states. The development policy prescriptions of modernization theory flow largely from the a-historical tenets of bourgeois neoclassical economics and essentially amount to a tautology. That is, "market society" (read capitalism) is blithely assumed to be synonymous with economic growth (development). As the telos of history "modern" (again, meaning capitalist) societies come into being as market economic intercourse expands and levels of savings and investment rise to facilitate deployment of available advanced technologies. According to modernization theory, in a world of independent states, international relations among states play no role in shaping development prospects. World development, quite simply, will proceed optimally when trade among independent states is based upon market rational prices and comparative advantage (the view that countries should specialize in producing goods for which they have factor—land, labor or capital—suitability).

By the mid1960s, however, well after decolonization had largely been completed the world over, modernization theory was beset with a credibility gap as it increasingly became evident that development characteristic of the dominant capitalist states was not occurring in what had become known as the "third world",[7] beyond the capitalist heartland. Taking up the challenge of explaining why this was the case were a raft of critical/ radical theories of development. Instructively, these drew upon internal critiques of the two opposing traditions of economic thought—mainstream bourgeois economics and Marxism. Let us look at the internal critique of mainstream economics and modernization theory first. Latin America had in fact experienced decolonization a half century or more prior to that of the rest of the third world. Insights gained from the study of Latin American development as such entered the public domain and the wider development debate through the work of the Economic Commission for Latin America

(ECLA) created as a regional body of the United Nations (UN) in 1948.[8] Under the aegis of ECLA director Raul Prebisch, a view emerged of an increasingly asymmetric world economy in which the configuring of global trade according to dictates of mainstream economic textbooks conferred advantages upon the already industrialized economies. That is, specializing in raw material production became a road to serfdom for the third world rather than one of shared benefits of industrial progress. It led to an international economic structure of wealthy "center" economies exporting industrial goods, the prices of which tended to rise, and impoverished "peripheral" economies of the third world exporting raw materials and foodstuffs subject to falling prices, and to a process of "unequal exchange" with the center. To counter this, the ECLA advocated that third world states seek to deploy foreign investment in efforts to diversify their economies through import substitution industrialization (ISI) supported by state policy.

We need not devote time to discussing the obvious mainstream bourgeois economics critique of the ECLA argument. The ambivalence in the empirics of the ECLA position at the juncture of the 1950s, when their thesis was first advanced, no longer remains as history has clearly exposed the road to serfdom for most third world economies "specializing" in raw material production as well as modalities of unequal exchange operating beneath the veneer of so-called comparative advantage. More trenchant, however, was critique from the radical Left which questioned ECLA claims that multinational corporations (MNCs) were a benign force for transferring technologies as third world countries soon discovered whole sectors of their economies usurped by MNCs. As well, the early efforts of ISI foundered on shoals of burgeoning debt at the precise point at which the process of substituting domestic production for imports turned from that devoted to production of light consumer goods toward capital goods and the goal of full-scale industrialization.[9]

Ultimately, it was through the interfacing of ECLA analysis with Marxism that radical critique of modernization theory was rendered more potent. But Marxism had also to be put through a process of internal questioning. The problems Marxism faced originated in the fact that it was saddled with its own unidirectional theory of history—historical materialism (HM)—which, with varying degrees of ascribed necessity (a signal point of controversy in Marxist circles), held that the evolution of human society was marked by broad epochs of historical development or "modes of production", through which all societies passed, culminating in socialism. Further, HM was largely accepted as the master environment for the development of other regions of Marxist theory and research. Thus, Marx's economic study of capitalism in his *Capital* was recruited as simply a sub-theory of historical materialism, a sub-theory which purportedly confirmed the prognosis of historical materialism.

Linking Marxian analysis of international accumulation, as it had been developed by theorists of imperialism, to ECLA work, proceeded through the writings of Paul Baran[10] and involved a challenge to the received linear view of capitalist development. Baran argued that the post-WWII economy had entered a monopoly "phase" in which capitalism was no longer characterized by dynamism but by stagnation. Baran was also a pioneer in focusing Marxian eyes on the third world directly. He maintained the so-called backwardness of third world countries was not a vestige of pre-capitalist modes of production but followed from capitalist development itself. Further, that capitalism as a "world system" was not a homogeneous entity but a hierarchical structure in which more developed countries exploited less developed ones by siphoning off part of what he refers to as their "economic surplus"; the loss of which then imparts to those states all the economic features modernization theory interpreted as backwardness. Finally, if capitalism could no longer guarantee development of much of the world then the inescapable solution for development was for the third world to follow a socialist path.

It would be the writings of Baran, then, which led to the formulation of what constitutes one of the major enduring approaches to development studies—*dependency theory*. Here, I am using dependency theory as an umbrella term for critical theories of "underdevelopment", "unequal exchange" or "world system". Without going into conceptual wrangling amongst approaches, dependency theories share the following assumptions: First, they seek to anchor the study of development within understandings of the economic logic of capitalism. Dependency theories claim this logic not only engenders class division and significant social inequalities in "national" capitalist contexts but, in world economic interaction between developed and less developed states, yields economic outcomes in the latter qualitatively different from what capitalism produces in the former. In effect, the interaction spawns a "world system" marked by glaring and persistent social division and inequality. This insight enters a *unit of analysis* question into development theory and problematizes international relations. Second, dependency approaches characterize the capitalism of the third world largely in terms that reflect what they perceive as its peculiar economic orientation vis-à-vis the world economy and developed states ("dependent", "extroverted", "peripheral" and so on); and then contend that this particular orientation is at the root of persisting third world underdevelopment (what modernization theory had misread as backwardness). Third, dependency approaches dismiss outright neoclassical economics' theory of comparative advantage and free trade: they view the latter as providing ideological cover for the unequal exchange occurring in international economic intercourse between dominant producers and exporters of industrial goods and the economies of the world based on primary production. Fourth, the policy implications of dependency theory involve some measure of "delinking" from the world economy to build an "introverted" capitalism under the banner of ISI (ECLA never advocated delinking) or, in the most the radical incarnations of the theory, build a socialist economy as urged by Baran. This placed a spotlight upon the *state*—its' economic or class character, international orientation, and so on—as the organized force of development policy direction.

While dependency theory observations on the reproduction of world economic asymmetries characterizing global capitalism are compelling, dependency approaches would soon be taken to task over their conceptual adequacy. First, the simplistic switching of the unit of analysis from national to international capitalism was questioned given how it concentrated development studies at the "level" of world system at the expense of understanding varied "situations" of development.[11] Second, Neo-Marxist critics saw dependency theory as abandoning vital insights of Marx on divergent social relations and class configurations central to Marx's notion of modes of production. Neo-Marxist research in the development field sought to refine Marx's general framework of HM to deal with what they perceived as "articulations" of modes of production marking third world development conditions at both the "level" of the nation state and on a world scale.[12] Third, the increasing influence of post-structuralism and postmodernism in Western academies led to attacks on the very enterprise of critical development studies. From what became known as the "impasse debate" sprang arguments that all approaches animated by Marxism shared the same commitment to "necessity", in that the particular historical outcome, whether underdevelopment or development (or some mix devolving from articulations of modes of production), necessarily flowed from the historical unfolding of capital, or could be "read off" the capitalist mode of production, or stemmed from the "needs" of developed capitalism and/or the capitalist world system. As well, postmodern critics maintained Marxism was burdened by a commitment to "meta-theory", in that notwithstanding differences in geographical locale, the historical sequencing of development or the levels of aggregation being considered, Marxism sought to explain the varied processes of development through a single overarching theoretical structure. (To be sure, Marxists within the development field did protest the foregoing as unfairly tarnishing a diverse tradition with the same brush, and contended that new emergent approaches within Marxist theory were consciously attempting to avoid earlier pitfalls).[13]

Another problematic issue confronting the Marxist development research agenda has been its theorizing of socialist development given the view attributed to Marx that socialism was the culmination of a process of historical development and was institutionally prefigured in the development of capitalism. Under conditions where capitalism had not developed to any significant degree one question that arose related to the development of the productive forces both in the sense of their technological advancement as the basis for generalized abundance, and that of their "socialization" so as to render them amenable to economic planning as per the schema of HM. A second question concerned the working class—its proportionate size, role and influence, and formation of its class consciousness—in the development process. To caricature here a series of complex arguments,[14] Marxists maintained a) that the existence of a socialist world system meant that the "highest social order" had already been reached, therefore every society did not have to follow the evolutionary path through capitalism; b) that in situations where socialist revolutions occurred in the third world, the "transition" to socialism—involving management of the facets of economic development that capitalist development would "normally" have undertaken, the fostering of working class consciousness and solidarity with other social classes, and the ensuring of the socialist pedigree of the whole process—could occur under the auspices of Marxist-Leninist political parties imbued with proletarian class consciousness; and c) that where no socialist revolution was on the immediate agenda, Marxists could support strategies of "national liberation" and forge alliances with social classes deemed progressive from the point of view of indigenous "national" capitalist development.

This theorizing of socialism, as with Marxist animated theories of development in general, was similarly subjected to postmodernist attacks on so-called meta-theory as well as postmodern rants against Marxian "essentialism", "class reductionism" and so forth. However, the retreat from broad based support for critical/Marxist theories of development and growing disenchantment among even radical intelligentsia of third world countries themselves with critical approaches as such was driven by a concatenation of factors among which postmodern theories of knowledge played only one part. First, from the early 1980s neoliberalism, which had been gestating in the US as a hegemonic ideology and set of policy exhortations, was foisted on the world. The enabling mechanisms for this had been put in operation largely under the political radar (including that of US politics) throughout the 1970s. Of key significance here was the demise of the Bretton Woods monetary system (BWMS) which had enshrined the US dollar as world hub currency on the condition of maintenance of exchangeability of dollars for gold and the relatively fixed valuation of other major currencies to the dollar. To the issuer of the currency of the realm, of course, there always accrue so-called "seigniorage" benefits. Under the BWMS and its twin global governance institutions, the World Bank (WB) and International Monetary Fund (IMF)—then charged with such tasks as reconstruction of post WWII ravaged economies and alleviation of IMF member states' balance of payments difficulties—along with the global regime of capital controls and US pumping the world with much needed liquidity for long term industrial investment projects, seigniorage benefits enjoyed by the US as issuer of the world's hub currency were kept within bounds. In fact, it was the protective cocoon of the BWMS that supported both, the high wage, high profit, Keynesian welfare state, automobile societies of North America, Western Europe and Japan in their "golden age" of capitalist growth, as well as and the catch-up dream of ISI developmental states across the third world.

Faced with the increased competitive prowess of Western Europe and Japan in the key consumer durable industries central to capitalist post-WWII growth, a burgeoning trade deficit, and looming fiscal deficit from its overseas military adventures (these, such as the Vietnam War, fuelled a misallocation of investment and resources away from the civilian economy, leading to further diminutions in US competitiveness), the US engineered a series of global "coups" that would see the US dollar increasingly held as world reserve currency even as its anchoring to gold was severed. This was replaced by a new Treasury Bill IOU (T-bill IOU) standard of global reserves which cemented US monetary seigniorage for only the cost of printing dollars.[15] Integral to US dollar seigniorage were several processes that unfolded under the aegis of neoliberal ideology and US state neoliberal compulsion. Most importantly, there occurred the passing of levers of global finance into the hands of a rising phalanx of private transnational banks (TNBs) and financial intermediaries. This "financialization" however, was never an independent variable in the global economy placing symmetric constraints on all states and their increasingly disempowered "national" banks but a core component of US dollar-based hegemony. With the world awash with dollars from US global militarism, the "petro-dollar" arrangement brokered by the Nixon administration[16] and dollars streaming from the hollowed out US consumer durable industrial edifice seeking new profitable investment outlets, Wall Street became the center of dollar-based credit and international (increasingly short term) dollar-based financial arbitrage. Third world states' ISI initiatives benefited for some time from the ready availability of internationally loan-able funds, particularly given the spiraling dollar inflation of the 1970s. But with the unilateral raising of US interest rates by Paul Volker at the beginning of the Reagan presidency, the third world spun into debt crisis and the ISI dream was shattered for perpetuity.

It was not *just* a question of the ISI aspirations of third world economies being dashed by the US unilateral interest rate hike that was directed toward supporting the dollar as global currency under conditions of US industrial decline—though, we may note here, by the summer of 1982, commencing with Mexico, a wave of interest rate hike-induced debt crises swept across the third world with 27 countries requiring debt rescheduling by fall 1983. Even by 1996, cumulative output of the third world still had not recovered to the 1979 pre-debt crisis level.[17] Rather, the unilateral raising of interest rates by Volker strangled "economic nationalist" developmental projects the world over, including those of the US and most other Organization of Economic Cooperation and Development (OECD) economies. High interest rates wielded as part of the neoliberal policy package of *moneterism* and *supply side* taxation[18] may have quelled US inflation, and as noted, propped up the dollar and its attractiveness as world reserve currency, but the edifice proved highly inimical to industrial investment and the high wage employment attendant to that sector, and it further undermined the role of the Keynesian state in supporting the high mass consumption/mass production economies characterizing advanced capitalist development in the post-WWII period. In short, shorn of its BWMS cocoon and under the gun of neoliberal policy offensives, developmentalism in the post-WWII period, as it had been first constituted under the Marshall Plan which reconstructed Western Europe, was relegated to the dustbin of history by the late 1980s.

Development Theory, Globalization and the Washington Consensus

Returning to our point above of the concatenating of factors which undermined allegiances to radical/Marxian approaches to development, the fact is, these factors also contributed to the emergence of what may be felicitously conceptualized as a peculiar *surrealism* in development thinking as a whole. Besides the question of neoliberal-impelled undermining of conditions that made for post-WWII golden age development in both "national" and international economic spaces, another factor alluded to above was the unceremonious unraveling of the SU. This event further fed the neoliberal hysteria as embodied in former British Prime Minister Margaret Thatcher's assumptive dictum that there is no alternative (TINA) to the market and capitalism. To the demise of the SU must also be added the rise of the so-called Asian economic "tigers"—South Korea, Taiwan, Singapore and Hong Kong. The global significance of this clutch of Asian tigers ascending in the world economic hierarchy to the forefront of international competition resided not only in the way they sprang up from a third world mired in debt and industrial contraction but in the effort the neoliberal-hijacked BWMS institutions, the WB and IMF, devoted to painting their rise as an outcome of adherence to neoliberal so-called "free market" principles and policies.[19] The claim that the Asian "miracle" was bound to the market tied into yet another factor in the hegemonic neoliberal ideological rendering of the state of the world economy; this being the view that economic growth under market principles is optimized in the third world not through ISI but via so-called export-oriented industrialization (EOI). It was then the coming together of all the foregoing that in a large part made up what by the mid-1990s was being referred to in common parlance as globalization: Finally, what became codified as the "Washington Consensus"—the neoliberal ideological view of "the market" as synonymous with economic growth a-la-modernization theory—emerged as *de rigueur* development policy of powerful industrial states and international institutions toward the third world.

In beginning to unpack the ultimate significance of the Washington Consensus as development mantra through the waning years of the 20th and early years of the 21st centuries, we have to be clear: neoliberalism was never really about an epiphany of the market in national and international economic spaces notwithstanding the shrill ideological chants of its supporters or the credibility it attained from Nobel Prizes being showered upon its core academic proponents.[20] While the neoliberal agenda dubbed "privatization" did constitute a massive divestiture by governments of enterprises they had (in many cases successfully) run, the passing of these into hands of giant MNCs that operated like SU-style command economies can hardly be viewed as a return to laissez faire. So-called "deregulation" also did not amount to marketization but a reregulation designed to support MNC power as the strength of organized labor and efficacy of worker rights and protections were eviscerated.

"Liberalization" played out largely in the domain of finance as touched upon already. Internationally liberalization meant the elimination of capital controls on fund movements for short term arbitrage, the emergence of a "dirty floating" exchange rate regime which opened the door to rampant speculation and the unhinging of international finance from the "real" economy of production and trade, the opening of the worlds' stock markets and creation of stock markets in states where these had previously not existed or had been under tight "national" control regimes (this process inaugurated the labeling of third world states as "emerging markets"), and the introduction by newly empowered financial intermediaries of a welter of exotic financial instruments for lending and borrowing ("securitization" is the operative descriptive term for this process and derivatives an umbrella category for those instruments). Domestically, liberalization meant the rewriting of rules for what varying categories of funds such as those held by insurance companies and pension funds were allowed to do in terms of investment for the vast pools of social wealth they held. It also meant the changing of rules that governed the activities of institutions like banks, transforming them from boring but safe keepers of peoples' and business savings that lent out money to garner interest, to speculating arbitragers in their own right. Because of the unhinging of finance from the substantive economy of wealth and material goods production as the former had fed into the kind of economy Smith and Marx understood as capitalism, our use of the term "market" to describe neoliberal policy impacts here seems misleading and the notion put forward by the late Susan Strange of a *casino* economy far more apropos.

On the question of the Asian tigers as embodiments of market generated development outcomes, it has to be immediately pointed out that the development experience of trading entrepôts or "city states" such as Singapore and Hong Kong can hardly be upheld as general development models given that neither ever faced the daunting hurdle of transforming agricultural societies with a sizeable rural populace and semi-feudal ruling class into a modern capitalist society with independent farmers a proletariat jettisoned from the land, and an indigenous industrial bourgeoisie. Singapore has been a clear case of state-directed development since the ascension to power of the quasi-authoritarian People's Action Party led by Lee Kuan Kew following its mid-1960s separation from Malaysia; Hong Kong remained a British colony until the handover to China at the close of the 20th century. South Korea and Taiwan's development also had little to do with the capitalist market. Being on a signal fault line of the Cold War the anticommunist allegiance of both to the US (as was the case with Japan) paid extremely handsome economic dividends. From billions of US dollars in economic aid (both military and civilian) through the demand bonanza of the Vietnam War, South Korea and Taiwan were able to surmount obstacles of capital formation that plagued other third world economies in the move to heavy industrial ISI.[21] Further, as the neoliberal policy package was being forced upon Latin America and other areas of the third world as a condition of maintaining creditworthiness, to the mid-1990s the US absolved

South Korea and Taiwan of that significant constraint on their continuing maintenance of pre-neoliberal market eschewing developmental dirigisme; and the giant US market remained relatively open to Korea and Taiwan's exports. It was therefore precisely the persistence of post-WWII modalities of development in both states, though particularly in South Korea, cocooned internationally by US policy (in lieu of the BWMS), which led to their competitive world economic ascendency in consumer durable production (with the rise of even an indigenous automobile industry in South Korea) and the attainment by South Korea of full scale industrialization—really the *only* exemplar of this from the entire third world.[22]

Given the feeding into what in common parlance is dubbed globalization of the view of neoliberal policy change in OECD states and the so-called Asian miracle (the purported template for third world development) as driven by market processes, where does this leave the conceptualizing of globalization when, as has been illustrated above, it is clear that neither ideological pillar of globalization has much to do with the capitalist market? The fact is, as pointed out above regarding the notion of financialization, globalization is not an independent world economic variable operating as a natural force, symmetrically constraining the activities of all states. Without burdening the discussion here by wading into arcane debate over globalization[23] we can state unequivocally, that capitalism has always had an international economy or global dimension to accumulation from its inception. What is important for analysis is to assess the differing forms the global dimension of accumulation has assumed and to make determinations on the extent to which capital accumulation is actually internationalized in a specific capitalist era. A key differentiating feature of the post-WWII international dimension of capitalism is that while it was trade in light consumer goods such as textiles that characterized the mid-19th century world economy dominated by Britain, and export of portfolio or finance capital from advanced industrial states to colonies in the early 20th century "stage" of imperialism (including white settler colonies), the post-WWII economy was marked by the internationalization of production—this including foreign direct investment (FDI), international subcontracting, licensing, management agreements, and so forth—which opened the possibility for a genuinely international division of labor for the first time in the history of capitalism. And, within the context of internationalization of production characteristic of the global dimension of accumulation in the post-WWII period, world trade became increasingly intra-industry and intra-firm and dominated by large MNCs. The operations of TNBs fit in here to support MNC global endeavors and long-term investment strategies. In short, in both qualitative and, for that matter, quantitative terms,[24] post-WWII capitalism was highly "global" while simultaneously facilitative of the array of developmental projects constituting the "national" economies largely of the OECD, though in the third world as well.

So what changes under the impetus of so-called globalization? To some extent this question has already been answered in broad brush strokes:

the architecture of global governance, to borrow in-vogue buzzwords, which had maintained the requisite stability in a highly internationalized world economy for relatively balanced growth of the worlds' major OECD economies (as "balanced" as attainable under capitalism, that is), and held some potential as a cocoon for capitalist heavy steel and consumer durable production development in the third world, was unraveled. This leads to a follow up question: what are the forces that yielded this outcome? Again, we have given a partial answer. It was neoliberal-impelled financialization and so-called liberalization which burst asunder the post-WWII architecture. We have touched as well on the role the US played in the foregoing processes. But we need to delve further into the precise reasons for US policy here. As explained in greater detail elsewhere,[25] the US arrived at a strategic crossroads by the late 1970s: it could orient its economy toward an existence as one consumer durable production competitor amongst several in the "free world" it had taken great effort to foster, or it could pursue an alternate course in which it maintained global dominance through dollar seigniorage but shed much of its post-WWII industrial production edifice. Remember, the weight of the US economy in the world was immense, approximately 25% of global GDP. The directions an economy of that size took could not but impact strongly on the world economy given the level of internationalization of economic intercourse already noted. The relinquishing of competitive lead in key consumer durable and associated consumer electronics industry was first reflected in the bloating US trade deficit of the 1970s and 80s. Secondly, from the mid-1980s, the ever-increasing hollowing out of US industrial export sectors and subsequent economic weakening was reflected in plummeting tax revenues and a growing budget deficit. By 1985, the US thus became a net debtor nation to the rest of the world. By the mid-1990s, the capital account began to fall into deficit (that is, the US economy derived less income from US investments abroad than income accruing to foreign investment in the US). The ramifications of what was becoming a multi-billion dollar total current account deficit (soon to be a trillion dollar one) where the US imported more than it exported, saved less than it invested, spent more than its income was that the US transubstantiated into a *global economy* dependent upon the world for producing goods its citizens demanded, money its government required for international and domestic policy endeavors and investment money for its businesses financing.

In short, globalization is in fact a sexed up term for the way the US extricated itself from the predicament it faced over the maintenance of global hegemony. The follow up question here is therefore: what was the impact upon global development prospects of the emergence of the US as a global economy and where does the Washington Consensus fit into this schema? Let us pick up the story by considering the extensive internationalization of production characteristic of the post-WWII economy. The thrust of US MNC FDI through the BWMS decades, though extensive, was always to supplement domestic production and turned largely upon so-called "tariff jumping" to secure access to markets otherwise difficult to penetrate by producing "in" them. As the US economy struggled during the 1970s, in part due to vigorous competition from Western Europe/Germany and Japan,[26] US MNC FDI began to supplant domestic production and was increasingly directed toward the servicing of global markets with internationalized production. By the mid-1980s, US and other OECD MNCs not only accelerated the playing off of varying states regulatory regimes in a frenetic drive to lower costs through predatory relocation of marketable productive capacity but, aided by the information-computer technology (ICT) revolution through which they could exert ever more centralized control over global production while divesting themselves of the actual business of making things ("flexibility" is the buzzword here), MNCs strategically fragmented the global labor force as they disarticulated global production into what are dubbed (yet another buzzword) "value chains" (these reflecting the fact that global trade is now dominated by flows of components or sub-products).[27]

Remember, the transfiguration of international production is temporally juxtaposed with so-called financialization, the euphemism for the world economic process through which US dollar seigniorage based global hegemony crystallized. Financialization, however, was not just about the geospatial centering of the new world of casino-economic financial games on Wall Street and related satellites such as London. With the gigantic US economy running massive trade deficits, those states—initially Japan—running huge trade surpluses with the US were regimented into "saving" or "investing" their dollar earnings in US dollar denominated assets such as the aforementioned T-bill IOUs. The holding of global savings of surplus trading states in the currency of the world's major borrower from the earliest days constitutes a massive loan-subsidy to the US. This ample liquidity lubricated US credit and other markets, in turn supporting a "domestic" credit regime in the US of lower interest rates and easy borrowing. Over the neoliberal decades of the 20th century and into the 21st century several nuances marked this international state of affairs. First, the tsunami of currency speculation at the center of what has been euphemized as financialization forces most third world states to hold huge dollar reserves (as it is the dollar against which the bulk of currency "trading" occurs). Some are held in domestic banking systems, the rest in US-based financial instruments. This further adds to the foreign "credit" the US is able to draw upon for the cost of running a printing press. Second, because international financial transactions are increasingly conducted in dollars, when the participation in international trade and investment of a given third world state expands, it is impelled toward an external orientation of its economy to gain means of dollar payment. This requires either borrowing dollars or selling more goods for dollars than it buys. Across the neoliberal 1990s, therefore, dollar foreign exchange reserves grew by 235.8 percent. And, at the close of 2000, the share of total global foreign exchange reserves held by the third world including the so-called emerging markets (largely dollar, though other key currencies as well), increased to almost 60 percent of the world total.[28]

Let us look at how export-oriented industrialization fits in here and justify our dubbing of the Washington Consensus development perspective as surrealistic. The "I" in EOI is a misnomer. With MNCs controlling the commanding heights of the global economy, having disarticulated production into internationally dispersed value chains to service key global markets at the lowest possible cost, the very foundation for creating indigenous "national" industrial systems across the third world has been eviscerated. Those states that have achieved some success in clawing their way up the development ladder by laying their hands on benchmark technologies are also those most in debt to TNBs and other private global financial intermediaries[29] that enforce neoliberal policy dictums on these states as conditions of maintaining creditworthiness. Further, while much discussion in the mainstream business press of late has focused on so-called "offshore" practices of global finance (the manipulation of principles of extra-territoriality to evade "national" regulatory and taxation regimes for financial transactions), nothing has been said about the fact that MNC disarticulating and global dispersal of production has in a studied fashion blazed the same trail with the relocating of the business of making things in this world to so-called export-production zones (EPZs). These EPZs marking today's internationalization of production and geospatial locale for the world's marketable productive capacity from China to Sub-Saharan Africa to Mexico are effectively apartheid enclaves separated through offshore principles of extra-territoriality from the host economy.[30] What is important to recognize with regard to development prospects for the third world is that the EPZ phenomenon, both in terms of the sorts of labor forces employed and relations of production that hold in EPZ operations as well as the range of goods produced and technologies deployed for that, foster/perpetuate a major disjuncture in the "national" economy.

We should not lose sight of the animating factor in the transfiguring of international production: the transition of the US to a global economy dependent upon the world for the goods its citizens demand; such under conditions where the US divested itself of much of its mass production edifice and the high wage jobs at the core of that. The export orientation of the third world and other states demanded by Washington Consensus policy of course does not apply to the US. But across the world EOI is plied by vigorous neoliberal policy enforcement (by the US and global institutions controlled by it) of deflationary imperatives. Wages in EOI sectors are thus destined to remain painfully low perpetually forestalling the kind of economic symbiosis through which "growth" translated to *development* and full-scale industrialization in the major OECD economies and South Korea.

The Dearth of Radical Critique in Development Theory

We will examine macro aspects of the international impact of neoliberal Washington Consensus policy in the closing section of this chapter. Here we return to questions of development theory to ask how what was in a large part a recycled variant of modernization theory maintained such a long run? Why has this approach been taken so seriously in academic development policy and studies circles when—in sharp contradistinction with its precursor of the 1950s and the historical circumstances of the original's emergence—the actual possibility of development in the third world (in the capitalist context as inferred by modernization theory, of economies akin to those of the OECD mass consumption golden age) is virtually nonexistent?

It is worth saying something here firstly about critique of neoliberal policy springing up from within mainstream political science and economics:[31] Of note is the gestation of theories of "institutions" in development thinking as a way of countering neoliberal ideology of development as springing solely from "the market". A large part of the institutional analysis stemmed from comparative research on OECD economies treating questions of so-called "models of capitalism". In a sense, this literature reflected a broad resignation among erstwhile radicals (and a new generation of Left liberals or "statists") that with the demise of the SU capitalism remained the only game in town and it was time to choose the "best" (most "progressive" yet "competitive") variety to now live with. Though the debates were conducted at a high level of technical and scholarly sophistication, substantively they were spurious because their cross-national research orientation proceeded oblivious to the fact that the US, the purported "market" model in the debate, was not only hardly a market economy but definitively not a *national* economy. The US is a global economy, as defined above, whose institutional profile depends on dollar seigniorage-based commandeering of global savings to finance its business investment and government expenditure, and the marshalling of slave-like modes of labor control from China to Sub-Saharan Africa and Mexico to satisfy demand of its citizens for material goods under conditions of zealously enforced price deflation.

Much the same can be said about the refocusing on "democracy" and its governance institutions into mainstream development debate (and the launching of several new academic journals as part of the effort). Discussion in my view tends to be highly formulaic and a-historical as it ignores the complex issues and phasing in the institution of *universal* suffrage in the US and across the OECD itself (universal suffrage took between a half and full century to realize in most countries and followed the ascendency of a bourgeois class, the power of which was rooted in "national" capitalist economies; neither of the forgoing being conditions marking the third world today). One would do well to dust off Samuel Huntington's *Political Order in Changing Societies* to grasp why the original modernization theory, though a-historical in its own right, never descended to the nadir of technocratic sterility of today's debate. And to the extent questions of institutions and democracy factor into what is now referred to as the "post-Washington Consensus", it amounts to much too little too late.

Another tangent driven by disenchantment of largely third world radical intelligentsia with Marxism as well as the co-opting of a range of social science disciplines by postmodernism the world over (as alluded to above) was the breeding of perspectives that may be captured under the rubrics of "post-development" and "post-colonial" theories of development. For these approaches, the problem was never capitalism as a mode of production or world system, the relative efficacy of so-called market and state/institutional structures in development, and so forth but the "discourse" of development itself which was taken to be an "invention" of the US and its "free world" allies during the Cold War.[32] A genuinely liberationist agenda in this view demands the "unmaking" of development and the third world as discursive practices and realization of a post-development era in which the principle of "difference" is enshrined and local empowerment fostered. While some of the exhortations for social movements emanating from post-colonialism dovetail in important ways with analysis and proposals for progressive change in the third world put forward by environmentalist and feminist scholars,[33] in the end it is the pillorying of so-called meta-theory which perpetually blunts what critical edge postmodernism and its post-development progeny had. That is, to fully grasp the world economic totalizing force of what is euphemized as globalization requires precisely the sort of structural theory that postmodernism eschews.[34] It is indeed no accident that as postmodern, post-colonial celebrations of the "local" and culture/language delimitation of knowledge captivated academia neoliberal ideology reigned supreme at a macro international level. Arguably symptomatic of the paucity of theory in the strong sense being applied to understanding of so-called globalization is the way globalization is targeted by the global (sic) anti-globalization movement. As a recent study makes abundantly clear,[35] while rather innocuous meetings of international governmental organizations have been turned into media events of youth and police in running street battles, the protests challenge what are essentially formal aspects of the neoliberal edifice rather than its substantive undergirding; not much critique is leveled at capitalism (in the extended structural crisis it has been mired in) or the international machinations of the US and key allied governments that supported the tendencies referred to as globalization.

Marxian analysis, where allegiance with Marx's work and vision of a socialist future as the kingdom of freedom was maintained, had always continued, though largely on the fringes of (or more often exorcized from) public debate. There exist three key areas in which advances have been made in the refining of the Marxian research agenda: First, there is its cross-fertilization with "critical realist" theories in the philosophy of science. Postmodernism extrapolated from "conventionalist" critiques of positivism (the latter posit how no direct correspondence exists between our theories and a mind independent material reality; rather results of scientific investigation are "created" by us with instruments, concepts and/or thought schemes we deploy) to the view that there is no "real", mind independent world from which we can take soundings to assess the adequacy or truth of our thought schemes viz. their subject matters. There are *only* those schemes, texts, discourses, and so forth each generating their own "world". For Roy Bhaskar, postmodernism and its progeny constitute a case of the "epistemic fallacy";[36] that is, the provocative but erroneous belief that in answering the epistemological question of *how* we know—for postmodernism knowledge proceeds solely through a multiplicity of thought schemes—we simultaneously answer the ontological question of *what* there is to be known. In bringing ontology back in, critical realism argues that while experiment and other knowledge endeavors (such as the conceptualizing of development) do operate with socially and historically constructed cognitive resources the very intelligibility of these depends on there being something to experiment *on* or study. And the fact that whether through experiment or otherwise we cannot implement our thought schemes *just as we please* (will unmaking discursive phrases of this planet like *third world*, replacing this with global south, emerging markets and so on, unmake the hunger, destitution, poverty and so forth marking lives of this part of humanity or the structural conditions perpetuating such?) points to the existence of a world independent of our minds.

Secondly, Marxian analysis has rectified theoretically impoverishing tendencies in its economics/political economy research agenda which flowed from the misapprehension of the cognitive sequence in Marx's work;[37] that led to views of Marxism as advancing a teleology of development and socialism parallel to what modernization theory held about capitalism. Marxian economics, it has been demonstrated, is not a meta-narrative of the sort postmodernism rants against, as its concern is with but one subset of human social relations studied under historically delimited conditions. Its power emanates from the way it *informs* other research domains within Marxism—including that of historical materialism, a discrete theory which has a different subject focus from it—not in its subsumption of variegated regions of research under a single overarching epistemological or methodological umbrella. Marxian economics is not teleological because its primary mission is to apprehend the peculiar material anatomy of *capital*. Questions of the historical trajectory or historical development of capitalism, new work in Marxian political economy argues, necessarily involve study at different "levels of analysis",[38] a conclusion Marx, given his temporal emplacement, could not possibly have arrived at (though Marx's work in *Capital* did theoretically foreground such a conclusion). Marxian economics, in other words, precludes from the outset any form of theorizing that sets out in any way to "read off" historical outcomes from capital as attempted by formative "conventional" Marxist writings in the development field. This, of course, is not to deny that capital is deeply implicated in the constitution of the global political economy—its geospatial inequalities, modalities of exploitation and oppression, and so on—only that a comprehensive Marxian analysis of such in the development field, involving levels of theory and study of the changing configurations of the international dimension of capital, has yet to be undertaken.[39]

Thirdly, through re-conceptualization of the cognitive sequence in Marx's research agenda (as Marx himself certainly conceived it, though so many of his followers readily lost sight of it) Marxian approaches to socialism have also been refined considerably from simplistic views of capitalism constituting the "conditions" of socialism. The paradigm of what was dubbed "developmental socialism"[40]—socialism that in practice entailed the development of modalities of capitalist production organization—could not but produce the most unpalatable social outcomes: partly because developing societies were getting varying doses of, just that, capitalism, and in the case of China (or the Soviet Union), for example, a stunted variant of capitalism, but also because this was coupled with the most odious authoritarian modes of social control—something that was inevitable given the perceived task of "channeling" capitalist development to develop socialism. Similarly unpalatable, and operating with the same premise, is the so-called TINA position foisted on the world. This view, that given the current neoliberal economy enveloping the globe, socialist initiatives must wait on capitalist development again becoming conducive to the development of socialism. This perpetually condemns socialism (and the struggle for it) to some indiscernible future, and in my view, further opens the door to the emergence of modern forms of "barbarism" which Marx *himself* believed might supplant socialism as the post-capitalist alternative, while socialists are unwittingly sitting on their hands waiting for capitalism to build socialism for them. As maintained and discussed at length elsewhere, if socialism is to constitute an historical advancement over capitalism (and pre-capitalist societies) in terms of the socio-material betterment it offers for the reproduction of human material existence, then creative thinking about socialism should *begin* with the basic theory of capitalism—Marx's project in *Capital*—as the benchmark for conceptualizing socialism as the "antithesis" or "institutional opposite" of capitalism. We must develop an ontology of socialism[41] with a focus upon what must be *undone* in our economic lives dominated by centuries of capitalism and decades of neoliberalism. This ontology must then be given institutional expression with an eye to realizing socialist goals and debate within that context on what it means to be "developed".[42]

The Poverty of Global Neoliberalism

While global attention remains transfixed upon the solvency of major banks, insurance companies, automobile corporations and so on, primarily in the US though generally across the OECD, little consideration has been given to the fact that the neoliberal policy package which drove trillion dollar GDP economies to the brink of insolvency, and we are not finished yet, has been ravaging third world billion dollar economies (that is "billion" as in ten or maybe eleven digits) for decades. There exist three extremely troubling tendencies I wish to draw attention to which antedate the current Wall Street centered malaise. It is important to also say something in this section about debates on global poverty based on pre-malaise data. Finally, the section will conclude with a glimpse at what the current economic depression portends for the third world.

First, while there are temporal and quantitative variations among OECD economies, it is nevertheless the case that the historical pattern of development from the beginning of the 20th century up to the so-called golden age of capitalist growth has entailed increases in employment in the industrial sector of economies paralleled by a decrease in employed population in agriculture.[43] What we have witnessed under Washington Consensus tutelage for third world development is a dramatic increase in service sector employment where the shift of employed populations out of agriculture is no longer into industry but into services. In 2006, according to the ILO, services eclipsed agriculture as the predominant sector of global employment and currently represent 42.7 percent of all jobs in the world. And, the vivid picture painted by ILO figures is that the employment shift directly from agriculture to services, bypassing industry in stark contradistinction with the historical tendency of capitalist development, is representative of even the most poverty stricken states in South Asia and Sub-Saharan Africa—the latter region in which employment in industry has never risen above 10 percent of employed population.[44]

Second, the historical experience of development in today's advanced OECD economies involved the shift of populations from agriculture to urban areas and the absorption of the newly created workforce by expanding industrial growth. According to the United Nations (UN) as of 2005, 48.6 percent of the global population lived in cities with the figure for the non-developed countries of the world being 42.7 percent of people; that more than double the entire third world urban population of 1950.[45] Urbanization across the neoliberal decades has exploded however not as an expression of manufacturing growth but "radically decoupled from industrialization". To take Africa as a case in point, under conditions of stunted manufacturing and impoverishment of agriculture, it has nevertheless maintained an annual rate of urbanization of between 3.5 to 4% , this higher than the average 2.1% rate of urbanization in major European cities during the mid 19th century growth spurt of formative global capitalist industrialization. And, absent the absorptive capacity of industry which in the advanced OECD underpinned capitalist economic growth and development, rampant urbanization is producing "megaslums" of recycled building materials, open sewers, human squalor and destitution. It is estimated that there exist over 200,000 slums in the world with 30 of the largest megaslums in 2005 containing over a half million inhabitants each. It is indeed instructive that the much touted so-called new emerging markets of Brazil, India and China have the largest proportionate slum populations: Brazil, 51.7 million slum dwellers; India, 158.4 million (55.5% of its urban population); China, 193.8 million.[46]

The "employment" shift into services and the urban "tsunami" (though unlike a natural force the latter has been compelled by neoliberal policy) coalesce in but another disturbing trend: the burgeoning of what the ILO refers to as "vulnerable" or "informal" work as the main form of sustenance of third world populaces. This category of worker certainly includes the almost half billion workers toiling for less than $1 per day and a good component of the 1.3 billion earning $2 or less a day. It encompasses what the ILO dubs "contributing family workers", largely characteristic of subsistence agriculture around the world where family members often remain "unpaid" for labor. The swelling ranks of "own account" workers providing those ubiquitous third world services run the gamut from street corner shoe shining to massage parlors. It is in the megaslum environs where this pool of surplus humanity rubs shoulders with the "formal" sector as global outsourcers relocate production to places such as China or sub-Saharan Africa (the latter where virtually all work tends to be informal, making slave-like conditions of formal employment for the likes of Wal-Mart seem to be a "dream"[47]).

The foregoing trends provide the backdrop for debates currently raging over the eliminating of poverty by neoliberal policies. These are a statisticians dream and largely revolve around the creation of an artificial currency known as purchasing power parity (PPP) dollars and the measuring of absolute poverty set at $1 per day or less.[48] What critical analysis brings out here is the inadequacy of PPP measurements given the way these seek to establish commensurability between vastly different consumption patterns such as the consuming of services in the advanced capitalist states and the preponderance of meager incomes devoted to procuring a minimal caloric intake in the third world. Where agreement does exist in critical analysis is that where aggregate statistics indicate some reduction in global poverty the conclusions derive from reducing poverty and creating of a middle class of consumers in China and India.[49] But, as is pointed out, if it is indeed economic development of those two states on which global poverty reduction is based then it should be with the sorts of policies and indigenous circumstances through which poverty was actually reduced there that development studies must concern itself rather than with neoliberal jargon about "markets".[50]

If the foregoing trends from the neoliberal "good" years hardly portend what may in any reasoned judgment be delineated as development, the malaise which has unfolded since 2007 has only increased the plight of third world peoples. As this book was going to press the UN produced a substantially revised forecast of the debilitating impacts of the global neoliberal crisis for the third world and all indications are that before end 2009 the UN, IMF, ILO, WB, and other governmental organizations will be prompted to deliver further downgrading for the world economic situation. In the so-called "baseline" scenario world per capita income is expected to decrease in 2009 by 3.7%. In 60 third world states per capita income is expected to decline and only 7 countries in the third world as a whole are forecast to have growth rates sufficient to contribute to poverty reduction.[51] The Food and Agriculture Organization of the UN estimates that the number of malnourished (hungry/starving?) people in the world leaped from 848 million in 2003-05 to 963 million in 2008. And while wealthy states had pledged $12.3 billion at a mid-2008 summit to alleviate hunger only $1 billion had been disbursed by year end;[52] this while trillions of dollars were being pledged to global banks and private financial intermediaries on the losing end of gambles in the neoliberal casino.

Over the 2009-10 period unemployment worldwide is projected to rise by 50 million, though this figure could easily double, according to the UN. Between 73 and 103 million people are expected to fall into poverty with the greatest impact in East and South Asia. Again, however, the UN notes this to be an underestimation (India is the case where much of the renewed poverty will occur). There is direct evidence of the dynamic consumer goods export sectors currently shedding jobs and the workers either entering the ranks of unemployed or finding their way back to the rural areas they had earlier migrated from. In China alone 20 million workers had lost jobs by the end of 2008. The crisis-induced trend toward shedding of jobs and reverse migration contributes further to expansion of the informal economy we noted above and will take years to reverse—up to 2015, it has been estimated,[53] though this hinges on an impending economic recovery which still seems distant.

A summer 2009 meeting of the UN Economic and Social Council, that incidentally upped the tally for crisis spawned poverty to 130-155 million human beings, added to the litany of Wall Street meltdown sparked ills of high and erratic food prices, rising unemployment, diminutions in global growth and trade—the specter of climate change and its exacerbating of all the economic problems faced by the world. Where it sees further strife emerging as a result of the aforementioned is in the area of what is referred to as "social cohesion".[54] In the developed states we have already seen the eruption of social strife and protests in countries as varied as France, Greece, Britain and Iceland.[55] In the third world protest over jobs will be combined with social struggles over food as the growing incidence of violent food-agriculture related protests indicate. In fact, with developed states and the wealthier third world so-called emerging market states using the global crisis as leverage to gain access to food supplies in vulnerable countries by purchasing land and usage titles ("land grabbing" as it is dubbed)[56] it may be that global starvation will preempt environmental Armageddon as the concluding chapter in the neoliberal saga unless powerful social collectivities emerge to force change.

Part I

BRIC and the Neoliberal "Emerging Market" Myth

Introduction

Brazil, Russia, India and China, collectively referred to by the acronym BRIC, have been at the forefront in mainstream business press forums as key geospatial poles of economic growth and as destinations for high-return-hungry investors. Information on such so-called emerging markets focuses predominately on macro growth rates and on the vibrancy of core economic sectors that business analysts have singled out. Television programs promote views of economic vibrancy in BRIC states with exposes on glittering night life and mega shopping malls featuring all the well known brand name outlets; such ensconced in new steel and glass megalopolis urban capitals. Yet realities of life for the bulk of populaces in BRIC states are quite different. In Part 1 of this book three BRIC states—Brazil, India and China—are treated in terms of their development record under global neoliberalism and their future development prospects under the threat of rotating neoliberal economic crises, the most recent unfolding from 2007.

In Chapter One Paul Cooney argues that the actual achievements of economic development in Brazil have been the diametrical opposite of what neoliberal policy architects predicted. Cooney picks up Brazil's development story at the juncture of the 1982 third world debt crisis which prompted a major economic policy shift among third world states away from import substitution industrialization (ISI). The chapter chronicles Brazil's journey under neoliberal and Washington Consensus tutelage through what he sees as the main phases of neoliberalism, culminating in what Cooney refers to as "late neoliberalism" which paradoxically was pursued by ostensibly center-Left governments. The chapter concludes with a clear examination of the conditions currently existing in the Brazilian economy and its future prospects under the cloud of the unfolding Wall Street-sparked meltdown.

In Chapter Two, Ananya Mukherjee Reed examines the interplay between the basic contradictions of global neoliberalism and problematic conditions of development in India—the latter including India's gapping social class and caste divisions, persisting travails in agriculture and regional diversity. She goes on to deal with questions of poverty and social inequality reduction in India under the aegis of neoliberal policy. Mukherjee Reed concludes by asking some pointed questions about what development means in the neoliberal context and suggests alternative meanings of development along with discussion of the potential for social groups in India to mobilize to implement alternative visions of development.

In Chapter Three, Minqui Li recognizes the dynamism that has marked China's meteoric rise in the global neoliberal economy. However, the central concern of his chapter is with what he views as the key impediments to China's dynamism enduring into the future. Minqui traces the process of neoliberalism's rise in China and the extent to which the Chinese economy has come to depend for its vibrancy upon export markets—predominately that of the US. His analysis then turns to deep-seated problems of China's growth trajectory that are only now becoming visible—working class discontent and the depletion of global energy resources coupled with the environmental costs of deploying existing resources integral to China's hothouse development.

Chapter 1

"LATE NEOLIBERALISM" IN BRAZIL

SOCIAL AND ECONOMIC IMPACTS OF TRADE AND FINANCIAL LIBERALIZATION

Paul Cooney Seisdedos[1]

Introduction

Starting with the debt crisis of 1982, many developing countries began to make a structural shift in their economies. The dominant perception was that the development model of import substitution industrialization (ISI), which had prevailed in the majority of Latin American countries from the 1930s–1970s, had reached its limit and was exhausted. From then on, the neoliberal model of development came to dominate.

Neoliberalism arose as an ideology in the middle of the twentieth century and came to dominate economic policies worldwide during the 1980s.[2] There were several dimensions or aspects involved with the rise of neoliberalism: ideological, political, theoretical and the real economy. The main factors which facilitated the rise of neoliberalism in Latin America were the debt crisis of the 1980s, the strong influence of the IMF and the role of the Washington Consensus. The Presidents of Mexico, Argentina and Brazil (Salinas de Gortari, Menem, and Collor, respectively) employed a rhetoric which defended reforms as necessary in order to pursue a modern economy and subsequently implemented neoliberal policies in their countries. These policies included the liberalization of trade and finance, privatizations and labor flexibilization.

After twenty years of the dominance of these neoliberal policies, it important to assess the reality in Latin America with respect to the neoliberal claims or promises. Indeed, the achievements in economic growth have been far less—if not the exact opposite—of what neoliberals predicted. The general results for Latin America have been low rates of GNP growth, low wages, an increase in unemployment and poverty for the majority of Latin–American populations, not to mention financial crises and even depressions.[3]

It is important to note that the transition to neoliberalism took place in different periods across the different countries. For the majority of Latin America, this shift took place during the first half of the 1980s, but in the case of the Southern Cone, for example (Argentina, Chile and Uruguay), this change occurred after the military coups of the 1970s. Finally, in the case of Brazil, the shift to neoliberalism occurred only as of 1989 when Collor took office and it is therefore referred to here as *"late neoliberalism"*.

This chapter begins with an evaluation of the ISI period followed by an analysis of the transition to the neoliberal model in Latin America in general, and then looks at the particular case of Brazil. Although the shift toward neoliberalism began with the government of Collor, the most significant changes took place during the period associated with the Economics Minister and then President Fernando Henrique Cardoso: 1994–2002. After analyzing the implementation of various neoliberal policies for the period beginning in 1990 and up until the present, this chapter examines the socio-economic impacts on Brazil as a result of the trade and financial liberalizations. In addition to presenting several macroeconomic measures, such as rates of GNP growth, foreign direct investment (FDI), and foreign and internal debt, an evaluation is made of several key socio-economic indicators: real wages, unemployment, poverty and inequality.

The Period of ISI (Import Substitution Industrialization)[4]

After the crisis of 1929, a profound transformation took place with respect to the pattern of accumulation in Brazil. The economy had been following a model of an agro exporting country, with minimal industry. Shortly afterwards, however, industry began to gain autonomy and a new development model was adopted in Brazil: import substitution industrialization. This model was also being pursued by other countries in Latin America, such as Argentina and Mexico, as they attempted to achieve greater economic autonomy after the Second Great Depression, especially given the reduced role played by the US and Europe with respect to the international economy.

The basic idea of ISI is to strengthen national industry by reducing imports of manufactured goods and producing them locally. Brazil pursued the ISI model beginning with the Revolution of 1930 led by Getúlio Vargas after the crisis of 1929–1933, first for light manufacturing, by transferring a large proportion of the surplus generated by agriculture—particularly coffee—to subsidize manufacturing industry.

A significant result was the domination of industry by São Paulo with respect to national markets. The integration of the national market advanced at an accelerated pace, although the national percentage of production in São Paulo grew from 33.8 percent in 1919 to 48.9 percent in 1949. However, this did not imply a regressing or stagnation in the national periphery or hinterlands, since all the other regions had significant rates of growth for industry in this period as well. Nevertheless, the regional imbalance did produce several problems for the Brazilian economy from then on, especially in the North and Northeast regions, where the level of industrialization remained low.

In spite of major advances in areas like São Paulo, during this first stage of ISI the process of industrialization remained limited and dependent on the export sector in order to continue growing. During Vargas' second period (1950–1954) the development of heavy industry began to intensify and from 1956–1960 heavy industry was finally established in Brazil. This period is characterized by the attempt by the national state to reformulate economic strategy. New mechanisms of economic policy and planning were put into place to improve infrastructure: energy, transport, and other strategic industries.

In this sense, both direct and indirect state incentives were important for the infrastructure, strategic industries and the auto parts industry, the latter laying the foundation for the future automobile industry. Overall, the manufacturing sector grew at an annual rate of 6.3 percent between 1928 and 1955, with its percentage of GNP growing from 12.5 percent to 20 percent during this period.

Another important factor that contributed to this development in Brazil was the establishment of new financial institutions formed during the period of ISI. These included the Agricultural Credit Program (*Carteira de Crédito Agrícola*) and the Industrial Bank of Brazil (*Banco Industrial do Brasil*), both established in 1937; and the National Bank of Economic Development (*Banco Nacional de Desenvolvimento Econômico*) formed in 1952.

Just as Vargas is associated with the takeoff of the first stage of industrialization, the presidency of Juscelino Kubitschek (1956–1961) is associated with the deepening of industrialization. Kubitschek's famous program was called the Plan of Goals (*O Plano de Metas*) promising to advance the equivalent of 50 years of progress in only 5 years. The main strategic areas targeted in this plan were energy, transport, construction, steel and other basic industries. A crucial part of this overall development strategy was the construction of the new capital in Brasilia, aimed at reducing the overwhelming predominance of the South and Southeast in Brazil's economy. Finally, two other areas in which Kubitschek aimed to make major improvements were foodstuffs and education. Unfortunately these latter two achieved much less success.

The areas which achieved major advances during Kubitschek's government were the hydroelectric plants, navy construction, automobiles, electrical material and heavy machinery. These became the base for production goods in the country. During the period of 1956 to 1962, GNP grew significantly, at an average annual rate of 7.1 percent, strongly related to the rate of investment which reached 18 percent of GNP in 1958–59. However, the low rate of growth of exports and the increase of imports caused a growing trade deficit and higher rates of inflation and eventually led to a balance of payments crisis.

During the 1960s and 1970s, the military government accelerated industrialization, with high tariff barriers. The government of Geisel (1974–79) began an ambitious program for heavy industry, known as the Second National Development Plan (PND II– *Plano Nacional de Desenvolvimento II*). When it began, the IMF was encouraging Brazil to take on foreign debt, but by the end of the 1970s, the IMF did a 180 degree turn and Brazil's industrialization programs were forced to stop or be setback due to the monetarist shock (see the following Section).

The growth of GDP during the decades of the 50s, 60s and 70s was very strong, especially during the period known as the "miracle" (*o milagre*) from 1967–1974, when the rate of growth was over 11 percent. Even when the ISI model was in decline in the 1970s, the rate of GDP growth was 6.6 percent, which is three to four times the rate of growth achieved during the neoliberal period (See Figure 5 below for a comparison of GNP growth rates). The next section examines the factors which led to the general shift from ISI toward neoliberalism in Latin America.

Transition from ISI to Neoliberalism

During the 1970s, several economic problems arose that were associated with ISI and the role of the state in the functioning of the economy. The dominant problem was the balance of payments crises, reflecting persistent trade deficits as well as problems of fiscal management and corruption. According to Saad–Filho (2002), the three main problems associated with ISI in Brazil were: (1) the fiscal crisis of the State, (2) the alleged inefficiency of the manufacturing and services (especially financial) sectors, and (3) the difficulty in promoting a sufficiently dynamic national system for innovations.[5]

Neoliberals maintain that it is better to reduce the role of the state in order for the economy to function more efficiently, especially public enterprises; thus the call to privatization. This is part of the general critique of the developmentalist state, with the associated industrial policy and specifically the model of ISI, which limited the role of transnational corporations (TNCs) in third world countries. Advocates of laissez–faire or a free–market economy argue that ISI promoted inefficiency and contributed to slower growth.

However, despite the claims by neoliberals that economic growth during the ISI period was limited because of the lack of "freedom" for capital, growth in fact was stronger during the decades dominated by ISI compared to those dominated by neoliberalism, as shown in Figure 5 below. Most mainstream economists considered the ISI model to be exhausted and there was a need to eliminate subsidies and institutional support for industry. It could be argued that it was a particular form of ISI, one which was overly dependent on the TNCs, which exacerbated the problems of the trade balance.[6]

Petrodollars, the IMF and the Shift from Industry to Finance

During the decade of the 1970s, a great deal of capital seeking higher profits than that which industry could yield became available, thus resulting in a significant transfer of capital from industry to financial markets. This was primarily due to the accumulation crisis in the First World, but also due to the high price of oil which generated excess petrodollars. International financial markets played a particularly strong role from the late 1970s through the 1980s and 1990s and continue to up until the present day, and there has also been a shift away from foreign direct investment (FDI) and towards more speculative investment.[7] After the increase in the price of oil in 1973, the excess of petrodollars were being recycled by international banks and through the IMF and World Bank into developing countries, increasing the external debt of many of these countries. In some cases, such as Brazil, Mexico and South Korea, this debt increased by a factor of 3 to 5 times, and was used for the development of industry. In just six years, between 1973 and 1979, Brazil's debt quadrupled from US $12.6 to US $50 billion (see Figure 2 below), with borrowed funds further facilitating the expansion of Brazilian industry. In summary, the abundance of petrodollars combined with the lack of traditional investment opportunities facilitated the debt expansion for many countries spurring on industrialization.

The Debt Crisis, the IMF and Structural Adjustment Programs (SAPs)

Unfortunately, as a number of countries of the third world[8] were deepening their level of industrialization and building up infrastructure often with support of loans from the IMF, the World Bank or the IDB,[9] the rules of the game changed, as monetarists came to hold sway and push toward austerity and structural adjustment programs. During the 1980s, this influence led to imposed recessions both in the core economies but particularly in the "global south", especially after the Mexican debt crisis of 1982–83. For Latin America as a whole the 1980s were known as the "lost decade" and in the case of Brazil, from 1981–89 annual GNP growth was a mere 2.2 percent. The IMF used the debt crisis as leverage for pushing countries to adopt SAPs (Structural Adjustment Programs) or, in other words, neoliberal policies.

The three basic pillars of neoliberalism are arguably trade liberalization, financial deregulation and privatizations of public enterprises, with the flexibilization of labor considered as a fourth. The first two of these pillars will now be considered, as they constitute the focus of this chapter.

Financial Liberalization

Financial liberalization has tended to be associated with policies which attract or accommodate foreign capital. It has often been argued by mainstream economists that one major obstacle for developing countries was the low rate of savings, and that in order to achieve adequate levels of investment efforts were needed in order to provide a healthy environment for foreign capital.[10]

There are several policies associated with financial liberalization. The most significant is the relaxation of the minimum of 51 percent for the national share of investment in any given national firm, thus allowing foreign capital to clearly be the majority owner for national firms. Financial liberalization also includes deregulation or elimination of controls with respect to repatriation of profits and royalties, tax breaks or exemptions. Another major policy shift associated with improving the environment for foreign investment is the strengthening of the local currency.[11] This is seen as necessary in order to calm foreign investor's fears of suddenly having their assets denominated in *pesos* or *reais* drop sharply in dollar terms because of a devaluation of the local currency. This is often achieved through the combination of high interest rates and overvalued exchange rates, which has been the case for several Latin American countries in recent years.[12]

However, an overvalued currency is cause for concern, especially when an unanticipated external shock takes place and a crisis of confidence ensues, such as the currency crisis of 1999 in Brazil (see below). In such cases, it is not clear whether the devaluation or the fear of devaluation will cause a crisis; consider the cases of Mexico in 1995, Brazil in 1999 and Argentina in 2001. Furthermore, an overdependence on foreign investment is not something truly desirable, given the ever–present threat of capital flight, especially without capital controls in place.

When considering foreign direct investment, it is crucial to distinguish between portfolio investment and investment in new physical plant and equipment. If portfolio investment dominates, due to such a high level of liquidity, a minor shift or fear of a shift can lead to a rapid and devastating capital flight, such as in the cases of Mexico in 1994 and Argentina in 2001.[13] In addition, there is empirical evidence of financial deregulation being strongly correlated with capital flight and corruption.[14]

Trade Liberalization

In spite of the predominance of finance during the present period of neoliberal globalization, the push for free trade seems to be the true mantra of *laissez–faire* advocates. In general, when developing countries eliminate or reduce tariffs, national industry is negatively impacted because of the problems of competing with first world TNCs. It is much more difficult to compete against TNCs which have the most advanced technology and therefore much lower costs without protective tariffs. It is therefore a myth that through the elimination of tariffs, there will be an "even" playing field, in spite of claims by the defenders of free trade. Developing countries need to resolve the problem of promoting and developing their own technology (R&D) in order to avoid the dependence connected to importing high–tech and advanced technology, which tends to be the most expensive imports in terms of foreign exchange.

In most of the discussion around free trade, scant reference is made to the historical record, namely, that none of the advanced economies

(G7+) achieved success by pursuing the free trade model advocated today, but rather did so through a combination of incentives for nascent national industry and with significant tariff and non–tariff barriers. The strongest examples are the U.S., Germany, Great Britain, Japan and South Korea.

As opposed to following a free trade approach for development, the most developed economies practiced policies which the Washington Consensus assured developing countries to be a formula for failure. According to Chang,

> A closer look at the history of capitalism, reveals a very different story ...when they were developing countries themselves, virtually all of today's developed countries did not practice free trade (and *laissez–faire* industrial policy as its domestic counterpart) but promoted their national industries through tariffs, subsidies, and other measures.[15]

Chang shows that despite their rather strong stance of encouraging other countries to adopt free trade, the US and Britain "...were in fact often the pioneers and frequently the most ardent users of *interventionist* trade and industrial policy measures in their early stages of development."[16] Unfortunately, the hypocrisy of countries such as the US and institutions such as the IMF and World Bank has not been sufficiently challenged by the countries that are suffering the consequences thereof.

Late Neoliberalism in Brazil

Although the monetarist *Plano Cruzado*[17] was implemented in 1986 and there was also the reform of the financial system in 1988, it can be argued that Brazil only began pursuing the neoliberal model in earnest as of the 1990s when the government of Collor came to power.

Collor de Melo

Between the end of the dictatorship in 1985, the experience of the debt crisis in the mid–1980s, and the problems of hyperinflation at the end of the 1980s, Brazilians were ready for a change as reflected in the more progressive Constitution of 1988. After Lula and the PT (Partido dos Trabalhadores—Worker's Party) won the first round of the election in 1989, it seemed that a shift to the left was finally about to take place. However, thanks to manipulation by the media, and the alleged US's meddling, Lula and the PT's victory was postponed, and the conservative Fernando Collor de Mello pulled off the second–round victory.

Though later than many other countries in Latin America, Brazil was finally making the shift toward neoliberalism. During the short–lived administration of Collor,[18] the neoliberal policy of most significance was trade liberalization, which was implemented gradually starting in 1990. The impact of the shift in import tariffs on domestic industry and employment was stark. The decline of average tariffs from over 40 percent to less than 15 percent in just 6 years is evident below in Figure 4 in the section discussing the impact of trade liberalization for Brazilian industry. Starting with the Collor government, at the end of 1991, several administrations continued neoliberal policies aimed at controlling inflation and attracting foreign capital.

O Plano Real

A major problem for Brazil, like other Latin American countries, was hyperinflation, which, having exceeded 2000 percent in 1994[19] was the principal justification for the *Plano Real (Real* Plan). In addition to introducing a new currency (the *Real), the Plano Real* involved programs that included fiscal reform, elimination of inflation indexation, an overvalued and semi–rigid exchange rate, high interest rates, and a large inflow of foreign capital, much of which was speculative. As Rocha aptly describes in her 2002 article on "neo–dependency" in Brazil:

> The Plano Real, however, was much more ambitious in conception than a mere scheme for stabilization. From the outset, its central premise was that only by slashing inflation could an attractive investment climate be created for foreign investment by multinationals in Brazil.[20]

The rationale was that significant flows of foreign direct investment (FDI) were necessary for Brazil to achieve long–term growth, and that the *Plano Real* as the Cardoso maintained—would also improve productivity and effectively help national industry by achieving competitiveness of Brazilian exports on the world market.

The government argued that "a healthy investment climate to attract foreign investors" could be achieved through the elimination of inflation. Indeed, after reaching monthly rates of 50 percent in June 1994, rates of inflation fell to 6 percent in July of 1994 thanks to the *Real* Plan. So in that sense, it was a success. The Cardoso government, which began in 1995, argued that inflation had to be lowered to attract foreign investment and that such FDI would help finance the deficit in the balance of payments, and modernize industry and technology, thus improving productivity and the overall level of competitivity of Brazilian exports. This was quite a tall order given FDI's sullied history for the Third World, but this argument continued to have currency, despite the inevitable failure, as seen below.

Brazil experienced an unprecedented financial liberalization during the 1990s; a major feature of which was the encouragement of short term funds. Accommodating foreign capital became the main emphasis in an economic policy which was based on an overvalued currency, trade liberalization and high rates of interest. As in the cases of Argentina and Mexico, this kind of financial liberalization was key for the shift to the new model, but the increase in FDI also increased the external vulnerability (see section below). The deregulation of the economy was responsible for Brazil's new insertion in the world economy. In fact, Brazil went from having the third largest trade surplus in the world during the 1980s—only behind Japan and Germany—to having an economy with a trade deficit, immediately after the *Real* Plan was adopted.

De Oliveira & Nakatani (2007)[21] argue that instead of promoting growth the *Plano Real* proved to be the opposite. Growth for Cardoso's first term was just 2.6 percent and an even lower 2.1 percent for the second term, similar to the first years of the Lula government, which was 2.6 percent. In fact over the period 1996–2005 the average growth rate has been just 2.2 percent. It is even worse when considering GDP per capita growth in Brazil—only 0.7 percent for the same period.[22]

Cardoso's Government

Even though Collor was the first Brazilian president to initiate the shift toward neoliberal policies,[23] it was really Cardoso, as economic minister, who was key in the implementation of the *Plano Real* described above. And although Collor achieved the initial trade liberalization and some deregulation, it was Cardoso's presidency that clearly put Brazil solidly on the neoliberal path. The shift to accommodate foreign capital was unequivocal, with major influxes of foreign investment as well as imports shortly after he came to power.

Foreign Direct Investment

As clearly reflected in Figure 1 below, the net flows of foreign direct investment increased significantly from a mere US$2.1 billion in 1994 to US$10.8 billion in 1996, more than a 5–fold increase in just 2 years. Volatile portfolio investment constituted a significant part of this increase: 46.5 percent of the total in 1993, then 58 percent in 1994, 45.9 percent in 1995 and then declining to 32.4 percent in 1996.[24] After Congress eliminated several constitutional restrictions in 1995, this flow increased even more, growing to over US$32 billion by 2000. However, between 2000 and 2003, this flow plummets down to just over US$10 billion and then surges back up from 2004–2007 reaching over US$34 billion in 2007. Such volatility calls into question the logic that FDI flows will reduce Brazil's external vulnerability and insure stability and economic growth.

The *Plano Real* also attracted short–term speculative funds, reaching a net total of some US$23 billion. In fact, in addition to one of the highest rates of interest worldwide, the government permitted absolute freedom of capital movement and particularly advantageous tax–exempt mechanisms known as CC5s, which are bank accounts for non–residents with free access to floating exchange rates.[25] In fact this is a significant aspect of the context which led to the currency crisis of 1999.

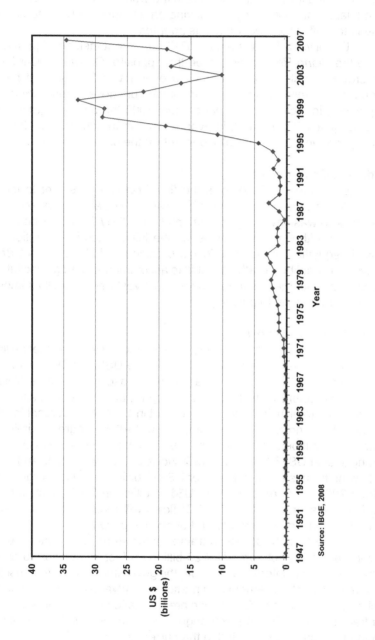

Source: IBGE, 2008

Figure 1: Foreign Direct Investment in Brazil: 1947–2007 [26]

The Currency Crisis of 1999

After the economic crisis in Russia during 1998, like in the case of the "tequila effect" caused by the Mexican crisis, the Brazilian economy felt the impact of another external shock. As Rocha (2002) describes it:

> This time international confidence was only restored—temporarily— when the US orchestrated an IMF bail out of $41.5 billion to postpone the now inevitable currency collapse till after Washington had made sure of Cardoso's re–election in October 1998.[27]

However, after the election it was only a few more months before the inevitable collapse in the form of an intensive speculative attack on the *real* in January 1999. Billions of dollars a day were taken out of the country, thereby forcing the Cardoso government to let the *real* float on world markets. The exchange–rate anchor that had been the centerpiece of the *Plano Real* was undermined, and $50 billion in foreign reserves were lost in an attempt to prevent the inevitable devaluation: an eventual loss of two fifths of its value with respect to the dollar. According to De Oliveira and Nakatani:

> External vulnerability and the international financial crises of the 1990s brought down the economy in late 1998. After the currency collapse in early 1999, macroeconomic policy was changed, with three main priorities: low inflation, free–floating exchange rates, and generation of primary surpluses to avoid more debt.[28]

In spite of the crisis of 1999, the neoliberal approach remained intact, both for the remainder of the Cardoso government and into the Lula administration, contrasting sharply with the election rhetoric critical of Cardoso's policies.

Lula's Government

After losing three consecutive elections, Lula and the PT finally won an election in October 2002. Despite the platform of the PT describing their commitment to social justice and worker's rights and criticisms of the policies of the Cardoso government, there was more of a continuity of the policies pursued by the Lula government than a break with the past. Yet the infiltration of neoliberal ideas within the economic policy formulations of the PT go back to the 1990s, so it was not really a case of the PT shifting its perspective once it came to power. As 2003 progressed, there was general disillusion among Brazilian progressives, as the possibility of serious change dropped off the horizon, in spite of the PT's campaign promises. Nevertheless, the Lula government implemented a number of social programs, albeit on a limited scale, in order to counter or ameliorate the worst aspects of neoliberal policies.

External Vulnerability,[29] *Foreign Debt and Internal Debt*[30]

The results of the policies that combined an overvalued *real* with extremely high rates of interest can be seen as a success from the point of view that, in the short run, it minimized external vulnerability, thanks to significant increases in foreign reserves and FDI. In addition, there was a reduction of the foreign debt from US $241 billion in 1998 down to US $188 billion in 2005, which then went back up to US $240 billion in 2007, as seen in Figure 2. Since the end of the Cardoso administration, the foreign debt as a percentage of GDP fell from 45.87 percent to 21.28 percent in December 2005. In the same period, the foreign debt service fell from 10.09 percent of GDP to 6.11 percent. However, in order to achieve these improvements, Brazil has been reducing external debt at the expense of increasing internal debt, thereby giving the appearance of reduced external vulnerability.

In fact, however, the internal debt is being increased substantially and at rates of interest significantly higher than the foreign debt being paid down. The rate of external debt tended to be around 4 percent, while the rate of internal debt is contracting at almost 13 percent annually.[31] Therefore, the shift from external to internal debt is a situation that is actually worsening the overall indebtedness for governments in the future.

The internal debt grew from 13.9 percent of GNP in 1991 to over 51 percent in 2006, which was a significant increase. One of the major increases took place during the first years of the *Plano Real*, when it went from 20.8 percent in 1994 to 39.2 percent in 1999, after the currency crisis. During the Cardoso government from 1999–2003, it showed a relative stability. With the exception of 2004, the public internal debt grew continually during the Lula government from 41.2 percent at the end of 2002 to 51.6 percent of GNP in October 2006,[32] which implied a real increase of 25 percent in just four years. This increase was not as drastic because it was accompanied by a drop in the external public debt as a result of the overvalued *real* and the strategy of accumulating international reserves by the Central Bank. It was therefore possible to reduce the net debt of the public sector during this period.

The net public debt (external and internal) grew significantly from 32.5 percent of GNP in 1994 to a maximum of 57.3 percent in 2002. Although its percentage of GNP decreased slightly in recent years, the absolute value continues to grow. Figure 3 below shows the strong growth of the internal debt from roughly US$600 billion to US$1600 billion during the period 2001–2007, and the increase of internal debt is much greater than the decrease of external debt.

The nature of internal debt is that it tends to be short term and valued at higher rates of interest, and accommodating, in particular, foreign investors. The problem created by this phenomenon is that the burden taken on by the government—and therefore the Brazilian people—implies a worsening of the debt situation overall. It is therefore critical to examine the basis behind the shift from foreign debt to internal debt, identifying the primary beneficiaries and the probable losers. The former tends to

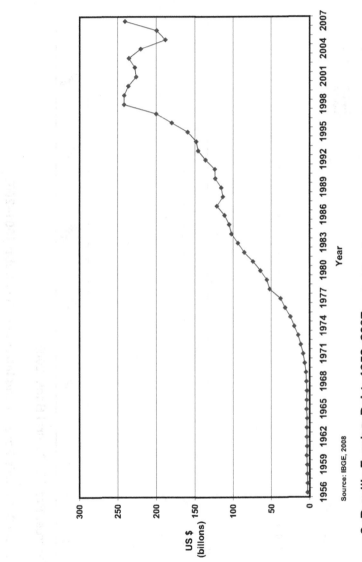

Source: IBGE, 2008

Figure 2: Brazil's Foreign Debt: 1958–2007

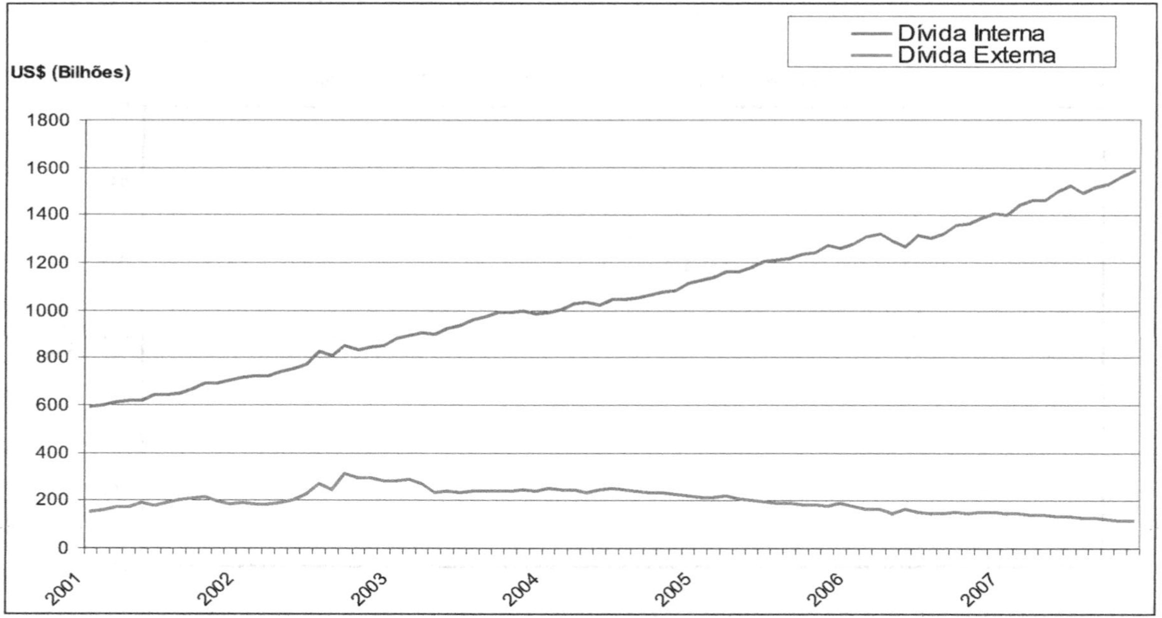

US$ (Bilhões)

— Dívida Interna
— Dívida Externa

Source: Brazil's Central Bank, 2007

Figure 3: Brazil's Foreign and Internal Public Debt: 2001–2007

correspond to foreign investors and the Brazilian elite, while the latter is the great majority of working class Brazilians.

For example, as the financial crisis in the US was worsening in October 2008, causing a growing uncertainty on world markets, Brazil lost over 10 percent of its international reserves in just a few weeks. Since that time, Brazil's economy appears to have entered a recession, as many other countries have during the present world economic crisis. In terms of GDP, Brazil suffered one of the largest drops in GDP in the fourth quarter of 2008: –3.6 percent. In terms of Brazil's labor market, which is further discussed below, formal employment is at its worst level in 10 years, and those requiring unemployment insurance reached a record level—17 percent, as unemployment increased 14 percent between October 2008 and January 2009, reaching 15.1 percent for the six major metropolitan areas as of March, 2008. Although it is difficult to forecast the near future, a worsening of the situation is expected for Brazil in the short term. Before speculating further on the impact of the current world crisis on Brazil's economy, the socio-economic impacts of trade and financial liberalization up to the present will now be considered.

Socio-economic Impacts of Financial and Trade Liberalization

A major concern for the Brazilian economy is the extent to which it is pursuing a trajectory oriented toward the interests of TNCs operating in Brazil, whether they are industrial or financial firms, often at the expense of national interests. As a result of the trade and financial liberalizations, national industry has more difficulties in competing successfully. First, with the highest or close to highest rates of interest in the world, the costs of borrowing are greater, and therefore reduce the competitivity of national firms. Second, the elimination of tariffs implies a far more difficult terrain in which to compete against TNCs within Brazil, far from the "level playing field" claimed by "free trade" advocates. Third, TNCs are often granted far better terms than are national firms: various regulations or taxes are relaxed for TNCs or foreign investors, but not for local firms. Finally, with an overvalued currency, imports are much cheaper and it is more difficult for Brazilian products to compete either at home or in world markets.

As national industry encounters more problems, this has repercussions for wages and profits and therefore, income in general. With a decrease in the overall output level of Brazilian manufacturing, there will be a decline in both manufacturing jobs and a lack of growth of real wages for manufacturing employees. For example, Brazil lost more than one million industrial jobs during the period 1989–1997 alone. Such declines are consistent with relatively stagnant real wages and a significant increase in the informal economy. Thus, even if unemployment may begin to decline, the tendency is that better paid jobs in Brazilian manufacturing will be replaced by precarious, lower–paid informal work, which is not a positive trend for the Brazilian economy.

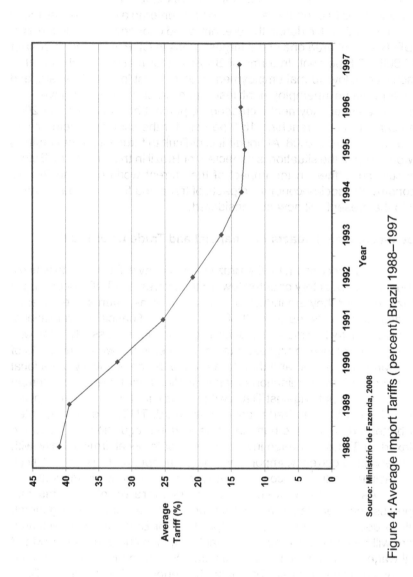

Source: Ministério de Fazenda, 2008

Figure 4: Average Import Tariffs (percent) Brazil 1988–1997

Therefore, an increasing preoccupation, as was the case of Argentina, is whether Brazil is beginning to reverse the process of industrialization, which it began in the 1930s, and becoming more oriented toward agro–exports and less oriented toward manufacturing industry.[33] The statistics of the percentage of GNP attributable to industry have not shown a clear tendency for a decline, although there has been increasing concern among Brazilian economists.[34] In fact, Brazil's ranking in terms of competitivity and industrial capacity and industrial exports has been falling compared to other developing countries during recent years.[35] For example, between the years 1989–1999, Brazilian manufacturing exports as a percentage of world exports declined from roughly 0.8 percent down to 0.5 percent, while Brazil's exports of raw materials grew from around 2.2 percent to more than 3 percent of world exports.[36]

The clearest measure with respect to trade liberalization is the reduction in average import tariffs, which fell from more than 40 percent in 1988 down to only 13 percent in recent years (see Figure 4 below). The worst example is that of capital goods which have tariffs approaching 0 percent, with certain exceptions. This basically makes it impossible for national high–tech firms to survive within Brazil.

Prior to the outbreak of the world crisis, the Lula government has enjoyed a period of quite high prices for *commodities* on the world market in recent years, and thus, in spite of disadvantageous policies for domestic firms, has been able to maintain a trade surplus. However, as a result of global recession, these positive results were reversed briefly in January 2009, though followed by a slight rebound thanks to commodity markets in early 2009.

Another major neoliberal shift was the move toward privatizations, which allowed an increasing number of foreign firms to increase their investment and effectively buy up Brazil's national patrimony. In various sectors of the economy, there was a notable increase in the degree of internationalization of production. The presence and domination of TNCs was most notable in the following sectors: foodstuffs, automobiles, computers, pharmaceuticals, hygiene and cleaning, plastics and rubber among others.[37] As national industry encounters problems it leads to a spreading of problems for other parts of the Brazilian economy: a decline in employment, wages, and income, and the overall capacity for the economy to grow.

Growth

As pointed out by De Oliveira and Nakatani, although the Lula government seems to have achieved the economic fundamentals in accordance with the IMF and the Washington Consensus this has not led to significant growth.[38] In fact, for the period of 1996–2005, Brazil only grew at an annual rate of 2.2 percent and during 2005 as the world grew at a rate of 4.3 percent, Brazil only reached 2.3 percent. Nevertheless, during the last couple of years of the Lula administration, growth has been improved, reaching between 4–5 percent annually for 2006–2007. Yet, as

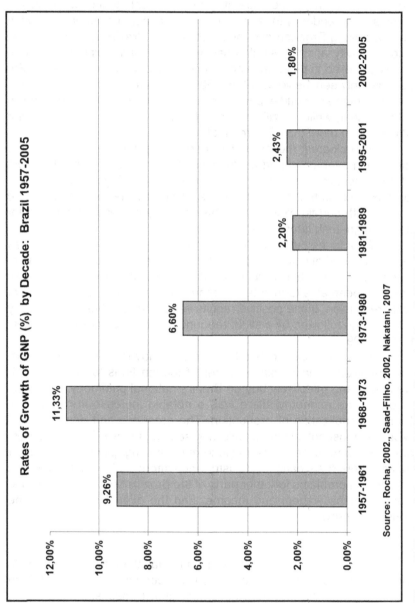

Figure 5: Rates of Growth of GNP by Decade: Brazil 1957–2005

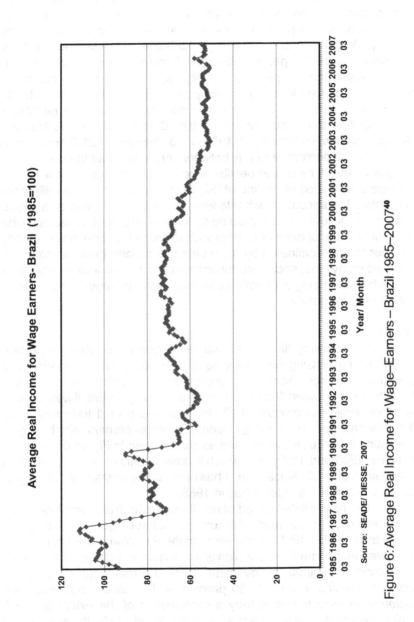

Average Real Income for Wage Earners- Brazil (1985=100)

Source: SEADE/ DIESSE, 2007

Year/ Month

Figure 6: Average Real Income for Wage–Earners – Brazil 1985–2007[40]

just mentioned, in spite of an international situation much more favorable than during the years of the Cardoso administration, growth has only been minimally better.

The advocates of neoliberalism argued that the ISI model led to stagnation, and that through trade and financial liberalization, higher rates of growth, productivity and wages would be achieved. The reality is that the neoliberal period had much lower rates of growth than that of the ISI period, as can be seen in Figure 5 below. The first three columns correspond to the ISI period, with annual growth rates of 9.26 percent, 11.33 percent and 6.6 percent, respectively. In contrast, the last three columns correspond to the neoliberal period. Overall, the growth rates of the ISI period are more than triple the rates during the latter neoliberal period. During the period known as the "Brazilian Economic Miracle" (*Milagre Econômico Brasileiro*), 1968–1973, the annual GNP growth rate reached 11.33 percent, which is between four and a half to over 6 times the growth rates for the three neoliberal periods considered. Yet even if one considers the period of decline of ISI, 1973–1980, when it was allegedly exhausted, the annual growth rate was 6.6 percent, which is on average three times the level achieved during the neoliberal period. Thus, using the conventional benchmark of GNP growth rates, the ISI period was clearly superior to that dominated by monetarism and neoliberalism. However, there are many other socio–economic aspects to be considered other than GNP when assessing economic well–being, such as wages, employment, poverty and inequality.

Wages

In a country like Brazil, wages is one of the most important variables for assessing the well–being of the majority of the population, and unfortunately, wages have been suppressed for decades, if not centuries. Nevertheless, between 1955 and 1986, the real wage in Brazil was growing at a rate similar to productivity.[39] However, the overall trajectory since then has changed. The average income for wage–earners, which roughly corresponds to the real wage, and as can be seen in Figure 6 below, fell between 1985 and 1992, after which it grew slightly until 1997, and then fell again until 2002. Since then, it has been stable or stagnant at roughly 50–55 percent of the value it had in 1985.

During the initial period of neoliberalism in Brazil, with Collor and then Cardoso, it is not much of a surprise that average wages remained below their level in 1985. However, with the PT (Workers' Party) coming to power, many anticipated a significant increase, instead of continued stagnation or minimal improvement. Thus, the real wage for Brazilian workers remains at roughly 50 percent of the value it had when the *dictatorship ended!* This is truly a confirmation of the extent to which maintaining neoliberal policies is a much greater priority for the government than the interests of workers in Brazil today, in spite of a government led by the Worker's Party!

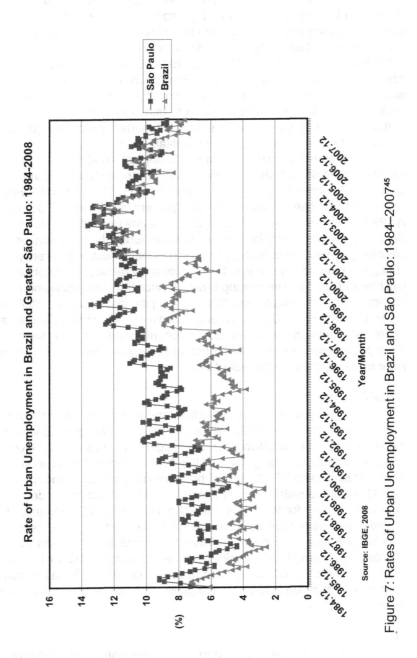

Figure 7: Rates of Urban Unemployment in Brazil and São Paulo: 1984–2007[45]

Unemployment and Underemployment

As discussed above, the combination of high interest rates, the overvalued *real* and the trade liberalization which began in 1990, brought about the elimination of firms with high costs and low profitability and a concomitant increase in the rate of unemployment,[41], growing from less than 5 percent in 1990 up to almost 14 percent in 1999, as can be observed below in Figure 7. Between 1990 and 1997, 1.9 million people lost formal jobs in industry and roughly another half million in services. Between 1990 and February 1999 3.2 million people lost their jobs. The employment situation clearly became more precarious, whether we consider job losses or the growing dependence on the informal market, which has grown to as high as 50 percent in certain metropolitan areas.[42]

Although the Brazilian Institute of Geography and Statistics (IBGE) has expanded its definition of unemployment, progressive economists tend to have more confidence in estimates by DIEESE or SEADE[43] which estimated total unemployment to be 14.2 percent in 1998 and 18.3 percent in 1999.[44] Independently of which data source one uses, there has been a clear tendency for unemployment to increase during the neoliberal period beginning in 1990, although there has been a clear reduction in recent years during the Lula administration. This tendency of reduced unemployment has now switched to a worsening situation since the world economic crisis became manifest in September 2008. During the last quarter of 2008 and the first quarter of 2009, Brazil has lost between one and one and a half million jobs, and as mentioned above, unemployment for the six major metropolitan regions reached 15.1 percent in March 2008, with continued increases expected for the rest of 2008.

Social Programs

From a progressive perspective, one of the few positives of the Lula administration was the *Bolsa Familia* program, designed to improve the situation for the Brazilian poor and indigent. It is basically an income transfer program, providing roughly US$ 40–80 a month for the poorest of Brazil, totaling some R$ 27.7 billion, between 2003 and 2007 and reaching over 11 million households. It combined several other programs designed to provide money for food, gas and schooling for Brazil's poorest. This program was also seen as instrumental in the reelection campaign of Lula in 2006, when the number of families receiving the transfer almost doubled: increasing from 6.5 million families in March 2005, to 11 million families in March 2007. In addition to reducing poverty it was perhaps even more significant in reducing inequality as it was aimed at the lowest income strata.

Inequality

For convenience and popularity, the dominant measure of inequality—the Gini coefficient—is considered for Brazil. In 1976, the Gini coefficient for Brazil was 0.62, and this value was only surpassed during

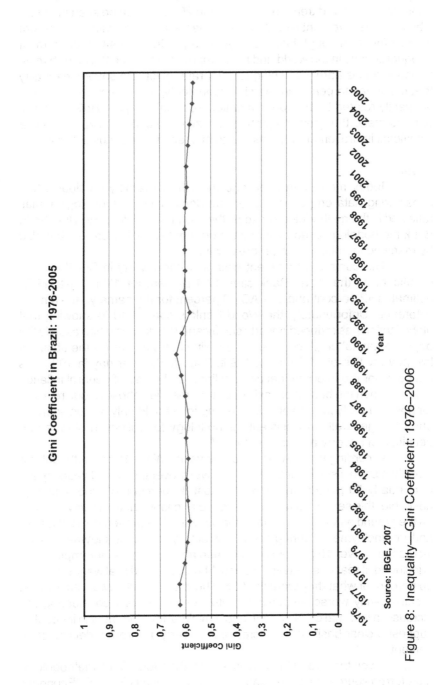

Figure 8: Inequality—Gini Coefficient: 1976–2006

the period of hyperinflation in 1989 (0.635). Since then there has been a generally downward trend to reach 0.57 in 2005. As can be seen in Figure 8 below, the movement over thirty years has been slight, with some recent improvement. Although just 4 or 5 years ago, Brazil was the fourth most unequal society in the world and it has improved to be the 9th or 10th most unequal, this is hardly anything to celebrate, given the severe inequality that continues to persist in Brazil. Undoubtedly, this recent improvement is directly related to the above-mentioned social program *Bolsa Familia*, unfortunately, the great majority of Brazilians have not experienced a significant improvement with respect to their economic status or livelihood.

Poverty

Today more than ever, one must be extremely cautious when considering data on poverty, given the dominance and ideological bias reflected in the methodology used by the World Bank. Not only is the World Bank methodology used by many government statistics' offices, but also by many economists, even progressives.

The contrast of different estimates for poverty in Brazil is quite significant as the World Bank cites 17.4 percent for 1990, while IPEA estimates 42 percent and ECLAC 48 percent for the same year—a huge difference. Unfortunately, the World Bank is committed to showing that globalization has reduced poverty significantly worldwide when exactly the opposite has taken place. The three main criticisms are (1) the absurdly low poverty line of $1.25 in the US in 2005 (US$1 per day in 1985), as the basis for the international poverty line, (2) the use of general inflation indexes when the basket of basic goods, namely just those goods relevant for poor or nearly poor people's consumption should only be considered[46] and (3) a generally inconsistent methodology for collection of data and definition of poverty across countries.[47]

According to IPEA, which employs the World Bank methodology, there has been a significant decline in poverty over the last 30 years, going from nearly 50 percent in 1976 to almost 30 percent in 2005. Although desirable, this seems quite dubious, once one looks at the reality in Brazil on the ground as well as considers the statistics just presented: real wages and unemployment. During the last twenty years unemployment alone increased to over 10 percent and as seen above, once underemployment is included, it reaches between 12 and 14 percent, and real wages are only 50 percent of what they were in 1985. Therefore, much lower real wages, a significantly worse employment situation, especially considering the increase in informal employment, and a minimal improvement in inequality, suggest a clear basis for an increase in poverty, far from a decline of 20 percent.

Given the strong bias involved with the World Bank methodology, a preferred source of poverty data for Latin America is ECLAC (Economic Commission for Latin America and the Caribbean), which is shown in Figure 9 below. Despite the fact that poverty grew during the 1980s in Brazil, a reduction is evident since the 1990s. Given the introduction of social

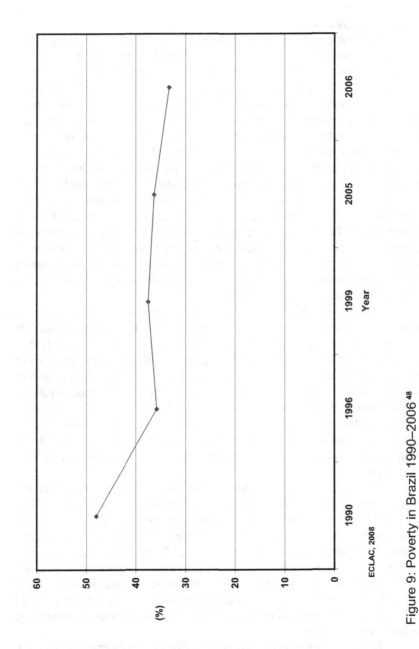

ECLAC, 2008

Figure 9: Poverty in Brazil 1990–2006 [48]

programs aimed at alleviating the situation for the poorest in Brazil, it can be argued that these improvements are more related to such social programs which aimed to counter the most deleterious impacts of neoliberal policies.

Winners and Losers

In evaluating the overall impact of the financial and trade liberalizations implemented in Brazil as it shifted toward neoliberal policies through the 1990s, it is crucial to identify the main beneficiaries and those that were socially excluded or experienced a worsening economic situation.

The neoliberal macroeconomic polices of increasing the rate of interest and an overvalued exchange rate were designed to increase and accommodate foreign capital coming into Brazil. In addition, there has been significant deregulation, reduction of taxes, and easing the process of repatriation of profits, royalties, etc. Thus, it is clear that the TNCs and foreign financial corporations operating in Brazil have benefited substantially. Brazilian banks have also clearly benefited, achieving record high profits in 2006 and 2007. The Brazilian elite which have investments in the Brazilian stock market (BOVESPA) and in international financial markets have also benefited substantially from the neoliberal macroeconomic policies. Although much of the elite were initially critics of a PT government, they have faired quite well in general since the Lula government came to power in 2003.

In addition to Brazilian banks, the IMF and other international banks have clearly benefited from Brazil's neoliberal turn. For example, Brazil is maintaining its primary surplus at a rather high level, approximately 4–5 percent of GNP, in order to ensure the payment of the *foreign debt*, even higher than originally requested by the IMF. Unfortunately, this implies that by putting aside money to pay debt service and accommodate foreign banks, there is less money available for *social programs*. As described above, the shift from external toward internal debt is increasing Brazil's external vulnerability and is benefiting those that own this debt while compromising future generations of Brazilians that will have to pay for it through taxes.

The main social program under the Lula government has been the *Bolsa Familia* program, as discussed above. Its budget during 2003–2007 was $27.7 billion, while that paid out to foreign bankers was R$263.3 billion. Thus, service for the foreign debt was almost ten times what was spent to alleviate poverty temporarily. In fact, what Brazil truly needs is a jobs program to reduce unemployment and improve real wages in order to make a serious dent in addressing its perennial problem of income and wealth inequality. Such contrasts provide an unfortunate though sobering insight with respect to the true priorities of a government allegedly representing the interests of workers.

Although there has been record profitability for Brazilian banks, the situation for the majority of Brazilian manufacturing firms is another story. In order for Brazilian manufacturing to become more competitive, many firms went out of business or had to lay off many workers, as reflected in the drop in manufacturing employment, and also in the minimal growth of Brazilian workers' wages, if not a decline. In addition to the problem of under and unemployment, well-paid employment remains quite difficult to find in Brazil, and the growth of jobs has tended to be much stronger in the informal sector. It can be argued that this latter and non–desirable result is associated with globalization in Brazil as in so many other countries.

Conclusions

This chapter began by examining the period of import substitution industrialization in Brazil, as was the case in other countries of Latin America. The expansion of industry during this period went through two stages: first light industry followed by an expansion of heavy industry. In spite of these advances and quite significant growth, eventually a number of problems surfaced during the 1970s. Afterwards, the various dimensions of neoliberalism were considered and how it came to dominate economic policies across the globe and particularly in Latin America. Evidently, the accumulation crisis of the 1970s, the growth of petrodollars and the promotion of third world countries' indebtedness played a role among other factors. Undoubtedly, the debt crisis at the beginning of the 1980s was a key moment in the shift from ISI to neoliberalism. The debt crisis provided the leverage necessary for the IMF and the World Bank to force many countries to adopt neoliberal policies, namely, privatizations, and trade and financial liberalizations. However, Brazil made this transition much later than most other countries, as it only took place with the arrival of Collor in 1989, and for this reason the term "late" neoliberalism was used.

Although the neoliberal transition started with Collor, the more substantial shifts began with the *Plano Real* as well as other policies implemented during the Cardoso government. Despite the advances made in reducing inflation, the problems of neoliberal policies became evident with the outbreak of the currency crisis of 1999. Afterwards, the continuity of neoliberal policies under the Lula administration was considered, through identifying certain changes and minor improvements, regarding social programs. This was followed by a discussion regarding the socio–economic impacts of the financial and trade liberalizations. As seen above, the neoliberal period in Brazil experienced much lower rates of growth than the ISI period: roughly between one quarter and one third of the rates during the ISI period. There was also a major reduction in wages during the neoliberal period, leading to Brazilians earning half of what they earned at the end of the dictatorship back in 1985. Unemployment and underemployment has clearly worsened in this period despite a slight improvement in the last few years, followed by a worsening situation since the end of 2008. Lastly, though inequality has diminished slightly and poverty moderately, it is difficult to argue that the overall situation for the majority of Brazilians has improved under neoliberalism, and whatever slight gains were achieved may be quickly reversed as a result of the present crisis.

As the most serious world recession in decades continues, the

Brazilian government and media are doing their best to avoid discussing the possibility of a worsening economic crisis in Brazil. Before considering Brazil's current vulnerability, it is worth considering the serious neoliberal crises which have already occurred in two other major Latin American economies, namely, Argentina and Mexico. Argentina experienced its worst economic crisis ever in its history in 2001–2002 and also suffered two waves of deindustrialization. Mexico experienced its second worst crisis ever in the mid–1990s. After evaluating the results of the Brazilian trajectory to date one should consider the possibility that Brazil will experience a more profound neoliberal crisis similar to Argentina and Mexico, despite whatever differences there may be between them.

Neoliberal crises have become too common since the mid-1990s. They are generally linked to finance, debt and capital flight. Although Brazil reduced its foreign debt and increased its reserves, it continues to be the second largest debtor in the world, after the United States. In addition, what initially appears as a reduction in external vulnerability—the shift from external to internal debt—may in fact be accomplishing exactly the opposite. Another major concern is the lack of capital controls in order to prevent a serious run on its currency or a surge in capital flight in the event of a deepening world recession.

The reality of crises is that they have a clear class dimension, and thus those most negatively impacted are the most vulnerable in society, namely the working poor and unemployed. Although a PT government should be implementing policies favoring workers, the majority of policies are geared toward accommodating the interests of both foreign and national elites. Thus, in the event of a serious neoliberal crisis, unfortunately, the majority of the Brazilian population, not the elites, will be the ones paying the price for years to come.

Chapter 2

NEOLIBERALISM IN INDIA

HOW AN ELEPHANT BECAME A TIGER AND FLEW TO THE MOON

Ananya Mukherjee Reed

The story goes like this. After the British left India in 1947, Jawaharlal Nehru, a fiery orator and a charismatic politician much enamored with "socialism", became India's first prime minister. Upon assuming office, he established "socialism" in India. Under his leadership emerged a massive state apparatus which took over the "commanding heights" of the economy. This state apparatus came to be ruled by a "Brahminical" anti-business rent-seeking bureaucracy which rigidly regulated accumulation and enriched itself by extracting resources from business. The development of capitalism suffered and economic growth sagged. A highly talented business class, which had consolidated itself under the difficult conditions of British colonialism and had supported the nationalist movement, was robbed of the opportunity to offer its talent to the cause of growth, development and poverty reduction.

After Nehru's death, his daughter Indira Gandhi continued this iron rule of "socialism" and went even further (for example, she nationalized the banking system in 1979). Then in 1984, from the rather unfortunate circumstances of her assassination, emerged a new, young leader who waved his magic wand and liberated India's repressed capitalist classes from their chains. He was Indira Gandhi's son Rajiv Gandhi. Though he had no political experience at that time, what he did have was precious: he belonged to India's young elite who owed no allegiance to the so-called "socialism" of his grandfather and was committed to the new mantra of private enterprise, elite consumption, high technology and globalization. He thus set in motion a series of wonderful events as soon as he assumed office. With his economic populism for the elite, he helped unleash the latent powers of consumption of the so-called Indian middle class: the excessively slow "Hindu" rate of growth achieved under the repressive state began to give way to higher growth and higher profitability. The tiger had begun to roar.

There was, however, a cloud in this silver lining: the transition to this higher growth path was predicated on an unprecedented regime of debt and deficits: debt grew from 36 percent of national income in 1980-1 to 54 percent in 1990-1. A fiscal crisis inevitably followed. In addition, the balance of payments crisis also came to a head. In June 1991, India was left with just enough foreign exchange reserves to finance imports for two weeks or so. Then came the assassination of Rajiv Gandhi, and intense political and economic upheaval emerged as its consequence. Out of this crisis emerged immense opportunity. Under the able leadership of Dr. Manmohan Singh who was then the Finance Minister, India opted for a loan from the IMF (Singh was also Governor of the Reserve Bank of India during Rajiv's expansionary period). Structural adjustment and economic reforms soon ensued. And such was the quality of leadership and the supply of entrepreneurial talent that India soon emerged as a global economic powerhouse. Even amidst the current financial crisis, India is projected to grow at 6-7 percent, a much lower growth rate than in the recent past, but high nonetheless compared to the recessionary trends elsewhere. In October 2008, it successfully launched its first moon mission at a cost of approximately $86 million. In November 2008, India entered into a civil nuclear deal with the United States (and subsequently with France) signifying full membership in the elite circle of nuclear prowess.

The story of the rise and rise of India has become a powerful symbolic representation of what neoliberal globalization can do for a nation ravaged by a cumbersome "state". As soon as the state "withdrew", a "miracle" unfolded: growth rates shot to 9-10 percent, poverty decreased from 36 percent to 28 percent; incomes in the organized private sector doubled in a space of ten years; foreign exchange reserves swelled to $36.6 billion, foreign investments grew from $103 million in 1990-1 to $23 billion in 2006-7 and so on.[1] Most importantly, India's political and economic position in the world improved dramatically. This was most evident as I watched the unraveling of the financial crisis. India's Prime Minister Dr. Singh was thus the uncontested star of the special G-20 summit on the financial crisis, America's key nuclear partner as well as its fast emerging partner in the War on Terror.

How are we to interpret this complex of events? In what follows, I attempt one such interpretation by focusing on three related aspects. The first concerns the miracle story itself, and the fractured nature of the miracle. We then go on to examine the second myth: the nature of the state in India. While anyone with any knowledge of India will never contend that India was a socialist state, there exists some serious debate about the nature of state, its "interventionist" incarnation and the nature of its alleged "withdrawal" in the neoliberal era. My main argument in this regard is as follows. While there are significant differences between the regulatory regimes in the two phases, the latter does not represent a "withdrawal" of the state from accumulation, just as interventionism did not represent "state control" of accumulation. What each of these regimes represents are different projects of accumulation and legitimation, corresponding to two different phases in the development of capitalism. In both phases, the state's role has been proactive and essential to accumulation. While its neoliberal configuration has resolved some of the contradictions of the earlier regimes, it has produced new contradictions. How are these to be resolved? The final set of questions concerns the possibilities of transition beyond neoliberalism. We explore these questions by examining the struggles and contestations which have emerged in neoliberal India. Such contestations follow one of two broad "logics". The first embodies a logic *of redistribution* where change is sought to alter market outcomes for disadvantaged groups, without altering underlying institutions and social relations. The second can be seen to embody a *logic of transformation* where social relations, in particular, class relations within institutions of the state and the market are embedded, are challenged. It is important to avoid the pitfall of regarding either of these two logics as "more" or "less" "radical" (or 'more or less possible') than the other. Marginalized social groups may often articulate demands for redistribution. Governments and elites respond to such demands swiftly, either to stall pressures for more fundamental transformation or for electoral gains. The task of progressive politics in such situations becomes rather complex: while demands for distributive justice cannot be trivialized, the danger that they obscure broader projects of transformation also cannot be ignored. This potential conflict between redistribution and transformation has become particularly significant at the current conjuncture and, I believe, is one of the greatest challenges of progressive politics in the neoliberal era.

In what follows, I present a balance sheet on neoliberalism in India. I then go on to explore some aspects of resistance to this neoliberal project. In the final section I consider the implications for development and the potential for social transformation.

Neoliberalism in India: An Abbreviated Balance Sheet

As I mentioned above, the shift to the neoliberal model began with Rajiv Gandhi's regime in the eighties. Its pace accelerated significantly with the finalization of the IMF loan in 1991 and since then has continued under different governments. It became particularly defined under two regimes: the National Democratic Alliance (1999-2004), a coalition led by the Bharatiya Janata Party (the BJP) and the United Progressive Alliance (UPA), led by the Congress. The UPA has been in power since 2004 and elections are due in 2009. The UPA was formed as a coalition of several parties, with support from the Left Front (which comprises an alliance of nine Left parties). All members of the UPA adopted a Common Minimum Program in May 2004.[2] The program sought to balance the divergent mandates of the Left and the Congress until finally the Left withdrew its support in July 2008 over its opposition to the Indo-US Nuclear Deal. In what follows, we examine briefly the economic successes of the NDA and UPA periods

As of 2007-8, India's Gross Domestic Product (GDP) at Purchasing

Power Parity (PPP) was estimated at US$ 5.16 trillion (or US$ 3.19 trillion, depending on estimation methods). With the first estimate, India is the third largest economy in the world after the United States and China, while with the second, it is the fifth largest (behind Japan and Germany). Per capita income at the nominal exchange rate is currently estimated at US$ 1,021 (as such, India is categorized as a low income country by the World Bank).

Table 1 adjacent gives the overall rates of growth as well as sectoral rates. As I noted above, India has experienced some spectacular rates of growth in recent times even though growth rates of different sectors has been quite uneven. The worst performer has been the agrarian sector, which has grown very marginally. While its sectoral share has fallen continuously from 36.4 per cent in 1982-83 to 18.5 per cent in 2006-07, more than half a billion people (and 52 per cent of the workforce) still depend on it for employment and livelihood. Its slow (and at times negative) growth rates have therefore caused much distress in the countryside.

By contrast, both the services sector and the industrial sector have grown well. The Information Technology component of the service sector (in particular outsourcing-related activities), has been growing at more than 30 percent annually with an aggregate revenue of $ 64 billion in 2008. It currently generates direct employment for 2-2.5 million people, indirect employment for another 8-9 million and constitutes 5.5 percent of India's GDP.[3]

Yet another much celebrated aspect of India's economic growth has been the growth of the Indian corporate sector. Table 2 below presents some data on the largest of Indian corporations, as published annually by the Reserve Bank of India. The set represents approximately the largest 2000 public limited companies (i.e. those listed in the stock exchanges). As we see here, their financial performance has been quite commendable. Very recently, the Reserve Bank has also begun to publish data for financial companies (which have recorded a phenomenal 91.6 percent growth in after-tax profitability between 2006-7 and 2007-8).

The most critical part of India's corporate success has been its global dimension. As of 2008, seven Indian companies were listed in the Global Fortune 500 (interestingly, five out of the seven are public limited companies with the Indian government as the majority shareholder; see Table 3 below). Fortune also ranked Ratan Tata-led Tata Steel as the company with highest revenue growth of over 353 per cent between 2007 and 2008.[4]

The Tata Group, which has historically been one of the largest business houses in India, has also emerged as the first Indian multinational (MNC), yet another marker of the global face of corporate India (Table 4 below presents basic data on the Tata Group). Tata Steel's acquisition of the Anglo-Dutch steel company Corus has positioned Tata as the fifth largest steel manufacturer in the world. Tata Motors, another one of Tata group's ventures, recently acquired Jaguar-Land Rover (JLR) for $2.3 billion.[5] Tata is of course not the only overseas investor—Indian companies in every major industrial sector have overseas acquisitions.[6] In 2006, private capital

Table 1 Rate of growth of GDP at factor cost at 1999-2000 prices (per cent)

	9th Plan (1997-02)	2002-03	2003-04	2004-05	2005-06	2006-07	10th Plan (2002-7)	
Agriculture & allied	2.5	-7.2	10	0	5.9	3.8	2.5	2.6
Manufacturing	3.3	6.8	6.6	8.7	9	12	8.6	9.4
Trade & hotels	7.5	6.9	10.1	7.7	9.4	8.5	8.5	12.1
Transport & communication	8.9	14.1	15.3	15.6	14.6	16.6	15.3	
Financing, real estate, housing	8	8	5.6	8.7	11.4	13.9	9.5	11.7
Community	7.7	3.9	5.4	6.9	7.2	6.9	6.1	7
GDP	5.5	3.8	8.5	7.5	9.4	9.6	7.8	8.7
Some additional data (growth over previous year)								
Rate of growth of food grain production				-7.0	5.2	4.2		0.9
Index of Industrial Production				8.4	8.2	11.6		9.0
Rate of growth of foreign currency assets in US $ million				26.2	7.0	29.4		57.9

Source: Based on *Economic Survey 2007-8*, Government of India, p. 5, Table 1.3

Table 2 Key Financials for largest Public Limited Companies, Financial and Non-Financial

Non-Financial Public Limited Companies	1990-91 to 2002-3	01-02 and 02-03	% change between year to year				
			02-03 and 03-04	03-04 and 04-05	04-05 and 05-06	05-06 and 06-07	06-07 and 07-08
Sales	11.7	10.8	18.5	25.2	16.9	26.2	18.3
Profits Before Tax	11	43.5	52.9	52.2	24.4	46.1	21.9
Profits after Tax	9.7	43	55.9	53.8	24.2	45.2	26.2
Financial companies			2003-4	2004-5	2005-6	2006-7	2007-8
Gross profits			18.3	29.5	64.8	26.3	54.5
Profits before Tax			37	36.9	69.8	27.5	52.9
Profits after Tax			23.1	41	75.7	24.6	91.6

Source: Reserve Bank of India

Table 3 Indian companies in the Global Fortune 500, 2008

Name of Indian company	Global Fortune 500 rank	Revenue US $ millions	% of shares owned by Government of India
Indian Oil	116	57,427	80
Reliance Industries	206	35,915	
Bharat Petroleum	287	27,873	54.93
Hindustan Petroleum	290	27,718	51.1
Tata Steel	315	25,707	
Oil & Natural Gas	335	24,032	84.23
State Bank of India	380	22,402	59.73

Source: Global Fortune 500, 2008
http://money.cnn.com/magazines/fortune/fortune500/2008/

Table 4 Financials for the Tata Group

Year	2006-07 (US $ billion)	2005-06 (US $ billion)	% change
Total revenue	28.8	21.9	31.51
Sales	28.5	21.4	33.18
Profit before tax	4.0	3.0	31.7
Profit after tax	2.8	2.1	33.3
Total assets	25.2	18.0	40.0
International revenues (including exports)	10.8	6.8	58.8
Total shareholders	2,923,688	2,302,446	27

Source: Tata Group website [7]

outflow from India exceeded the inflow of foreign direct investment. In 2008, the amount of overseas investments in mergers and acquisitions stood at $26 billion and in the UK alone is reported to have generated almost 4000 jobs.[8]

Let me conclude this section with some data on the expansion of personal wealth and net worth that has occurred in India over the recent past. In 2007, the wealth of the 40 richest stood at $351 billion, up from $170 billion in 2006. With India's GDP at around $1 trillion, that would mean he wealth of the 40 richest amounted to approximately 30 percent of the national income (at market exchange rate). In relative terms the net worth of billionaires in China and the US comprises 3 and 11 percent of their GDP respectively). [9]

Poverty, Unemployment and Inequality

The conventional wisdom about India is that its remarkable economic growth is somehow "trickling" down, and if it is not, moderate redistributive measures can accomplish that task. While there are hardly any arguments against taking steps to ameliorate the vast, unprecedented and unacceptable levels of inequality that we currently see in India, any such measure can at best be partial unless the basic premises of neoliberal globalization are altered.

As I mentioned above, one of the important claims for the success of neoliberal growth in India is that poverty has been significantly reduced. While early claims of poverty reduction have been established to have been exaggerated, there is general agreement now that a palpable reduction in poverty has occurred (roughly from 36 percent in 1993-4 to 28 percent in 2007-8). According to the World Bank, India's poverty rate as a share of the total population went from 60 percent in 1981 to 42 percent in 2005, while the actual number of the poor increased from 420 million to 455 million during the same period (this uses the new poverty line at $1.25 a day).[10] However, the average real disposable incomes and consumption levels also remain abysmally low and unequal (see Table 6). According to the same World Bank report, mean consumption of the poor ($ per day) increased from $0.84 in 1981 to $0.93 in 2005. The government's own data shows that as of 2006-7, in an average household in India's 'miracle' economy, individual consumption was no more than about $12-$22 per month.[11]

Table 5 Indices of inequality in India

Indices	(%)
	3.6
Share of income or consumption, poorest 10%	
Share of income or consumption, poorest 20%	8.1
Share of income or consumption, richest 20%	45.3
Share of income or consumption, richest 10%	31.1
Inequality measures, ratio of richest 10% to poorest 10%	8.6
Inequality measures, ratio of richest 20% to poorest 20%	5.6
Gini index	36.8
Population living below $1 a day (%), 1990-2005	34.3
Population living below $2 a day (%), 1990-2005	80.4
Population living below the national poverty line (%), 1990-2004	28.6

Source: United Nations Development Program, Human Development Reports online database, http://undp.org/hdro

Not surprisingly then, the Global Hunger Index 2008 found the state of hunger in India to be "alarming" with 200 million people suffering from chronic hunger. India scored worse than nearly 25 sub-Saharan African countries and every other country in South Asia except Bangladesh. According to government's own National Family Health Survey (NFHS), 45.9 per cent of children under three are underweight, 39 per cent are stunted, 20 per cent severely malnourished, and 80 per cent anemic. As Utsa Patnaik had argued in her seminal essay *The Republic of Hunger*:[12]

> While everyone understands food shortage as in a drought, namely a physical output shortfall which curtails *supply*, it appears to baffle many that even more severe consequences can arise when the *effective demand,* the purchasing power of the masses falls, so that even though the physical supplies of foodgrains are there, people starve or move into hunger, owing to their inability to purchase food or to access food. The reasons for declining rural mass effective demand in the nineties to date are many, and are all connected with deflationary neo-liberal reforms combined with trade liberalization

Patnaik concluded that almost 75 percent of rural India fell below a minimal nutrition norm (i.e. number of calories people could afford to consume). She also pointed to the disturbing fact that the national poverty lines, which formed the basis of neoliberalism's claims of spectacular success, were set at such low income/expenditure levels that they could not meet the minimal nutrition norm.

The second critical feature of neoliberal growth is the increase in unemployment. According to the Planning Commission of India:

> Non-agricultural employment expanded rapidly at 4.7 per annum during 1999-2005 but this growth was entirely in the unorganized sector and mainly in low productivity self-employment. *Employment in the organized sectors actually declined despite fairly healthy GDP growth...* The wage share in our organized industrial sector has halved after the 1980s and is now among the lowest in the world. One reason for this is increasing capital intensity of the organized sector, another is outsourcing. An issue for policy research is why, despite our factor endowment, organized sector has been choosing to replace labour with capital at this scale and whether there are policy distortions that encourage this which should be corrected. [Emphasis added]

In addition, the Commission laments the "sharp increase in unemployment (from 9.5 percent in 1993-94 to 15.3 percent in 2004-05) among agricultural labor households which represent the poorest groups".[13] Between 1993 and 2000, employment growth slowed to 1.25 per cent per annum but accelerated to 2.6 per cent between 1999 and 2005 between (Economic Survey 2007-8:12).

As indicated by the Planning Commission, net new employment was generated only in the informal unorganized sector. It is estimated that 93 per cent of India's workforce is employed in the informal or unorganized economy. Two categories of workers comprise this informal economy—workers who work in the unorganized sector and informal workers in the organized sector. According to the National Commission for Enterprises in the Unorganized Sector (NCEUS): [14]

- The entire increase in employment in the organized sector between 1990-00 and 2004-5 has been of an informal nature, i.e. the formal sector is in a process of being systematically 'informalized' (p.4).

- 77 percent of the Indian population, about 836 million people lived below $2 a day in 2004-5 (this figure is in purchasing parity terms; in actual terms they had about 50 cents per day per capital to spend on consumption (p.6).

- Wages in the unorganized sector range from Rs.27 to Rs.70 per day (about 50 cents to $.2.50) and are highly gendered.

- A large proportion of unorganized workers remain outside the protection of the Minimum Wages Act (p.43). 85 per cent of all casual workers in rural areas and 57 per cent of them in urban areas earn below the minimum wage (p.48). Agricultural workers in rural areas were the worst off - with nearly 87 per cent of the men and 97 per cent of the women receiving wages below the notional minimum (p.45).

- Most workers worked for more than the legal 8 hours per day. There is one compulsory "holiday" in the week, which is unpaid.

- The overall condition of work across all categories was considered to be "deplorable".

With 93 percent of the workforce in this unorganized sector, it will come as little surprise that the increase in incomes across different categories of Indian workers has been highly unequal (Figure 1). As we see above, incomes of agricultural labor and self-employed non-agricultural labor have decreased between 1993 and 2003 while incomes in the organized private sector have seen the highest growth. The two categories of organized workers who have been well served constitute no more than 7 percent of India's workforce. This exclusive 7 percent comprises the highly educated and skilled professional classes, who also happen to come from the upper/ middle classes and castes. There is very little representation from certain social groups in this workforce. I discuss this below.

Neoliberalism has also seen a deepening of social inequality in India. As is well known, India has a vastly complex and unequal social fabric comprised of different socio-ethnic and socio-religious groups. After Independence, affirmative action was established for some of these groups in areas such as education and public sector employment. While such measures had some success, it remains clear that they have been hardly

**Figure 1. Indices of real per worker incomes
(1993-94=100)**

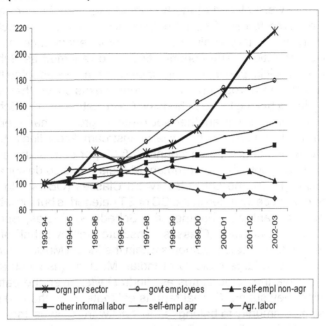

Source: Sen and Himanshu (2006)[15]

able to reverse established patterns of privilege. As such every commission set up by the government has recommended deepening and widening of affirmative action. In the eighties, a government-appointed commission (the Mandal Commission) opined that 52 percent of Indians belonged to "backward classes" and recommended proportionate affirmative action. This unleashed intense social conflict and backlash from the upper classes. A similar controversy was repeated more recently when affirmative action was recommended in state-funded institutions of higher education, in particular India's prestigious and internationally known institutes of technology and management. The arguments were not very different from those we have historically seen in the West, namely, that such policies would force a deviation from the criteria of 'pure merit' and compromise the quality of graduates. Absent from these discussions is the premise that merit itself is socially constructed and dependent on established patterns of privilege. I have examined these issues at length in my recent book.[16] Let me mention a few elements here, primarily to give readers an idea of India's social fabric and the complexity of the problematic of inequality.

There are at least eight religious communities in India. India's Muslim community, with a population of 138 million is the third largest Muslim community in the world and constitutes approximately 14 per cent of India's current population. The majority of Indians are Hindus, but as we know, not all Hindus are equal. Brahminical Hinduism espouses a system of social hierarchy comprising of four "castes". Historically, manual and menial laborers were placed at the bottom of the caste ladder and were subject to extreme forms of social ostracization such as untouchability. Untouchability was legally abolished in India at Independence, as was all forms of discrimination. The communities were renamed as Scheduled Castes (SCs) in official parlance, while social movements adopted the term *Dalit* (literally, the downtrodden). The current census shows that about 16 per cent of Hindus belong to the Scheduled Caste category. The Scheduled Tribes (STs) constitute yet another socio-ethnic group, characterized by similar forms of alienation from the social mainstream. According to the 2001 Census, the Scheduled Tribes account for 8.08 per cent of the country's population. In addition, the Government of India has also designated yet another social group—the Other Backward Classes (OBCs)—to include people who cannot be included in the SC or ST categories but exhibit similar patterns of disadvantage. Together, the Scheduled Castes, Scheduled Tribes and Other Backward Classes constitute well over half of India's population. Of late, radical movements within the Indian Muslim community have claimed that a large majority of Indian Muslims (as much as 80 to 90 per cent) have the same status as Hindu *Dalits*, given the patterns of discrimination they suffer. Official reports estimate more than 40 percent of the Muslim community to belong to the 'backward classes' (see Table 6 for a profile of *Dalit* Muslims and Table 7 for inequality in higher education).

Does neoliberalism and globalization present new opportunities for redressing this kind of inequality? Some argue that this is indeed the case since, as long as access (to education, labour markets etc.) is improved and merit rather than privilege becomes the basis of success, social inequality can be expected to diminish. This is not we have seen so far in India. We return to this below.

Table 5 Indices of inequality in India

Indices	(%)
Share of income or consumption, poorest 10%	3.6
Share of income or consumption, poorest 20%	8.1
Share of income or consumption, richest 20%	45.3
Share of income or consumption, richest 10%	31.1
Inequality measures, ratio of richest 10% to poorest 10%	8.6
Inequality measures, ratio of richest 20% to poorest 20%	5.6
Gini index	36.8
Population living below $1 a day (%), 1990-2005	34.3
Population living below $2 a day (%), 1990-2005	80.4
Population living below the national poverty line (%), 1990-2004	28.6

Source: United Nations Development Program, Human Development Reports online database, http://undp.org/hdro

Table 6 A Profile of Dalit (OBC) Muslims vis-à-vis other socio-religious categories, India, 2004-5

	Literacy[a] (%)	Graduate and above[b] (%)	Employed in the Public Sector (%)	Incidence of Poverty (%)	Low Income (All India) (%)	Middle Income (All India) (%)	High Income (All India) (%)
Hindu General Population	80.5	15.3			8.9	73.9	17.2
Hindu SCs/STs	52.7	2.2			28.6	65.1	6.3
Hindu OBC	65.7	3.2	8.3	27	25.9	72.6	1.5
Muslim General Population	66	2.4	2.7	35	29.3	66.2	4.4
Muslim OBCs	61.9	1.9	0.6	38	32.7	63.5	3.8
All other minorities	75.2	8.9			13.2	68.6	18.2
Total	67.3			28	22.9	69.8	7.3

Source: Compiled from *Social, Economic and Educational Status of the Muslim Community of India: A Report*, Prime Minister's High Level Committee, Cabinet Secretariat, Government of India, November, 2006. [17]

Social groups	Rural	Urban
ST	1.1	10.9
SC	1.2	4.7
Muslim	1.3	6.1
Hindu OBC	2.1	8.6
Sikh	2.8	25
Christian	4.7	23.7
Hindu-Upper caste	5.3	25.3
Other religons	5.4	31.5
All-India average	2.6	15.5

Source: Deshpanded and Yadav 2006.[18]

The Agrarian Crisis

Between 1995 and 2006 as many as 200,000 farmers committed suicide in India.[19] What caused this "epidemic" of suicides? A whole complex of (quintessentially neoliberal) policies has had this devastating effect on the agrarian sector: These include reduced agricultural investment, diminution of agrarian credit, withdrawal of agricultural subsidies, removal of minimum support prices and what is most disturbing, the opening of India's market to the subsidized agriculture of Western states under the aegis of so-called "free trade". A major protest by 50,000 farmers in Mumbai in 2005, for example, had demanded that agriculture be taken out "from the purview of the World Trade Organisation". They demanded further that there be "an increase in the import duty on agricultural commodities and reinstating Quantitative Restrictions to protect Indian farmers".[20] Compounding the problem of state withdrawal was the emergence of "predatory" profiteering in areas of credit, supply of seeds and fertilizers and marketing on the one hand, and the near-complete absence of non-agricultural employment alternatives on the other.[21] These policies were inflicted within a context of already existing agrarian vulnerability and inequality on the land. Recent National Sample Surveys show and increase in landlessness, with a very significant increase in landlessness amongst agricultural labor between 1987 and 2005.[22]

This agrarian crisis must also be seen in conjunction with the nature of growth in the non-agricultural sector that has occurred in the neoliberal period. Broadly speaking, the trend has been one of growing disproportionality between agricultural and non-agricultural growth— marked by a continuous fall in demand for agrarian output against rising input costs.[23] Driven primarily by services, recent non-agricultural growth has not generated much additional demand for agrarian production.[24] The meteoric rise of incomes for certain sections of the population has generated demand for high-end commodities, which has been met by debt-financed imports (rather than domestic production). On the other end of the economic spectrum, the purchasing power of low income households has fallen, with less money available for food. The virtual collapse of all public provisioning of (already inadequate) healthcare, education, transport and similar other needs and the necessity to secure them from the open market have reduced already low income streams to produce a devastating impact on food availability.

Situating the Miracle

India's much-celebrated miracle is thus a rather fractured one—a manifestation of the contradictions of neoliberalism. Two major elements define contradictions: (a) the persistence— and deepening—of the malaise of aggregate demand; and (b) the persistence of structural inequality between different social groups despite the adoption of a secular framework with non-discrimination and affirmative action. Can these contradictions generate possibilities for transformation? For this, we must first turn to history and the specificity of the Indian model of intervention.

As has been extensively argued, state interventionism in India was intervention *for* accumulation, planning was "planning *for* capitalism".[25] Intervention in this sense was rather successful, albeit fraught with its own contradictions. A modern oligopolistic corporate economy did develop in India during (and as a result of) the interventionist regime.[26] However, the architects of intervention neither intended nor were able to systematically link corporate growth and profits (which were consistently higher than many of their counterparts in different parts of the globe) to macro-economic growth, employment, productivity or wage gains for the majority of Indians.[27] Further, corporate profitability was not organically linked to innovations or expansion in domestic productive capacity, in particular the productive capacity of Indian labour; capital intensive technologies were preferred both in public and private sectors during the interventionist regime. Two major sources of profitability were market distortions and state support. The development of infrastructure, supply of cheap inputs and the nationalization and regulation of finance were amongst the key instruments for sustaining corporate profitability. Most importantly, despite the emergence of a large state apparatus, an efficient or adequate distributive mechanism for fulfilling even the most basic needs of India's people could not be established.

There were several consequences of this interventionist model. First, a fiscal crisis emerged, inevitably, as a result of the unidirectional transfer of public resources to the private sector; second, the dominance of oligopolies stifled small business and innovation; and third, the pattern of growth in both agriculture and industry failed to stimulate and widen the base of aggregate demand, while certain sections of the organized working classes and agrarian classes experienced a fairly high growth of disposable incomes. In other words, interventionism had successfully generated the appropriate conditions for a structural shift towards a more neoliberal form of capitalism: the state had performed effectively to set the stage for its own "withdrawal".

Thus, unlike in the West, in India the context for neoliberalism was not characterized by a crisis of profitability, but by a fiscal (and balance of payments) crisis as well as a deeper crisis of aggregate demand. While the political leadership needed solutions to these crises, business saw opportunity. The income growth of the upper classes offered tremendous market opportunities. Indian business was well positioned to profit off of the neoliberal restructuring that was occurring in the West (through measures such as outsourcing, export processing, lucrative sell-offs to global companies etc.). Neoliberalism provided the framework required to mobilize these opportunities; as well, it provided significant—albeit partial— resolutions to the crises of the state, by allowing it to legitimize its selective "withdrawal" from its economic role.

However, it is clear that this shift has not resolved the fundamental problems in the economy for the corporate sector, itself. For example, has the nature of corporate profitability changed? Are profits driven more by innovation and productive capacity rather than state support or market power? With respect to innovation, it is claimed that the emergence of the information technology in India is indeed a story of innovation driven growth. This view is, however, increasingly challenged, in particular by industry insiders. Analysis suggests that the spectacular growth of this sector, led by its role as the "back-office of the world" depends on wage differentials between skilled labor (vis-à-vis the North)—rather than substantive innovation.[28] This actual apathy with regard to radical innovation appears even more ironic in that in India, substantial public investment has been allocated towards the development of Research & Development (R&D) and higher education infrastructure over the last fifty years. However, this massive public investment has so far yielded only private returns. Its developmental returns are far from being realized.[29] Of course, this is just one instance of a larger disjuncture between private returns and social gains, even within the limits of capitalism.

Two factors are important in understanding the disjuncture between private returns and social (and developmental) gain. The first is the choice of technology, which still does not create opportunities for employment (especially in the organized sector). The second involves the exclusionary nature of India's education system, which prevents the majority from acquiring marketable skills and entering the organized sector. However, proposals for widening access through measures such as affirmative action have met with violent resistance from the upper classes. This elite resistance is not new: what is new is the state's increased vulnerability to the claims of the elite and its commitment to the logic of resolving inequalities via the market.

The contradictions of this market logic have become even more evident in the context of the financial crisis. Indeed, the Indian government has moved deftly with appropriate policy responses so as to prevent a major slowdown. Several bailout packages are under consideration, including one for the IT sector. Not only has this intervention been efficiently managed, the official position also repeatedly emphasized that the Indian financial system remains much more regulated than the global system, and hence much less vulnerable to crisis. In other words, the market logic *is* negotiable: by its own account, the Indian state has successfully negotiated this global logic, and has retained controls without sacrificing its growth momentum. Although the present government refused to acknowledge it, these negotiations with the global logic of neoliberalism were an outcome of mobilizations by various social actors, most notably the Left parties who had made major gains in electoral politics in the 2004 elections. (Incidentally, these elections were seen as a comprehensive verdict against the neoliberalism of the earlier government encapsulated in its infamous *India Shining* campaign.)

Strategies for Transformative Politics

The exploration above only reinforces what we already know: that the contradictions of neoliberalism cannot be resolved with "more neoliberalism". In other words, a return of the state in many of the areas from which it has been "evicted" is an obvious priority. However, if we take the state to be a balance of social forces (rather than a Weberian institution), then altering the underlying balance of social forces emerges as the key issue. While neoliberalism has shifted the balance of social forces in one direction, this shift has not occurred without resistance. Two types of resistance to neoliberalism have emerged. The first trajectory embodies demands for redistribution (such as demands for affirmative action, social security, employment guarantees etc.). Irrespective of their potential impact, all of these are in effect demands for a return of the state to areas from which it had withdrawn. The second trajectory reflects a more fundamental resistance to the role of ruling regimes during neoliberalism and a rearticulation of social relations. Ironically, the most visible example of this has been the resistance around the Special Economic Zones (SEZs), and in particular in West Bengal. As is well known, West Bengal has been ruled by a Left Front Government since 1977, with a particularly strong record of land reforms.

Let me highlight just a few aspects of the conflict over the SEZ projects as a full discussion is outside the scope of this paper. Two regions in West Bengal, Singur and Nandigram, were chosen as sites of two industrial development projects. Singur was chosen as the site for an automobile manufacturing project by one of the largest Indian corporate houses, the Tata group. Nandigram was chosen for a high-technology industrial and township complex with investment from an Indonesian investor (the Salem Group). In both cases, the Left Front government attempted to acquire substantial amounts of land, which engendered vigorous resistance. In Singur, those who stood to lose land were primarily absentee landowners, and as such, the size of the compensation package was their major area of contention. Many have argued that the fundamental plan of the Left Government was not flawed—in that it had sought to engender a planned transformation from a low-productivity agrarian structure to a high-productivity high-wage industrial one.[30] The bigger question concerns the completely unidirectional nature of the agreement between the Tata Group and the Left Front government of West Bengal. In approximate terms, the government was committed to invest about *double* the amount relative to the Tatas, and with no returns specified in advance (except for fairly vague promises of employment). The package for the Tatas also included comprehensive tax write-offs, rental and other subsidies with substantial costs to the public exchequer. This deal was struck at a time when West Bengal was in deficit and the Tatas were experiencing substantial revenue growth enabling them to acquire overseas equity.[31] Why was such a giveaway necessary? Surely, the Tatas could not have raised capital under similar terms had it ventured to do so through the market. An investor would clearly seek to safeguard returns, seek to obtain corporate and managerial control, and impose conditions on its investment. That the Left Front did not negotiate in the public interest left it vulnerable to political opportunists who mobilized public opinion and exploited the situation to their benefit.

The case of Nandigram is even more complex and punctuated with a horrible saga of violence.[32] At issue was a joint venture with the Indonesian Salem Group which would involve the acquisition of 14000 hectares of land and potentially affect 65,000 people.[33] Majority of the local population are dependent on subsistence agriculture, with few opportunities for commercial cropping or industrial activity.[34] Average annual incomes are close to or below the national poverty line. It is hardly surprising then, that fertile agricultural land would be so precious to a community such as this. Indeed, their strong resistance had led to a decision to shelve the project. Ironically, even that decision could not prevent a violent confrontation between the police, cadres of the ruling party and the local population, which again was exploited to the maximum by political opportunists. Innocent lives were lost and people were brutalized, displaced and harmed in a myriad of ways.

While Nandigram and Singur are read largely as a Left regime's attempt to implement its neoliberal vision of industrialization in the face of peasant resistance by taking recourse to violence when necessary, there are also deeper contradictions at play. First, Nandigram is direct evidence that neoliberalism everywhere is authored by states and governments—in this case a Left government with one of the best records of land reforms. It has also enjoyed unbridled power since 1977 with a strong rural base as well as a progressive urban middle class. Why did no other alternatives for structural transformation emerge in such a context? Are alternative development strategies possible? With its progressive history, its agrarian resources and a strong cooperative movement, West Bengal would appear to be an ideal context for transformative development. For sure, constrains would remain, transformation may have to incremental. But surely some negotiations with neoliberalism were in order? While there are many reasons behind the acceptance of neoliberalism, I wish to focus on what it means for development. I conclude by reflecting briefly on this question.

The Meaning of Development

It appears that governments, irrespective of their political leanings, see development as the development of capitalism. Under neoliberalism, this has meant the development of a *race-to-the-bottom* capitalism marked by a continuous and relentless relinquishing of all democratic control on accumulation. This obviously is not sustainable, which is why we see the reinstatement of some of the elements of public control as the multiple crises of neoliberalism unfold. There is little doubt that such re-regulation of capital is necessary, but is it sufficient for development? We have seen several models of regulation in the developing world, each fraught with contradictions. The much-revered developmental states of East Asia did implement a successful regulatory regime for the development of capitalism. Its success lay in ensuring that corporate growth was systematically translated into national economic growth, growth of the productive capacity of labor, and of wages. It was not without its dark side, however. In South Korea for example, it was accompanied by tremendous costs for the rights of workers, a highly oligopolistic model of capitalism, and little democratic control over the state or business. The Indian model of regulation on the other hand, was much less effective in regulating business and generating similar linkages to economic growth or wages. Except for certain small segments of the organized working class which enjoyed both growth in wages and political freedom, the bulk of Indian workers remained marginalized from the mainstream of industrial capitalism. The agrarian sector remained similarly unequal, in terms of land ownership and agrarian incomes, and is currently manifesting a crisis of immense proportions.

The key question, then, concerns the organization of social production and reproduction. How can production be organized such that the majority is integrated rather than marginalized, dispossessed or displaced? Unfortunately, the discussion of alternative production continues to be trapped into binaries like "socialism" and "capitalism", imagined as pure forms of tyranny of the state or the market. Yet, in reality, globalization has fomented myriad social struggles for establishing alternative forms of production, several of these in India.[35] Ecological and agrarian struggles, food sovereignty movements, the revitalization of the cooperative movement, the fair trade movement, the emergence of alternative financial organizations are all important alternative forms of production, and as such, critical elements of what Jessop has called *alter-globalization*.[36]

These alternatives can be understood in terms of three dimensions: the notion of social justice and inequality; the understanding of difference; and the notion of agency. Drawing upon the work of the critical feminist philosopher Iris Young and theorists of alternative development such as John Friedmann, elsewhere I have developed a detailed comparison of these alternative models with other models of development.[37] I will reflect on these briefly here. First of all, in these conceptualizations, justice, difference and agency are all understood in relational terms, i.e. as different configurations of social relations. Second, social relations are seen as relations between *collectivities*, such as class, gender, race, ethnicity etc. Third, and related, is a critical understanding of justice which is not limited to redistributive politics. Young has called this an "enabling conception of justice".[38] I have referred to a transformative paradigm, in the specific sense that it requires transformation of social relations that, as Young suggests, cannot be achieved through liberal models of redistribution. Fourth, and perhaps most important in this conceptualization is the notion of *social power*, as developed by Friedmann. Social power refers to power that emanates from the social relations of the marginalized, rather than from the organized institutions in the economy, polity or civil society. Friedmann names eight such "bases" of social power: defensible life space; surplus time; knowledge and skills; appropriate information; social organization; social networks; instruments of work and livelihood; and financial resources. While beginning with Friedmann, I have departed from his conceptualization somewhat. Friedmann argues for approaches to development that help citizens increase their access to the "bases" of social power. This, to my mind, assumes that development must occur first and the increase in social power (which Friedmann calls empowerment) will follow. I have suggested instead a different causality—or perhaps a rejection of unidirectional causality altogether which, I think, stands in contradiction to Friedmann's notion of empowerment. I propose instead that we see development *as* the mobilization of social power. The specific and material outcomes of development may, then, be varied, depending on the kind of mobilization that takes place. For our purposes of understanding development, I have suggested focusing on mobilizations which seek to alter relations of structural inequality.

How then are we to see the mobilizations against neoliberalism? In India specifically, I have alluded to two types of mobilization for social justice. The first involves demands for redistribution, which, unless accompanied by deeper structural change, cannot redress the fundamental historical patterns of inequality that are at the stake. The second, while successful in its resistance to a particular manifestation of neoliberalism, still leaves open the question of structural transformation from low-productivity subsistence agriculture and poverty. Perhaps the answer lies in the logic of the resistance itself. Its strength appears to have emanated from the deep insecurity felt by its people: they were threatened by the loss of their land, their only asset, with little or no possibility of gaining an alternative asset from the industrialization that was proposed.

What we see therefore is a fundamental antagonism between visions of development "from below" and institutionalized visions and practices of development "from above". As I have discussed elsewhere this antagonism can no longer be reconciled within neoliberalism, or even within more redistributive and "pragmatic" visions of development (such as the Millennium Development Goals). This is not to diminish the importance of distribution. After all, demands for distribution are claims to justice; they are also the demands around which people mobilize. At the same time, there is a visible understanding within resistance movements that the contradictions and synergies between demands for redistribution and demands for structural change have come to constitute the central challenge for progressive politics in the present conjuncture.

Chapter 3

LIMITS TO CHINA'S CAPITALIST DEVELOPMENT

ECONOMIC CRISIS, CLASS STRUGGLE, AND PEAK ENERGY

Minqi Li

Measured by purchasing power parity, China now accounts for 10 percent of world GDP (gross domestic product), about half of the current size of the US economy. Since 2000, China's share in world GDP has been growing at about 0.5 percent a year while the US share has been falling at about 0.3 percentage points a year. Under these trends, China could overtake the US and become the world's largest economy by around 2020.[1] Is China's economic rise sustainable? How will the class dynamics within China and China's changing position in the global capitalist economy affect the global class struggle?

China's dramatic economic rise rests upon an economic model that is based on export-led economic growth, intensive exploitation of the world's largest cheap labor force, and massive exploitation of nonrenewable fossil fuels. In the short and medium-run, as the US economy and other advanced capitalist economies fall into recession and stagnation, China is likely to suffer from a substantial slowdown in exports expansion and will be forced to reorient the economy towards domestic consumption. However, such an adjustment would in turn require a massive income redistribution from the capitalist class to the working class. It is by no means clear that the Chinese capitalist class would be willing or able to make the necessary concessions to secure its own long-term interest.

In the long run, China's capitalist development is likely to be confronted with two insurmountable obstacles. First, over time, the Chinese working class will inevitably become organized for economic and political struggles, and emerge as a powerful political force. The Chinese workers will necessarily demand a broad range of economic, social, and political rights, in addition to higher levels of material living standards. In response, the Chinese capitalist class could choose between repression and co-option. By then, the Chinese working class may very well be too powerful to be repressed, while co-option could turn out to be too costly for the capitalist class. Secondly, China's capitalist accumulation has been very energy intensive and depends heavily on the nonrenewable fossil fuels. A growing body of evidence now suggests that both Chinese and world production of fossil fuels are likely to peak in the coming decades. The depletion of energy resources and other environmental costs will impose another insurmountable limit to China's capitalist accumulation.

China's opening up to the global capitalist market and its dramatic economic rise have played an indispensable role in the global triumph of neoliberalism. In the coming decades, we are likely to witness the steady growth of the Chinese working class, as well as its class consciousness and its capability for organization. The renewed struggle of the Chinese working class could play an important part in the future global revolutionary movement and help to turn the global balance of power again to the favor of the global working classes.

China and the Triumph of Global Neoliberalism

During the 1950s and 1960s, the global capitalist economy experienced unprecedented rapid growth, widely known as the "golden age." However, by the late 1960s new contradictions emerged. High levels of employment, welfare state institutions, and the depletion of the rural surplus labor force changed the balance of power between the capitalist classes and the working classes. Labor militancy grew throughout the advanced capitalist countries and the semi-peripheral countries (such as Latin America, Eastern Europe, and Southern Europe). The profit rate suffered large and sustained declines, and revolutionary upsurges threatened to overthrow capitalist governments in many parts of the world.

In response, the capitalist classes organized a global counter-offensive. After a bloody coup that overthrew the democratically elected socialist government in 1973, the Chilean fascist government conducted the first monetarist experiment. In China, after Mao Zedong's death, the pro-capitalist forces took over political power. With Thatcher coming to power in 1979 and Reagan in 1980, monetarism and other neoliberal policies became dominant in the advanced capitalist countries. In the 1980s and 1990s, "structural adjustments" and "shock therapies" were imposed on the Third World countries and Eastern European former socialist states, with devastating economic and social consequences.

"Globalization" has been an indispensable component of neoliberalism. Through greater and deeper integration of the peripheral and semi-peripheral economies into the global capitalist economy in the form of trade and financial liberalization, capital from the advanced capitalist countries can be re-located to the periphery and semi-periphery where large reserves of cheap labor force are available and there is little political constraint on resources depletion and environmental degradation, thereby raising the global profit rate. China's dramatic economic rise needs to be understood in this context.

Neoliberalism has been a strategic attempt of the global capitalist classes to reverse the historical gains of the world's working classes, in order to lower the cost of wages and social spending and restore the profit rate. The neoliberal policies and institutions collectively constitute a strategy to undermine the bargaining power and organizational capacity of the working classes. But for this strategy to be successful, it requires not only the will and determination of the capitalist classes, but also certain objective conditions.

By depriving working people of their economic and social rights and lowering their living standards, neoliberal policies have led to surging inequality. They have destroyed the national economies in many countries and seriously undermined the political legitimacy of global capitalism. The neoliberal policies have also led to economic stagnation and violent financial crises. For the capitalist classes, neoliberalism represents a very costly strategy in political and economic terms, despite the fact that they remain the primary beneficiaries of its institutionalization.

For neoliberalism to be sustained and successful, a new global environment needs to be createdwhich, on the one hand, maintains the global balance of power favoring the capitalist classes for a prolonged period of time while, on the other hand, permitting the creation of certain conditions to address some of the inherent contradictions of the neoliberal global economy. It is in this respect that China's transition to capitalism and economic rise has played an important and indispensable role.

Maoist revolutionary theory and practice played a major role in the global revolutionary upsurge in the 1960s. The counter-revolutionary coup in 1976, in which the pro-capitalist forces took over political power in China, thus represented a major defeat on the part of the international revolutionary forces. With the defeat of the Chinese revolution and other revolutionary challenges (France in 1968, Chile in 1973, and Portugal in 1975), the global political initiative passed into the hands of the system's ruling elites, paving the way for the rise of neoliberalism.

By the 1990s, the Chinese ruling elites were ready to undertake mass privatization. Tens of millions of state sector workers were laid off. Those that remained employed were deprived of their traditional socialist rights, such as job security, medical insurance, access to housing, and guaranteed pensions. In the meantime, privatization in the rural areas has destroyed the rural public health care and education system, which had been very effective in the Maoist era to meet the rural population's basic needs. Hundreds of millions of peasants have become migrant workers working under sweatshop conditions. The defeat of the urban working class and the creation of a massive surplus labor force laid down the foundation of China's capitalist boom. By the early 2000s, China had become the center of the world's manufacturing exports.

China's economic rise has important global implications. First, China's deeper incorporation into the capitalist world-economy has massively increased the size of the global reserve army of cheap labor. In some industries, this allows the capitalists in the advanced capitalist countries to directly lower their wages and other costs by relocating capital to China. But more important is the "threat effect." That is, the capitalists in the advanced capitalist countries could and have forced the workers to accept lower wages and worse working conditions by threatening to move their factories or offices to cheap labor areas such as China, without actual movement of physical capital.

Second, China's low-cost manufacturing exports directly lower the prices of many industrial goods. To the extent unequal exchange takes place between China and the advanced capitalist countries, part of the surplus value produced by the Chinese workers is transferred to the advanced capitalist countries and helps to raise the profit rate in the advanced capitalist countries.

Third, as China's share in the world GDP rises, China has directly contributed to the acceleration of global economic growth and in recent years has become a major engine of the global economy.

Fourth, in recent years China has accumulated huge foreign exchange reserves. By investing most of the foreign exchange reserves in US dollar assets, China has played a central role in financing the US current account deficits. China therefore has acted as a major pillar of global capitalist stability.

China and the Global Economic Crisis

Under neoliberalism, working people in many parts of the world have suffered from absolute declines of living standards. "Structural adjustments" and "shock therapies" destroyed many national economies. Monetarist policies led to high real interest rates that discouraged productive investment and encouraged financial speculation. Thus, in the neoliberal era, global effective demand has been depressed and there is a strong tendency for the global economy to stagnate. Moreover, throughout the 1980s and 1990s, trade and financial liberalization led to large and unpredictable movements of speculative capital across national borders, threatening the global economy with increasingly more violent financial crises.

There was a serious danger that the neoliberal global economy could collapse and sink into a downward spiraling depression. The danger has not materialized largely because the world's largest and hegemonic economy—the US economy—has acted as the world's consumer of the last resort. The US has been able to grow more rapidly than other advanced capitalist countries, generating demand for the rest of the world.

However, as the US grew more rapidly than the rest of the world, US imports tended to grow more rapidly than the exports. As a result, the US has been running very large current account deficits. The US current account deficit now stands at about 700 billion dollars a year and the US net foreign debt stands at about 2.5 trillion dollars.

The US current account deficits must be financed by borrowings from the rest of the world. China has played a key role in financing the

US current account deficits and stabilizing the global capitalist economy. China's foreign exchange reserves have by now surged to nearly 2 trillion dollars, mostly invested in US dollar assets. If China had not been financing the US borrowings, the US dollar would have collapsed and ceased to be the world's major reserve currency.

Within the US, economic growth has been led primarily by consumption which accounts for 70 percent of the US GDP. As the US working class has suffered from sustained declines in real wage, the growth of household consumption has to be financed by increasingly larger household debt. With the burst of the housing bubble, the US debt-financed consumption can no longer be sustained. The US economy is now falling into a recession which, most likely, will be followed by persistent stagnation. The Euro-zone and the Japanese economy are also struggling with recession or stagnation.

China has relied upon exports expansion as its major engine of economic growth. With the advanced capitalist economies in recession or stagnation, it will not take long before China's exports expansion suffers a dramatic slowdown. Can China's economic growth machine manage to survive the developing global economic crisis?

China's Economic Challenge: A Reorientation towards Domestic Consumption?

A country's GDP consists of household consumption, government consumption, investment, and net exports (exports less imports). From 2000 to 2006, China's investment to GDP ratio rose from 35 percent to 43 percent. The exports to GDP ratio rose from 23 percent to 40 percent. Net exports as a share of GDP tripled from 2.4 percent to 7.5 percent. By contrast, household consumption as a share of GDP ratio fell sharply from 46 percent in 2000 to 36 percent in 2006, and government consumption share fell from 16 percent to 14 percent.[2]

Investment represents the building of capital goods and infrastructure, which are in turn used in the production of final goods. Much of the investment took place to expand the production capacity of the export sector. Thus, in terms of final demand, the Chinese economy in recent years has been primarily led by the expansion of exports.

China's economic growth has been accompanied by sharp increases in economic and social inequality. The workers' and peasants' income growth lags far behind overall economic growth, and nearly one hundred million people have to struggle with an income less than two *yuan* a day (roughly corresponding to one purchasing power parity dollar a day). In recent years, health care, education, and housing costs have surged, known to the Chinese working people as the "new three mountains" (the old "three mountains" referred to the pre-revolutionary forces of oppression such as imperialism, feudalism, and bureaucratic capitalism), imposing a heavy burden on ordinary working families' living budget. About half of the urban residents and nearly 90 percent of the rural residents have no access to any health insurance.[3]

Between 1990 and 2005, China's total labor income fell from 50 percent of GDP to 37 percent of GDP, a dramatic decline of 13 percentage points.[4] During the same period, household consumption as a share of GDP had fallen by about the same amount. So long as the Chinese working people continue to suffer from rising inequality, growing costs of living, and deprivation of basic needs and security, mass consumption is likely to be depressed.

How long can China's current model of growth be sustained? The US accounts for about 20 percent of China's export market. In 2007, the European Union as a whole (including the Euro-zone, the UK, and the new member states of Eastern Europe) actually replaced the US to become China's largest export market. However, for China to run large current account surpluses, some other economies have to run large current account deficits. The European overall current account balance has been in rough balance. From a global perspective, China's current account surpluses have been entirely absorbed by the US current account deficits. If the US no longer runs large current account deficits, then unless Europe starts to run large deficits, it will be very difficult for China to sustain its large trade surpluses.

China's excessively high level of investment results in massive demand for energy and raw materials. China consumes one-third of the world's steel and one-quarter of the world's aluminum and copper. China's oil consumption is less than 10 percent of the world total but since 2000, China has accounted for one-third of the world's total incremental demand for oil. China's massive demand has been a major factor behind the surging global costs of energy and raw materials.[5]

If the current level of investment is sustained for some more years, it would leave China with a massive amount of excess production capacity that is far greater than what is needed to meet the final demand in the world market and far greater than what can be supported by the world supply of energy and raw materials. China would then be threatened with a major economic crisis. For the Chinese economy to be restructured on a more "sustainable" basis (from the point of view of sustaining capitalist accumulation), the Chinese economy has to be reoriented towards domestic consumption.

The combined share of household and government consumption now stands at about 45 percent of GDP. If investment were to return to more "sustainable" levels (about 30-35 percent of GDP) and the trade surplus were to become smaller (0-5 percent of GDP), then the combined share of household and government consumption would need to rise by about 20 percentage points to 65 percent of GDP. But for consumption to rise, the workers' incomes and government social spending have to rise accordingly. It follows that there must be a massive income redistribution from capitalist income to labor income and social spending by the amount of about 20 percent of GDP.

Will the Chinese capitalist class be enlightened enough to undertake such a massive economic and social restructuring? Suppose the Chinese leadership is sufficiently far-sighted to understand that for the sake of the long-term interest of Chinese capitalism, it is necessary to make some concessions to the Chinese workers and peasants. Will the Chinese leadership have the necessary will and means to impose such a redistribution on the transnational corporations, the wealthy Chinese capitalists, and the provincial and local governments? These are some difficult questions for the Chinese capitalist elites to address.

Imagine that the Chinese ruling elites are willing and able to overcome these difficulties and carry out the necessary social reform, and the Chinese economy is transformed so that growth is led by domestic consumption rather than investment and exports. In that case, China should be able to sustain relatively rapid economic growth in the coming five to ten years. However, in the long run, Chinese capitalism will sooner or later run into two insurmountable limits.

The Rising Chinese Working Class: The Gravediggers of Chinese Capitalism?

China's transition to capitalism has played an indispensable role in the global triumph of neoliberalism. China's huge reserve army of cheap labor force has been a major factor in undermining the bargaining power of the global working classes. However, capitalist development has been transforming China's own social structure and a large proletarianized working class is emerging in China.

Table 1 presents China's changing class structure from 1979 to 1999:

Table 1 China's Changing Class Structure, 1978-1999

Social Class	1978	1988	1999
Bourgeoisie	1.2%	2.3%	4.2%
Labor Aristocracy	4.8%	9.5%	14.1%
Traditional Proletariat	20.1%	21.6%	23.1%
New Proletariat	6.5%	10.8%	14.6%
Peasants	67.4%	55.8%	44.0%

Source: Special Research Group of Chinese Academy of Social Sciences, "*Zhonguo Muqian Shehui Jieceng Jiegou Yanjiu Baogao* (A Research Report on the Current Structure of Social Strata in China)," in Ru Xin, Lu Xueyi, and Li Peilin (eds.), *Shehui Lanpishu 2002: Zhongguo Shehui Xingshi Fenxi yu Yuce* (Social Blue Book 2002: Analyses and Predictions of China's Social Conditions), pp. 115-132. Beijing: *Shehui Kexue Wenxian Chubanshe* (Social Sciences Academic Press). Bourgeoisie includes "state and social managers," "economic managers," and "entrepreneurs." Labor aristocracy includes "professionals and technicians," "clerks," and "self-employed." Traditional proletariat includes the workers in the industrial, commercial, and services sectors. New proletariat includes "peasant workers" and the unemployed. Peasants include the rural laborers.

From 1978 to 1999, the proportion of peasants in the total population fell from 67 percent to 44 percent. As a proportion of the population, the traditional urban proletariat increased from 20 percent to 23 percent, only by 3 percentage point. The relatively slow growth of the urban proletariat reflects the massive layoffs of the state sector workers in the 1990s. However, the new proletariat (which includes mostly the so-called "peasant workers," or the migrant workers who had their origins in the rural areas but are employed in the urban capitalist industries) expanded rapidly from 7 percent to 15 percent. Together, the traditional urban proletariat and the newly proletarianized workers combined accounted for nearly 40 percent of the total population. Since then, as urbanization has proceeded and more workers have migrated from the rural areas to the urban areas, China's proletarianized working class has further expanded.

Until now, the Chinese capitalists and the transnational corporations in China have been able to reap huge profits through the intense exploitation of China's massive cheap labor force. In the manufacturing sector, the Chinese workers' wage rate is about 5 percent of the US wage rate, 6 percent of the South Korean wage rate, 24 percent of the Polish wage rate, or 41 percent of the Mexican wage rate.[6] It is commonly known that sweatshop working conditions are pervasive in China. The Chinese workers do not have the right to organize for collective struggle and are provided with little legal protection.

However, capitalist development itself is now creating a new set of social conditions that could potentially lead to its own downfall. China's remaining surplus labor pool now is being rapidly depleted. A recent study of the Chinese Academy of Social Sciences suggests that China could deplete its surplus labor pool as soon as 2010. A demographic study predicts that China's working age population as a share of the total population will start to decline in 2010 and the absolute size of the working age population will start to decline in 2015.[7]

The historical experience of other countries suggests that as capitalist development depletes the rural surplus labor force, the relations of forces between the capitalists and the workers are likely to turn to the workers' favor. Over time, as the labor supply is further tightened and the second-generation migrant workers become more familiar with the urban environment and more conscious of their working class identity, the workers are likely to become more self-confident and militant. Sooner or later, the Chinese workers will organize more frequently and effectively for economic and political struggles.

If the history could serve as a guide, then in perhaps one or two decades, the bargaining power and organizational capacity of the Chinese working class could rise to the point that they could impose serious pressure on the capitalist profit rate and accumulation. What strategies will be available for the Chinese capitalist class? It could refuse to make any concessions and repress any potential workers' rebellion. However, in one or two decades, the Chinese working class is likely to have become much more powerful than now. If the capitalist class engages in an outright confrontation with the working class, it could very well trigger a social revolution that will bring down the capitalist class itself.

Moreover, as is argued above, Chinese capitalism can no longer rely upon export-led growth. To sustain long-term accumulation, the Chinese economy needs to be reoriented towards domestic consumption. While such a reorientation would help to address the problem of insufficient effective demand, the trouble is, it would require a massive income redistribution that could dramatically reduce the amount of surplus value available for the capitalist class. Economically, this could lead to another accumulation crisis as it drives down the profit rate. Politically, it is by no means clear individual capitalists would be willing to make the necessary sacrifice to save their collective class interest.

Are there any possible solutions to this dilemma?

In the capitalist world market, China is one of the semi-peripheral countries. In global commodity chains, Chinese capitalist businesses specialize mostly in low and medium value added activities. The limited value added available for the Chinese capitalist class means that not only that they cannot reap super profits as do the global monopoly transnational corporations, but also that there is limited space of maneuver to pursue society-wide compromise in class relations.

Thus, one possible strategy for the Chinese capitalist class is to make a serious attempt to upgrade China's position in the capitalist world division of labor, to establish technical and financial monopoly in certain global commodity chains, and to get a share of the transnational capitalist super profits. Such a strategy would require a very high degree of state intervention and a relatively effective state machinery. In other words, the state must be able to represent the collective interest of the capitalist class as a whole and effectively discipline individual capitalists. It is not obvious that these political conditions are present in China. More importantly, given China's enormous size, it is impossible for China to move up in the global commodity chains without seriously depressing the profit rate for the advanced capitalist countries as a whole. China's competition with the existing advanced capitalist countries could also lead to potentially explosive geopolitical consequences that could threaten to destroy the entire existing world system.

There is another possible strategy. The Chinese capitalists could look for certain areas in the world's periphery and relocate capital to countries where even cheaper labor force remains available and abundant. On the one hand, it is not obvious where in the world one can find a massive cheap labor force with a size comparable to China's that is readily available for capitalist exploitation (that is, in addition to the cheap labor force, the political, social, and material conditions also need to be favorable for capitalist accumulation). On the other hand, such a massive expansion of capitalist development in the rest of the world would certainly greatly increase the demand on the world's energy, other resources, and environmental space. In fact, the world's remaining energy resources may not be enough to sustain China's current pattern of growth much longer.

Peak Energy and the Limits to China's Capitalist Accumulation

China's economic growth has been heavily energy intensive and arguably the single most important factor behind the rapid growth of global energy demand and greenhouse gases emission in recent years. China now accounts for 15 percent of the world's primary energy consumption and under the current trend could overtake the US to become the world's largest energy consumer by 2010. China has already overtaken the US to become the world's largest carbon dioxide emitter and now accounts for one-fifth of the global emissions.

Domestic coal production accounts for 72 percent of China's primary energy supply. Domestic oil, domestic natural gas, hydro, and imports (mostly oil) account for 10, 4, 2, and 11 percent respectively. Nuclear energy and renewables together account for less than 1 percent. Thus, China heavily depends on the nonrenewable fossil fuels, especially coal, for its energy supply. [8]

As fossil fuels are nonrenewable resources, eventually they will be completely depleted. But long before the eventual depletion, the production of fossil fuels is likely to peak when about half of the ultimately recoverable resource has been exploited.

According to China's Ministry of Land and Natural Resources, China's remaining recoverable coal amounts to 200 billion metric tons.[9] China's cumulative coal production has been about 50 billion metric tons. China's annual coal production reached 2.5 billion metric tons by 2007 and has been growing at an annual rate of 10 percent since 2000. At this rate, China's cumulative coal production would have passed 150 billion metric tons by around 2020, suggesting that the production could peak before 2020.

The consensus among Chinese researchers is that China's domestic oil production is likely to peak around 2015, with the peak production level unlikely to be above 200 million metric tons (the current annual production is about 190 million metric tons).[10]

China's natural gas production now makes a small contribution to China's energy supply, but has been growing at 14 percent a year since 2007. The current annual production is about 70 billion cubic meters. The Chinese researchers estimate China's ultimate recoverable natural gas to be 10-13 trillion cubic meters.[11] With a 10 percent growth rate of annual production, China's natural gas production could peak by 2030.

China currently has a nuclear electricity generating capacity of 7 giga-watts. The Chinese government plans to expand the nuclear electricity capacity to 40 giga-watts by 2020. Nuclear electricity generation uses uranium, which is a nonrenewable resource. The German Energy Watch Group points out that the world's proved and possible uranium resources could last only 30-70 years at the current rate of consumption.[12] China's economically recoverable uranium is estimated to be 650,000 metric tons.[13]

If China's nuclear electricity capacity is expanded to 40 giga-watts, China's annual consumption of uranium will need to rise to about 9,000 metric tons. At this rate, China's domestic uranium resource will be exhausted in about 70 years.

The long-term potential of hydro electricity is limited by the available sites that are suitable for hydro development. Renewables, such as solar, wind, and biomass, now account for a very small part of the energy supply and are unlikely to play a major role in the foreseeable future.

Thus, in the coming decades, China will have to rely upon a massive increase in energy imports to sustain rapid economic growth. However, now there is growing evidence suggesting that the world production of fossil fuels is likely to peak in the near future.

In 1956, M. King Hubbert, an American geologist who worked for the Shell Oil Company, predicted that the US oil production would peak around 1970, a prediction that was later confirmed by the actual trajectory of the US oil production. Since then, many other important oil producers have reached the peak and their production has been in decline. The two most important European producers, Britain and Norway, peaked in 1999 and 2001 respectively. Mexico, which was the world's fifth largest producer, peaked in 2004. The current evidence suggests that Russia, the world's second largest producer, is likely to have peaked in 2007.

Colin J. Campbell, an Irish petroleum geologist, conducted a detailed study of the world's oil discovery history and pointed out that the world oil discoveries peaked in the 1960s.[14] The Association for the Study of Peak Oil and Gas Ireland estimated the world oil production peak would take place in 2008.[15]

Dave Rutledge, chair of the Division of Engineering and Applied Science at California Institute of Technology, studied the historical series of world oil and natural gas production and concluded that about one-third of the world's ultimately recoverable resources of oil and gas have already been exploited, implying a peak of the world total production of oil and gas around 2015. Rutledge also finds that the world's remaining recoverable coal is likely to be far less than the official reserves and that world coal production could peak in about ten years.[16]

As it is very unlikely for China to sustain rapid economic growth through growing energy imports from the rest of the world, China is likely, as domestic energy production peaks, to face insurmountable energy crisis beyond 2020. The Chinese capitalism has so far relied upon economic growth to alleviate social contradictions and maintain a certain degree of social stability. As China's economic growth collapses, China's existing political and social regime will not survive. This will certainly pave the way for a new upsurge of revolutionary struggle in China. Given China's crucial importance, such a development could greatly deepen the crisis of global capitalism and turn the global balance of power decisively to the favor of the global working classes.

Part II

RESISTANCE AND ALTERNATIVES TO GLOBAL NEOLIBERALISM

Introduction

The dawn of the neoliberal era was marked by the sanctimonious utterance of former British Prime Minister Margaret Thatcher, that "there is no alternative" (TINA) to neoliberalism and capitalism. Though much repeated by right wing conservative forces the world over, the fact is TINA was a fundamentally flawed and misleading dictum. In Part 2 of this book we will see that not only has global neoliberalism been resisted by vulnerable yet determined states but genuine alternatives have been maintained throughout the neoliberal decades—this notwithstanding the marshalling of the full wrath of neoliberal forces against them.

In Chapter Four, Al Campbell tells the story of Cuba's struggle to adhere to its founding socialist principles and popular programs in the face of the unceremonious unraveling of much of the rest of the Soviet bloc in 1989. Campbell does acknowledge that socialist strategy in Cuba requires an interfacing with the international economy. He exposes those components of Cuba's interaction with global neoliberalism where clear stresses on its socialist system emerge. However, Campbell also points in a very clear fashion to those elements of socialism in Cuba which act as bulwarks against capitalism. Ultimately, the question is not just one of defending socialism against capitalism and neoliberalism. Rather the real issue is the sort of development socialism offers the Cuban mass public vs. what has been the lot of the majority of third world peoples caught in the neoliberal maelstrom and the global race to the bottom the latter has perpetuated.

Chapter Five by Greg Wilpert chronicles the journey of Venezuela from the period of its nascent capitalist development under the aegis of a series of military dictatorships through to the ascendance to power of current President Hugo Chávez. Wilpert then contextualizes the policies of the

Chávez government in terms of the roles played by oil wealth and state-directed developmentalism in Venezuela's modern economic history. Wilpert displays that while there is some economic policy similitude with the past, the Chávez era development diverges in distinct ways from that and has thus fostered resentment among traditional elites. Further, based on close examination of key social and economic policies, the chapter demonstrates the extent to which the current Venezuelan model embodies non-neoliberal modalities of development. Wilpert also argues that the successes of Hugo Chávez are not predicated solely upon high oil revenues but on the way funds have been invested and in the programs Chávez initiated to enhance popular empowerment and citizen freedoms.

The setting for Chapter Six is the impacting of the 2008 financial meltdown on Africa. Patrick Bond maintains that African elites largely tended to ignore warnings from progressive scholars and activists about blind adherence to neoliberal ideological principles and economic policies. However, alternative voices were never completely silenced, and the current economic malaise opens the door to a fundamental rethinking of state policies toward finance, global so-called "free trade" agreements and corporate strategies in extractive industries. Bond further suggests how non-neoliberal anti-globalization economic and social policies engineered in Latin America could be successfully adopted in Africa. Yet, he makes it clear that the major impediment to a progressive agenda in Africa remains United States (US) global hegemony. Therefore, progressive policy makers in Africa must strive toward the delegitimization of US financial and military power to achieve their ends.

Chapter 4

CUBA: A PROJECT TO BUILD SOCIALISM IN A NEOLIBERAL WORLD

Al Campbell

Resources were not obtained by opening the economy to market forces, or by privatizing government property, or by trimming social expenditures. Different from other readjustment cases, it was not acceptable to apply market and neoliberal laws to restrict without limits the levels of consumption and investment. Such activities would have resulted in the absolute poverty of most of the population and the total loss of the ability to lead development in favor of the national interest.

José Luis Rodríguez,
Minister of the Economy and Planning[1]

Introduction

With the dissolution between 1989 and 1991of the non-capitalist Soviet international economic block that Cuba had been part of (COMECON), Cuba had to decide what new type of economic system to build. Unlike its former "socialist" allies, Cuba consistently maintained its intention not to allow a capitalist restoration.[2] By 1991 neoliberalism had become the dominant form of capitalism in both the First and Third Worlds. The post 1991 effects of global neoliberalism on both Cuba's narrowly defined economy and its broader (very linked) social project can be understood in the following frame: the intersection of 1) Cuba's rejection of neoliberalism as being incapable of bringing authentic social and economic development to Third World countries, 2) Cuba's commitment to look for new structures to build socialism, 3) Cuba's necessary extensive economic interactions with international neoliberal capital, and 4) the latter's inherent drive to reshape Cuba's economy and society in accord with neoliberalism's own intrinsic nature.

This essay will look at the following aspects of the interaction of the Cuban economy with global neoliberal capital since the demise of COMECON. Section two will briefly review Cuba's consistently maintained rejection of neoliberalism and capitalism, its commitment to building socialism and its recognition that certain "concessions" would have to be made to international capitalism to assure the survival of their project. Then section three will address the issue of "what neoliberalism is", to the minimal extent needed for the subsequent discussion of its effects on Cuba since 1991. Section four will give several quantitative measures of neoliberalism's influence on Cuba though its external channels, foreign trade and especially the much discussed foreign investment and joint ventures. Then section five will turn to what this author will argue is a much more important issue for the socialist future of Cuba, the possible effects of neoliberal ideology on the current reforms in the state-run main system of domestic production. Here the focus will be on the current discussion in Cuba concerning the functioning of state enterprises, which includes among other important aspects both a changing relation of the enterprises to the state and (perhaps) a changed concept of work motivation and justified remuneration. With all this as background, the sixth section will discuss several fundamental structural aspects of the Cuban economy that are incompatible with capitalism, that would need to be completely reversed for a capitalist restoration, and which are not currently under discussion as part of the considerations of economic reform. Section seven will then address one particular high-visibility aspect of the currently discussed reform process that some defenders of Cuba's socialist project consider particularly dangerous to that project. The chapter is then concluded.

A Declared Rejection of Capitalism and Commitment to Building Socialism

Literally hundreds of speeches and written articles from 1989 to the present by both political leaders of the Revolution and Cuban academics present Cuba's consistent position of rejecting a capitalist restoration as a desirable path for new growth and development for their country. The purpose of the following very small sample from those declarations is to both reflect their position and to give an indication of the reasons they give for their rejection. The first sample is a series of quotes from three speeches by Fidel. The first two come from just after the worst part of the economic downturn, while the third is from a speech two years later, so all three are early in the almost two decade period since the end of COMECON in 1991. The next sample represents the position of a broad and influential social group in Cuba, the CTC union federation that represents the large majority of Cuba's roughly four million economically active non-agricultural workers. The third sample comes from a little discussed independent survey by the Gallup polling company concerning the attitudes of ordinary Cubans toward a number of aspects of Cuban society. Again this was carried out very soon after the nadir of the economic downturn, when life in Cuba had been very hard for four years. The last sample jumps in time almost to the present, after many of the hardships of the special period had been left behind, and the discussion concerning the economic reforms that are occurring today was just beginning to unfold.

> Capitalism and social development always have been, always are, and always will be irreconcilable. Capitalism and plunder, plunder within and outside the country, are inseparable. Capitalism and unemployment are inseparable.[3] .... There will be no transition towards capitalism.[4] .... We had to establish joint ventures in a relatively short time period, we had to accept foreign investment, we had to do what we did in respect to the decriminalization of convertible currency .... We are aware of the inequalities that it created, the privileges it created, but we had to do it and we did it.[5]

> We have seen that all this opening we have made, this experience, has been a bag of problems, of contradictions, of daily headaches.[6]

> Capitalism as a system belongs to prehistory, even though we know that it rules in the world, and we know that it rules and how it rules, but it has nothing to offer people, one wolf wishing to devour another wolf, that's its sermon; a merciless selfishness that has nothing to do with what we would wish for human beings.[7]

At its five-year national congress in 1996 the CTC adopted 168 theses on the current situation and its tasks. Theses 15 to 37 constituted section II of the document, which was entitled "Our Strategy Does Not Lead to Capitalism," and argued that position.[8]

In 1994 fourteen Gallup pollsters questioned 1,002 randomly selected[9] adults on their attitude toward the revolution. Here we have a still broader group than the CTC, a statistical sample of the entire Cuban population of the time. Sixty-nine percent identified themselves as communists, socialists or revolutionaries, and hence were against the restoration of capitalism.[10]

At the December 2005 session of parliament ("National Assembly of People's Power"), Cuba's then Minister and President of the National Bank of Cuba, Francisco Soberón, gave a speech that was reproduced in full in the press. Its final line was "Socialism is not a conjunctural option for Cubans but rather the destiny that we have freely and irreversibly chosen."[11] Again, the reasons given for this position, in this case as part of a speech that argued Cuba would be adopting more market-like and market mechanisms in the near future, are of interest.

> .... we should begin by emphasizing that for its 46 years the Revolution has always tried, even under the most adverse circumstances, to assure the most equitable distribution possible, in accord with the morals of our Socialist system. ... In our Socialist system the environment of cruel insecurity has disappeared, and people have a good part of their basic necessities guaranteed, independent of their contribution to society. ... Comrade Fidel said on a particular occasion that the Revolution will not have reached its highest moral values until we are able to create much more as free humans than we are able to produce as slaves. ... Perhaps one of the most complex dilemmas that confront a Socialist revolution is to achieve efficiency in economic management without renouncing the politically strategic objective of creating a communist consciousness. ... In Socialism, which gives dignity to humans and frees them from alienating consumerism.... By expressing these ideas, one runs the risk that some will think that what we are trying to make understood is that people should work only for money. That would be a grotesque transfer to Socialism of the most vulgar relation that any ignoramus is capable of perceiving in capitalism.[12]

International opponents[13] of the Cuban social system have two obvious possible arguments as to why these universally maintained declarations by Cuba's political leadership do not preclude a transition to capitalism. The first is that the leadership is being duplicitous, deliberately misrepresenting its intentions to restore capitalism because that would not be politically palatable to the Cuban population. The second is that although they indeed intend as claimed to maintain their project to build socialism, by instituting the market-like reforms that they now are implementing, they have moved onto a "slippery slope" that will lead to the restoration of capitalism against their will.

The following two quotes reflecting these two positions come from the mid nineties, when an international debate erupted about whether the market-like mechanisms and markets introduced in Cuba at the time indicated or prepared the way for a restoration of capitalism. They are included at some length because they are exactly the discussion going on now concerning today's reforms. The *Economist* made the duplicity argument.

However, hardline speeches will deflect attention from a shifting ideology and a deepening of economic reform and social transformation. There are indications that the PCC congress {the fifth party congress of the Partido Comunista de Cuba in October 1997- A.C.} will include efforts by party ideologues to link the market reforms so far introduced to the idealistic socialism identified with the national hero, Ernesto "Che" Guevara.[14]

... [the congress] could yet herald a new phase in the economic reform process behind a cloud of rhetoric.[15]

The noted academic cubanologist and dedicated opponent of socialism, Carmelo Mesa-Lago, made the "slippery slope" argument.

But the dynamics of the reform call for further change. The government legalizes some of the economic activities that are taking place, although it tightly regulates them, and such a step is seen as a green light to expand those activities. Restrictions are ignored, and there is a move to new illegal operations. This, in turn, puts pressure on the government to grant another concession, which is followed by a further push toward the market. In his speeches at the beginning of the 1990s, Castro warned against the danger of a chain reaction or the snowballing effect of the economic reforms in the USSR and Eastern Europe that ultimately led to a market economy, but he felt confident that such a process would not take place in Cuba. Yet recent events suggest that history is repeating itself in the Caribbean.[16]

But by the end of 1997 the advocates of a capitalist restoration began to complain about the "stalling" and later the "abandonment" of the "reform process."[17] It is now a historical fact that the claims in the 1990s by the Cuban leadership that they would make concessions to global neoliberalism in order to survive, but that they would limit those concessions to an extent that prevented a capitalist restoration, are in fact what occurred. The arguments of duplicity or a slippery slope both proved false in that case. This should be borne in mind when considering the current reform process in Cuba.

Neoliberalism

Neoliberalism is today's capitalism.[18] It represents a change from the dominant form of capitalism of the 1950s and 1960s, and many aspects of it are best defined by its change from that earlier form of capitalism. A terse picturesque description is that it has restored "many of the most violent features of capitalism, making for a resurgent, unprettified capitalism."[19]

Keeping in mind the parable of the seven blind men and the elephant and accepting that there are many ways to describe neoliberalism, I will here characterize it as having two principal aspects. The first is an inter-class dimension: neoliberalism involves a much more aggressive attack by capital against labor. The second is an intra-class dimension: neoliberalism is characterized by a rise to hegemony of finance capital. But for the purposes of this essay, its surface manifestations are more important to note than its underlying essence.

The following are commonly associated with neoliberalism: i) free trade;[20] ii) free capital movements; iii) reduced government or equivalently "free markets", [21] including in particular financial deregulation and privatization; iv) increased labor market "flexibility"; v) "strong money" (low inflation) and the associated central bank policy of inflation targeting; vi) a changed corporate governance model and often "shareholder value."

According to this or any other reasonable description of neoliberalism, it is immediately apparent that Cuba is clearly not neoliberal. This of course is nearly universally accepted.[22] The more subtle issue is in what ways has global neoliberalism, which the Cubans have continually fought against, penetrated the Cuban development process. At the most extreme, the concern is whether global neoliberalism has been able to sew seeds in the Cuban development process that in time will grow to yield a capitalist restoration.

External Channels of Neoliberal Influence:
Trade and Foreign Investment

Trade

In 1987 Cuba conducted 72.0 percent of its merchandise trade with the USSR and an additional 16.3 percent with other planned economies,[23] leaving less than 12 percent of its trade with the capitalist world. In 2006, given that there were almost no planned economies left in the world, Cuba carried out essentially 100 percent of its trade with capitalist countries.[24] While this represented a big change in the nature and conditions of its foreign trade, how did this impact the nature of the production process in Cuba, and in particular, how much did it drive Cuba toward neoliberal or capitalist production?

During the 1990s Cubans wrote frequently about the changes this meant for the operation of their enterprises. In 1992 the Constitution was changed to allow a decentralization of the export and import processes, but markets were still explicitly rejected in favor of state control: "the State directs and controls foreign commerce."[25] While most imports now had to be paid for in hard currency, there was at first still a single state enterprise that dealt with all the foreign trade and so at first the process of imports worked for the enterprises essentially the same as before. Soon after the constitutional reform, however, numerous agents were empowered to import, including a number of big enterprises,[26] but there was nothing in this changed import procedure that required any significant change in the nature of their production processes. With exports there were more effects. Above all, exporting Cuban enterprises now had to become more "flexible." That is, completely contrary to the previous system of long term stable contracts, now to export it was often necessary to be able to shift the specifics of what was produced, to do so quickly and with higher quality than in the previous system, and to assure deliveries on time (which often involved the performance of other enterprises). These were difficult changes, a whole culture of production had to be changed. But even in these export-related changes, where the effects on enterprise operations were much greater, there was nothing that implied that the enterprises now had to operate according to the laws of capitalist accumulation.

Theoretically there is no reason to assume that trade will determine the mode of production of the people who trade. The loose idea that trading with a "more efficient" trading partner will cause one to adopt the "more efficient" production process is crude Social Darwinism.[27] The historical record demonstrates this same point. The Soviet Union traded for 60 years with capitalist countries without changing its non-capitalist production process. And as most progressive development economists argue, capitalist countries traded with pre-capitalist societies for centuries and in the end often had to resort to force to transform those societies to capitalism.

Foreign Investment

Contrary to trade, capitalist foreign investment does largely imply capitalism for the enterprises involved, and as such conceivably could represent a vastly greater threat to the process of building socialism. Any country attempting to build socialism therefore needs to treat capitalist foreign investment with many more safeguards than trade with capitalist countries.

Foreign investment in Cuba is essentially all in joint ventures. While it is now legal for foreign companies to completely own an enterprise in Cuba, in practice almost all joint enterprises remain at least 51 percent Cuban owned. Joint ventures went from 20 in 1990 to a high of 403 in 2002.[28] Currently the number has continued to fall from 258 in 2005 to 234 in 2006, but the capital involved has grown as the Cuban government has consciously moved from small, hard to monitor, strictly profit-driven joint ventures to larger joint ventures, especially with Venezuela and China, that are instituted more consciously as part of Cuba's overall development plan.[29] Among the joint ventures, the most discussed by both supporters and opponents of the Cuban system are those in tourism.[30] Foreign tourism was chosen as the fastest way to generate the foreign exchange Cuba needed after the collapse of COMECON, and it exploded throughout the 1990s. This author believes that there was no other way to generate that much foreign exchange that rapidly, and that without it the revolution might well have been overthrown. But the point of concern here is that shortly thereafter, there were a million relatively wealthy tourists coming to Cuba (2 million by the 2000s), spreading the image to many Cubans that capitalism bred wealth.

Three limitations have been key in preventing foreign investment in Cuba from carrying out the same important contribution to a transformation to capitalism that it played in China: i) the extent of foreign investment, ii) the extent of the non economic (i.e., political) control of foreign investment, and iii) the absence of the legal ability for the production model used in these enterprises to spread to the rest of the economy.

i) In 1996,[31] it was estimated that three percent of the national income came from joint ventures.[32] Consistently, in 1995 there were 105,953 workers in joint ventures out of a workforce of 3.8 million, or 2.8 percent of the workforce.[33] One gets just a slightly higher measure of their impact if one considers that they contributed an average of 8.2 percent to Gross Capital Formation between 1993 and 2002.[34] Even the commonly asserted claim that they at least were central to foreign exchange earnings is overstated: the value of their exports of goods and services as a percent of the value of all exports from 1993 to 2002 was just over 13 percent.[35] So while joint ventures made and continue to make an important contribution, they clearly have played a very secondary role in the entire economy. This in turn represents one important limitation on the influence of the neoliberal and capitalist ideas that they bring into the Cuban economy.

ii) Decree Law 50 in 1982 had legalized certain forms of joint ventures, but in fact no joint ventures were formed until the very end of the 1980s. The constitutional reforms of 1992 that were intended to reshape the constitution to accord with the new political-economic reality built the joint venture concept into Cuba's basic legal structure.[36] But the fundamental operational law for joint ventures today is Law 77 ("The Law of Foreign Investment") from September 1995.[37] Key for our considerations here are its provisions for authorization of foreign investment in chapter VIII: "Of the Negotiation and Authorization of Foreign Investment." First, it specified both the general goal for accepting such joint ventures, and indicated several specific operational implications of that goal. The general goal was to "carry out profitable activities that contribute to the strengthening of the economic capacity and the sustainable development of the country, on the basis of respect for sovereignty and national independence and the protection and rational use of natural resources."[38] Operationally, this has been held to indicate that the three central interests by Cuba in joint ventures are "financial resources, technologies and new markets."[39] Further, all proposed joint ventures (excepting some very small ones) must be directly approved by a very high group of the (elected) leadership of the Revolution, the Executive Committee of the Council of Ministers,[40] for both its social-political as well as its narrowly defined economic benefits for Cuba. Such a tightly politically controlled foreign investment procedure is markedly different from the "absence of capital controls" that is a well-known central aspect of neoliberalism. It prevents existing (capitalist) joint ventures from spawning new joint ventures in accord with, and to the degree determined solely by, their own desires—the rule of the law of the market.

iii) Central to the restoration of capitalism in China was that the capitalist practices imported with joint ventures were legally allowed (and even officially encouraged) to be duplicated in the private domestic economy, to the extent that non-state enterprises now constitute over 50 percent of that economy.[41] This is not legally possible in Cuba. There is no legal private property (individual or group) in industry.[42] A recent campaign in Cuba against illegal industrial production underlines that it is the intention of the new government of Raúl Castro not to allow such a spread of capitalism to domestic manufacturing.

These three considerations together indicate that, notwithstanding the real potential for capitalist foreign investment in general to continually expand the role of capitalist relations of production to the point where they come to dominate an economy, this is not happening at present in Cuba. To the contrary, Cuba is presently characterized by its restriction to a small part of the total economy, with a political process controlling any new projects and hence any possibility of its qualitatively expanding its role. Cuba has legal property forms in the domestic economy that make it impossible to reproduce there the private production relations from the joint ventures.

The Domestic Economy

While there are other concerns that could be considered in relation to the domestic economy, three of the most important issues frequently and currently[43] discussed as part of the 'transformation to capitalism' debate about Cuba are: i) self employment (*"trabajo por cuento propio"*), ii) the property relations in agriculture, and iii) the new management system in industry (*"perfecionamiento empresarial"*).

Self Employment: On September 8, 1993, Decree Law 141 was passed listing over 100 occupations as acceptable for self employment. Subsequently a number of additional occupations were added. Of particular importance and eventual controversial nature were the "small private restaurants" (*"paladares"*) made legal in 1995.[44] Participants were licensed and paid taxes.[45] Of key importance concerning their potential to contribute to a capitalist restoration was that these were to be private markets. In particular, the state would not set prices, but rather prices would be set according to what the market would bear.

It is important to get a rough feel for how much of the Cuban work force is self-employed. At the end of 1995 there were 200,727 registered self-employed workers, out of a total civilian workforce of 3,788,587, or 5.3 percent.[46] While that number has gone down some over the years since then, it is still broadly representative today. As such, it represents a very small part of the Cuban workforce. However, most commentators agree that for every licensed self-employed worker there are a number who work 'for him' in one way or another—unregistered assistants, people producing what he then sells, etc. There are no reliable public estimates, but if the number is as high as 2 (full time equivalents) as some reasonable commentators indicate, that would suggest around 15 percent of the economically active population is engaged in self-employment. One would get a still higher number if one considered all the people who did 'some work' and got 'some income' through this. Two key considerations about the importance of this type of work are the following. First, by all indications this number has not significantly changed over the last decade and hence we do not see a trend of self-employment expanding to replace state economic production as supporters of a capitalist restoration had hoped. But second, these self employment markets do in practice ideologically support in the consciousness of some Cubans the neoliberal 'markets *über alles*' position that planning cannot effectively provide individual services and that markets[47] are necessary for at least this type of economic activity. As such and notwithstanding the major limit on its role in the economy, self employment presents a particular challenge to the Cuban socialist project that must constantly be evaluated and addressed.[48]

Property Relations in Agriculture: There are two distinct 'market-like mechanisms' that have been used with the intention of increasing agricultural output. They are often mixed together in discussions as they are in practice, but they should be kept conceptually separate. One is to let agricultural producers sell part of their production directly to consumers on markets whose prices are determined solely by supply and demand. The other is to raise the price the state pays for goods it buys from producers at prices it sets.

On October 1, 1994, approximately 120 Agricultural Products Markets were opened,[49] with two to three times that many in existence today. Private, coop, or state producers can sell in these markets anything beyond the amounts they are required to sell to the state. One can immediately see how, notwithstanding the capitalist nature of these markets, the production process behind them is very far from being 'free market.' Only what is produced beyond the state contract can be sold there, and the state contracts are constantly re-evaluated on the basis of what an agricultural unit has produced in the past. If one increases one's output dramatically and hence has large amounts to sell on these agricultural markets (from which one will generate that year a revenue far above that of an industrial worker or state service employee), the next year the contracted amount will be raised, in accord with what this unit has now shown it can produce. This was publically discussed from the beginning as the way that these markets would improve not only distribution, but more importantly, agricultural production.

Five important considerations about these markets are the following. First, these markets will almost certainly significantly expand in the near future as it is nearly certain that the ration card will be eliminated.[50] Second, at present a number of important agricultural products are sold entirely to the state and not distributed through these markets, such as tobacco, sugar, milk, beef, and others. These latter are the products particularly involved in the "increase state prices" stimulus approach that has been talked about so much recently under Raúl. To begin with, at the National Assembly meeting in December 2006 Raúl directed the Cuban government to pay up the large debts it owed to its own agricultural producers. This was followed in Spring 2007 by beginning a process of raising the prices paid to the producers (but not charged to consumers) for a number of these products. As an example, milk and beef prices were tripled.[51] Third, the agricultural reforms contain a number of key non-market reforms as well as the market-like ones. Among these are a drive to put idle and underutilized arable land (estimated at 51 percent[52]) back into production and a program to decentralize the responsibility for assigning land to producers to the community level. Fourth, the combination of these market-like and non-market measures has succeeded in increasing the production of food. Caloric intake has returned to (and slightly increased above) its 1989 level,[53] and milk production is up 30 percent in the first quarter of 2008 over the same period in 2007. This has also affected the price of food. Prices in the agricultural markets of course are well above the (highly subsidized) prices of rationed goods, but they are well below the black market prices that existed prior to the opening of these markets, and equally important, they have been continually falling for over a decade. Finally, like the self employment measure, these successful results are leading some Cubans to embrace the ideological neoliberal 'markets *über alles*' position also in regards to agriculture and conclude that it can be stimulated only by market-like measures (notwithstanding that some of the measures involved in the success are non-market measures). Again, we thus have a practice that, even if accepted on net as appropriate for the revolution at its present conjuncture, must still be recognized it as containing a threat to the Cuban socialist project and therefore must be constantly evaluated and addressed.

The New Incentive and Management Systems in Industry: In the late 1980s Raúl began to design an improved system of enterprise management for enterprises run by the army. The model was explicitly adopted as the model for the whole economy in the early 1990s and further developed throughout the decade. In 1998 it began to be implemented as the system of "enterprise improvement" (*perfeccionamiento empresarial*). Put simply, its goal is to raise the productive efficiency of state enterprises, thereby enabling a predominantly (but not exclusively) state run economy to meet the population's need for goods and services.[54] The Cuban leadership believes this program has so far been fundamentally very successful. Carlo Lage said:

> The companies applying *perfeccionamiento*, being 28 percent of all companies with 20 percent of sales, account for 51 percent of all profits, 72 percent of foreign exchange earnings and are 50 percent more productive.[55]

With so far only about a quarter of the roughly 3,000 Cuban enterprises (and involving only a fifth of sales) operating in this improved fashion after

10 years, the Cuban leadership sees this as both a project that still has tremendous potential to further improve the Cuban economy, and as a project that will remain a central component of their economic program for many years to come.

As opposed to one of the pillars of neoliberalism indicated above, improved enterprise performance in Cuba is not pursued through driving down the workers' share of net output. Rather, at present three issues are stressed as key. The first is eliminating corruption and theft by both management and workers. This is not an issue involved in the return-to-capitalism debate.

The second issue is increased enterprise efficiency. One aspect of this is simply a more rational use of resources by management (including improved accounting). Again this is not an issue seen by either advocates or opponents of a return to capitalism as promoting such a return, though advocates generally claim increased efficiency would be a result of such a return. Raúl holds specifically that in a planned economy one can achieve such increased efficiency without capitalist markets. But another aspect of Cuba's concept of increased enterprise efficiency is that it will be furthered by "economic decentralization" and "increased enterprise autonomy." By this they mean that a significant number of decisions that were made in the Ministries before will now be made by the enterprise directors: Since a characteristic of capitalism is economic decision making by individual enterprises (or more precisely, individual capitals), this aspect on the surface can seem like a move in the direction of capitalism. In the next section which discusses the barriers in Cuba to a capitalist restoration, I will return to this issue and argue why in the institutional setting that exists in Cuba today this does not support such a restoration.

The third issue constantly proposed today as part of improved enterprise performance is "payment according to work."[56] Just like the last issue, on the surface this seems a pro-neoliberal reform. I will return in the next section to argue why, in the specific institutional structure of Cuba today, it is not—unlike the role it did play in the restoration of capitalism in China.

Barriers to the Restoration of Capitalism in Cuba

This paper does not make the claim that capitalism could not be restored in Cuba. There were barriers to the restoration of capitalism in China, as an example, but the government there eliminated those barriers and restored capitalism. The argument rather is that at present there remain major barriers to the restoration of capitalism in Cuba that would need to be eliminated for such a restoration, and as of the writing of this paper, there is no indication of any powerful or serious movement to eliminate any of these barriers.

The most immediate barrier one sees is that there is no legal structure for private productive capital accumulation. There is no limitation on wealth accumulation, but one cannot turn that into capital by hiring labor, exploiting it, capturing the surplus value, and accumulating that as continually expanding capital.

Three ways to overcome this fundamental restriction come to mind. The first is the Soviet Union and East Block's road, where the state-owned basic means of production were privatized,[57] that is, turned into capital. There is no discussion at all of this in Cuba. The second way is the Chinese road. Here private capitalist production, first largely as joint ventures with foreign capital and then as normal domestic capital, grew up over several decades while state owned enterprises (SOEs) declined. Here too, Cuban laws simply do not allow this. The joint ventures are with Cuban state enterprises, and domestically a private producer is either forbidden to hire labor or in some fields (for example, agriculture) restricted to hiring only a few employees. Again, there is no discussion at all of making the sweeping legal changes needed to allow any but the smallest scale capitalist operations. The third way is less clearly articulated, but represents a fear of some supporters of the Cuban socialist project—that the process of *perfeccionamiento empresarial*, especially with its increased enterprise autonomy, will somehow grow into capitalist enterprises. But even a superficial consideration of this process makes clear that in itself it cannot restore capitalism. Enterprises production is still nationally planned, individual enterprises are not free to set their product prices, individual enterprises are not free to set wages, and finally enterprises (not to speak of private enterprise owners, which do not exist) are not free to keep their profits, all of which are necessary for capitalist private production. Again, the existing system would need to be replaced (or "overthrown") to move to capitalism; it does not seem to be a process that could slowly evolve.

Stated another way, the large majority of the economy is state owned and planned, and Cuba's clearly stated intention is to make that state-owned economy more efficient, not to convert it to a private capitalist dominated economy by either the Soviet or Chinese roads. While again I make no claim that a complete reversal from their present anti-capitalist course could not occur at some future time, there is not even a preliminary discussion of it in Cuba at this time.

A related major barrier that would need to be eliminated for a restoration of capitalism is the state's near total control of the vast bulk of new investment. Here the state has two major control mechanisms. First, the majority of the economy is still state owned, and therefore the state makes the bulk of the domestic investment decisions (including the state's input into the investment decisions of joint ventures). Note that while enterprises are being given more autonomy on many issues including minor investment decisions, to date the state still controls major investment decisions. These are very often not made on the basis of individual enterprise profits or profitability, but rather on criteria such as import substitution, building chains of production, and so on (that is, as part of an economy-wide economic plan). Second, as already mentioned, all proposals for foreign capital activity in joint ventures are reviewed at multiple levels of the state, and each must receive the final approval from the highest political level, the Council of Ministers.

Another related barrier to a capitalist restoration is that there is no labor market in Cuba.[58] This takes us back to the now much discussed "payment according to work" brought up in the last section. The extent to which this represents a reflection of global neoliberal ideology in Cuba today is an important question.

It is worth noting that international champions of neoliberalism recognize these as essential barriers to their desired project of restoring capitalism in Cuba. The *Economist* wrote

> The central control of prices continues to restrict the scope for the allocation of goods, services and capital through the market mechanism.[59]

> Enterprise reform has progressed steadily but remains hampered by price and labor controls.[60]

The final barrier that would need to be overcome in order to restore capitalism, generally ignored by too narrow "economic analyses," is the most fundamental because of its social nature: the popular support in Cuba for the Revolution and the popular opposition to a system of Third World neoliberalism and capitalism. The Gallup results cited above indicating majority support for Cuba's non capitalist path reflect this fundamental social barrier to a capitalist transformation. Further, the Battle of Ideas[61] was launched in 2000 to make people, and especially young people, aware of what their social/economic system has brought them, which they would not have under Third World neoliberalism – something too easy to take for granted and to forget when one focuses on a system's shortcomings. This author finds from his at least yearly trips to Cuba since the beginning of the 1990s that the marginal effects on basic attitudes from the Battle of Ideas and the strong economic performance of Cuba for the last four[62] years have left the ratio of support to opposition at least as high as the two to one ratio reflected in the Gallup poll at the depth of the economic crisis in 1994.

"Payment According to Work"

The concern here is that this concept, now being strongly advocated in Cuba, may be the result of the influence of global neoliberal ideology and hence a danger to the process of building socialism. Here I will make two short and simple arguments: that in the context of Cuba it is not, and that, further, the concept is actually, as is repeatedly asserted by the Cubans, consistent with payment in a socialist[63] (but not a communist) economic system.

If one has competition among workers for jobs and enterprises that are free to set wages as low as they can get workers, then the formula "payment according to work" becomes a (circular) justification for enterprises driving down wages. Since one cannot in general actually measure the marginal contribution of any worker, enterprises accept the market ideology that markets set wages according to workers' marginal contributions. Then if labor market competition drives down the wages that workers are willing to accept, enterprises justify the lower wages as being set by the marginal contribution, which the labor markets are now showing is lower than previously. So the whole concept becomes part of the process of exploiting labor to whatever degree the class struggle allows. But since as argued in the last section, Cuba does not have labor markets nor can its enterprises set wages, the concept of "payment according to work" cannot play the same role in Cuba. Instead, it is promoted there with a dual goal. First, it is intended to stimulate workers to make a greater effort at work, both quantitatively and qualitatively ("work harder and work smarter"). It is just the latest form of the use of material incentives that have been used, along with moral incentives, over the whole course of the Cuban revolution. Over that time the partial use of material incentives has not contributed to a capitalist restoration. But beyond that, this corresponds to Cubans' sense of socialist equity, the goal that "everybody's living standard corresponds directly with their legally earned incomes, that is, with the significance and quantity of their contribution to society".[64] In this latter sense "payment according to work" is partially equivalent to what Marx called for in "Critique of the Gotha Programme." There Marx spelled out that in his vision of socialism each person could draw from society goods that took the same amount of labor time to produce as the person contributed labor time to social production.[65] This is the basis for the repeated claim by the Cubans that not only is this formula not a neoliberal import into their institutional framework, but further that it is consistent with their project of building socialism.

Conclusion

While I hold that the quote by the Minister of the Economy and Planning that opened this paper is both correct and centrally important, it is only half the story. The sweeping economic reforms of the economy after 1989 were indeed made contrary to the neoliberal recipe. But as the architects of those reforms themselves often acknowledged, concessions to the world dominant ideology and economic reality of neoliberalism had to be made. Stated differently, Cuba was not able to follow the road to building socialism it would have chosen if it had not been a small country in a neoliberal world. Cuban social/political/economic reality today (and tomorrow) must be understood as simultaneously consisting of both the following. First, global neoliberalism has affected Cuba's current reality in a number of ways. In addition to affecting Cuba's institutions, it is essential to keep in mind the impact of the illusions created by such factors as tourism, self-employment and the Agricultural Products Markets on the consciousness of (some of) the Cuban people, an issue which is centrally important for the transition to socialism. Second, up to the present, major barriers remain in Cuba's institutional structure and social consciousness that would have to first be eliminated before global neoliberalism could impose on Cuba its inherent goal, the abandonment of Cuba's project of attempting to build socialism.

Chapter 5

VENEZUELA'S OIL-BASED DEVELOPMENT IN THE CHAVEZ ERA

Gregory Wilpert

Introduction

Venezuela's oil-based non-neoliberal development model is usually dismissed as being a model that works only with a high price of oil and that even with high oil prices, critics say, it is unsustainable. According to this argument, Venezuela would never have enjoyed anywhere near its average annual 10 percent growth from 2004 to 2007 if it had not been for the tremendous increase in oil prices—by over 300 percent—and thus in oil revenues in this same period. Although this is certainly a very plausible argument, there is something different about Venezuela that would indicate that its economic growth is not solely due to its increasing oil revenues, but also has something to do with the way these revenues have been invested. For example, if one compares Venezuela's economic growth with that of similar oil producing countries (similar in terms of oil production per capita), such as Algeria, Libya, Iran, Russia, and Saudi Arabia, none of these enjoyed as high an annual per capita growth rate as Venezuela did between 2004 and 2007.

The hypothesis of this chapter is that Venezuela's tremendous economic growth of the past few years is not solely attributable to its growing oil revenues, but also to its pursuit of a development policy that sees development as the development of its citizen's capabilities and freedom. This view of development has been pioneered by the economist Amartya Sen,[1] who argues that development ought to be conceived as the development of people's capabilities to exercise their freedom and not just in terms of economic growth statistics, such as GDP growth. Key capabilities that an economy and government policy ought to promote to make real development possible include health, education, freedom to associate, freedom of expression, freedom of movement, among several others.[2]

Contrary to mainstream media reports on Venezuela, the Chavez government has extensively promoted the expansion of its citizens capabilities and has thereby also given its economic growth an additional boost that the other oil producing countries mentioned earlier have not been able to achieve. In what follows I will examine the different dimensions of Venezuela's capabilities approach to development by taking a closer look at five main policy areas: oil, non-oil, social programs, fiscal management, and economic democracy. Before we can turn to these policy areas, though, it makes sense to first take a brief look at economic policy before the Chavez presidency.

Economic Development Policy before Chávez (1908-1998)

Development under Dictatorship (1908-1958)

The dictatorship of Juan Vicente Gomez (1908-1935) was a crucial milestone in Venezuelan history mainly because the Gomez regime was the first to initiate the exploitation of oil, which was discovered in Venezuela in the early 20th century. Gomez opened the country to multi-national oil companies and within a relatively short time, by 1920, Venezuela became the world's largest oil exporting country. By 1935 oil exports constituted 91.2 percent[3] of the country's exports. Prior to that, the economy had been a traditional Latin American agricultural economy, based on cocoa, coffee, sugar, cotton, and tobacco production.

As oil became increasingly important, the country's economy shifted from agriculture to one in which oil production, commerce, and services dominated. While agricultural production made up one third of Venezuela's GDP in the 1920s, by the 1950s this had dropped to 10 percent. Now it is a mere 6 percent,[4] one of the lowest percentages in Latin America.

As a result of this decline in agriculture, Venezuela's landed elite, which is traditionally fairly strong in most of the rest of Latin America, lost its power very early in the 20th century. Also, the emphasis on oil and the country's inability to develop a strong domestic industry meant that no strong entrepreneurial class developed to replace the landed elite. Rather, since most economic activity went through the oil industry in one way or another, which was regulated by the state, the real center of Venezuela's power was based in the state itself. No domestic oil barons emerged either, though, because Venezuelan oil production was under the control of foreign oil companies from the discovery of oil until the early 1970s.[5]

It was mostly thanks to oil that Gomez was able to hold on to power for so long. With the help of oil, Gomez became Latin America's richest man and at the same time managed to consolidate state power like no one before him. He transformed the Venezuelan state into a powerful bureaucracy by inviting foreign oil companies into Venezuela and forcing them to negotiate with the government for the terms of their investment.[6] The political (and military) elites thus ended up dominating not only the state, but also the economy. A strong tradition developed in Venezuela that largely holds until today, in which it was taken for granted that the state would have a determining role in the economy. The main economic policy debates thus revolved around currency issues, tariffs, and how to spread the oil wealth.

When Gomez died in 1935, another general took over (General Eleazar Lopez Contreras 1936-41), who took some of the first steps towards democratizing Venezuela. Also, in response to protests, Gen. Lopez Contreras confiscated all of the Gomez' family's properties, an action that turned the Venezuelan state into the country's largest entrepreneur and landowner, owning banks, various industries, and enormous haciendas. According to one analyst, "This marked the beginning of the state's direct participation as a capitalist in the economy."[7]

Under Lopez Contreras and under the next president, Medina Angarita (1941-45), the Venezuelan state attempted to increase its share of the profits of the country's oil production. Despite resistance from the foreign oil companies, this was eventually achieved, so that by 1943 profits from oil production would be split 50-50 between foreign corporations and the state. In 1945, a pro-democracy coup overthrew the Medina Angarita and brought to power a ruling civilian-military junta that lasted until the first elections through universal suffrage took place in 1947 (only one year after universal suffrage was introduced in France and Italy). This first democratic government of Venezuela lasted only nine months, interrupted by another military coup in November 1948.

The 1948 coup eventually brought General Marcos Perez Jimenez to power, who ruled without challenge for six more years, until 1958. One of the main distinguishing features of the Marcos Perez Jimenez regime was that it constructed numerous public infrastructure works. According to Perez Jimenez, democracy was to be measured by its achievements and constructions instead of by elections.[8] It was during his presidency that the Central University of Venezuela, various major bridges, a steel mill, and freeways were built. This notion of government as the agent for construction of public works still pervades Venezuela today, when Chavez boasts about the projects his government is engaged in and when the opposition criticizes a supposed lack of public works projects.

Oil production increased steadily during the Perez Jimenez regime by, on average, 9.4 percent per year.[9] Between 1948 and 1958, the number of oil wells increased from 6,032 to 10,124[10] and production thus increased from 1.3 million barrels per day (bpd) in 1948 to 2.8 million bpd in 1958.[11] Combined with increasing oil prices, this meant a constant growth of state oil revenues and of GDP. As oil income boomed, agriculture declined and Venezuelans engaged in a massive land flight. As a result of the dramatic decline in agriculture, Venezuela experienced the most rapid urbanization process and is currently the second-most urbanized country in all of Latin America.[12]

Then, in 1957, an economic crisis hit Venezuela, largely due to falling oil prices, which many say contributed to the unpopularity of Perez Jimenez. Another reason for popular discontent was that while those associated with the government became ever richer, most ordinary people did not appear to benefit from the increasing oil revenues. The 1953 constitution, which Perez Jimenez drafted, required him to hold an election by 1958. Originally, he believed that by then, his public works program would allow him to win the election easily. However, it became obvious that this would not be the case. Finally, on January 23rd, the discontent made itself felt among the highest ranks of the military and several of Perez Jimenez' top officers asked for his resignation.

Democracy, Growth, and Oil: 1958-1978

From the end of the Perez Jimenez dictatorship in 1958 until the end of the first presidency of Carlos Andrés Perez in 1978, Venezuela's economy went through a period of steady expansion, almost entirely due to steadily increasing oil revenues. During this time period the Venezuelan state had sufficient revenues to build up one of Latin America's most extensive welfare states. Inflation held steady at one of the lowest levels in Latin America, at an average of about 3 percent per year, making this growth appear to be particularly solid.[13]

Carlos Andrés Perez (known as "CAP") won the presidency in 1973. His campaign promised great things for Venezuela, which, to a large extent, came true. The price of oil tripled almost overnight, going from $3.05 per barrel to 10.73 between 1973 and 1974 (in inflation and exchange rate adjusted dollars—the nominal price quadrupled).[14] During the Pérez presidency state revenues, thus, also nearly tripled and his government would eventually receive more revenues than all of the other Venezuelan presidencies combined since the dictatorship of General Gomez. By 1976 Venezuela had a per capita fiscal income that equaled that of West Germany. All of this new income was immediately plowed into social welfare programs, a minimum wage, massive infrastructure projects, and efforts to "sow the oil" in import substitution schemes. Efforts were made to launch a Venezuelan automobile industry and to build the world's largest bridge (over Lake Maracaibo). By 1978 economic growth had managed to reduce the poverty rate to 10 percent[15] and unemployment dropped to 5.6 percent.[16]

Another main focus of Perez's "Great Venezuela" program, as he called it, was the building up of domestic industry, particularly mining and petrochemicals, the nationalization of the country's oil industry, the consolidation of its faltering steel industry, and the expansion of its hydro-electric capacity. None of these plans were new, but their scope was. Also, public investment in basic industries was given much higher priority than social spending. While the previous Caldera government budget plan intended to spend 35.4 percent on education, housing, health, and government services, Perez' budget plan foresaw only 19.9 percent dedicated to these.[17]

Perez introduced numerous changes into Venezuelan society that would end up serving as precedents and would shape Venezuela for decades to come. These measures included the introduction of a minimum wage, the doubling of public employment in just five years, a freeze on firings, and tax breaks for private enterprise. The consequences of these policies for the economy were felt quite rapidly. Inflation and capital flight were among the first consequences, due to the increased purchasing power and the lack of goods to purchase. Also, the dramatic increase in state spending heated up Venezuela's chronic "Dutch Disease."[18] As the oil boom reached its peak in 1976, the Venezuelan state counted on oil revenues for 85 percent of the state's total revenues.

By 1976, it became clear that the oil boom would not last. Oil prices were declining and the Perez administration, in an effort to make the best of what it had already invested, decided to go into debt. With international lenders looking for ways to invest Middle Eastern petrodollars, Latin American countries like Venezuela were perfect targets for loans. Venezuela's debt grew dramatically, from 9 percent of GDP in 1970 to 49 percent in 1988 (a more than five-fold increase in relative terms) or from $964 million to $29.5 billion (a more than 30-fold increase in absolute terms) – the largest per capita debt in all of Latin America at that time.

Decline and Failure of Venezuela's Oil-Based Developmentalism (1979-1998)

A fundamental shift began in Venezuelan society once the oil bonanza began to wane and sputter to a halt. The end of Venezuela's golden years came with the next two presidencies, of Copei's Luis Herrera Campíns (1979-1984) and of AD's Jaime Lusinchi (1984-1989), which were quite unremarkable except for the fact that this was a period when Venezuela entered its 20-year economic decline. There were occasional oil booms in this period, such as during the Iranian revolution (1980) and the gulf war (1991), but by then the booms could not make up for the ground that had already been lost due to heavy indebtedness, increasing oil production costs, declining oil price, and population growth. The decline of per capita oil income and thus also of per capita GDP was steady and unprecedented in the world during this period.

Real per capita income suffered a massive and steady decline over a period twenty years, from 1979 to 1999, declining by as much as 27 percent in this period. No other economy in South America experienced such a dramatic decline.[19] Along with this decline, poverty increased, from 17 percent in 1980 to 65 percent in 1996.[20] Why did this decline in per capita real income and corresponding increase in poverty occur in a country that, as the world's fifth largest oil supplier, ought to be rich?

Paradoxically, it is precisely that which ought to make Venezuela rich, which made it so poor: oil. In addition to the typical Dutch Disease problem, the sudden increase of oil revenues in Venezuela caused a serious problem in the government's fiscal policies. That is, the oil boom created the illusion that the oil income would last for a long time to come. However, when the oil income began to decline in the late 1970s, it was not as easy to reduce government spending as it had been to increase it. The result was that the government gradually went deeper and deeper into debt. More importantly, interest rates for the foreign debt increased dramatically, so that between 1970 and 1994 foreign debt rose from 9 percent to 53 percent of GDP.

Compounding the declining revenues and the rising debt burden was a massive capital flight, largely in response to the declining economic situation and the impression that the government was unable to do anything to stop the decline. In 1982 alone, $8 billion left the economy.[21] To stem this capital flight, President Luis Herrera Campíns introduced a tiered exchange rate in 1984, to replace the single fixed rate that had existed until then. That is, foreign currency for essential imported goods could be exchanged at a lower rate than foreign currency for other types of economic activity. The devaluation was significant, though, and dramatically decreased the value of Venezuelans' wealth and incomes relative to the outside world.[22] Middle class Venezuelans, who had become used to going on shopping sprees in Miami, could suddenly no longer afford to do so. Other consequences of this economic decline were increasing unemployment (reaching 13.4 percent in 1984), a growing informal sector (reaching 54 percent in 1998), and a dismantled welfare state.

By 1988, while an unknown lieutenant colonel named Hugo Chávez was organizing a conspiratorial Bolivarian revolutionary movement within the military, Venezuela seemed to be at the brink of an abyss. That year, former President Carlos Andrés Perez campaigned on a promise to reinstitute Venezuela's glory days of the mid 1970s, and to refuse to accede to neoliberalism, or to bring in the IMF to help with the country's fiscal deficit. Perez easily won a second (non-consecutive) term in December 1988. However, three weeks after his inauguration in February 1989, Perez completely reversed his campaign promises and introduced a full package (known as "*paquetazo*"—package hit) of IMF-required neo-liberal measures, such as gasoline price increases, privatization, social spending cutbacks, and deregulation of prices.

The economic shock treatment hit the population with unprecedented force. However, since the most immediate measures of the *paquetazo* affected all Venezuelans evenly in absolute terms, they affected the poor more than anyone else in relative terms. A 30 percent increase in bus fares affects a poor person much harder than someone from the middle class. Protests against the IMF-mandated bus fare increases began immediately when the new fares were instituted in the morning of February 27, 1989. By noon, the protests became gradually more violent, with street blockades and the burning of tires on the streets. Soon thereafter these protests turned into full-blown riots, in which stores were looted, first in Caracas and, as word spread, to almost all other cities throughout Venezuela. The protests and riots appeared to be spontaneous and none of the country's political leadership, neither from the government or the opposition or the unions, made any declarations about it one way or the other. Also, the police merely stood by.

The government then proceeded to violently repress the protests and riots, bringing in the military, which, together with the police, shot at protestors and rioters indiscriminately. The repression continued for several days after the riots had ended, with military forces going into the poor neighborhoods, the "barrios," attacking people at random. Finally, when the shooting ended on March 4, the death toll according to human rights groups stood at nearly 400.[23] Other unofficial estimates, however, place the number of dead between 1,000 and 3,000. Weeks later, human rights groups would find mass burial sites in the barrios, with bodies too decomposed to identify. In essence, this was one of the bloodiest repressions of the so-called IMF-riots to take place in the 1980s and 1990s.

In the aftermath of the IMF-imposed "structural adjustment plan" that had caused the *Caracazo,* unemployment rose from 7 to 10 percent, the economy shrank by 10 percent, real salaries dropped by 11 percent, and inflation rose to 94 percent for 1989. On May 18, the AD-dominated labor union federation, the CTV, called for one-day general strike against the government it had originally supported. It is in this context of economic and political chaos that Chávez and his band of co-conspirators within the military launched a coup attempt on February 27, 1992 against one of the country's most delegitimized and repressive presidents. The coup failed, but Chávez's brief television appearance, in which he took responsibility for the failure and called on his fellow rebelling officers to lay down their weapons, catapulted him onto the national scene as a savior of Venezuela's oppressed. A second coup attempt on November 27 of that same year, was an even greater failure because of the greater number of dead (300 instead of 14).

As if Venezuela's economic and political situation were not bad enough, in late 1993, shortly before Rafael Caldera was to be sworn into office to serve a second non-consecutive term, a banking crisis erupted. The government decided to nationalize the bank's losses by bailing them out with newly printed money, amounting to 10 percent of the country's GDP, or $8.5 billion, while numerous bank managers and owners fled the country, along with some of the bail-out funds.[24] The result of bringing in so much newly minted currency was massive inflation, which was to reverberate through the entire Caldera presidency. The annual average inflation rate was thus 61 percent—the highest average in the country's democratic history.

The Caldera government futilely tried to gain control over the country's economic chaos, all the while oil prices kept dropping, reaching an all-time low of $10 per barrel in 1998. Caldera presented several very different economic plans during his presidency. The first of these plans tried to keep Caldera's campaign promise not to follow the neoliberal precepts. However, with inflation skyrocketing and oil prices plummeting, none of these worked. So, in the second half of his presidency Caldera, just as

Carlos Andrés Perez before him, switched gears and began implementing measures more aligned with neoliberalism, under a plan called *Agenda Venezuela*, which he presented in April of 1996. With this plan, he initiated the privatization of the inefficient state telephone company and began to explore the privatization of the state oil company. Also, gasoline prices were increased by 600 percent. Caldera's popularity plummeted, from 66 percent to 33 percent in a two-year period and Venezuela's political class faced yet another crisis of confidence.

This generalized disgust with Venezuela's political class because of their constant broken promises and their inability to solve the country's economic problems set the stage for a complete outsider to win the presidency in the 1998 elections. Hugo Chávez was, of all the candidates running that year, definitely the most outside the political establishment and the one who promised to bring about the most dramatic change, in the form of a "Bolivarian revolution." It should thus come as no surprise that he won the election with one of the largest margins in Venezuelan history, with 56 percent of the vote, to the 40 percent of his closest rival.

Return to Oil-Based Developmentalism or Something New?
Social and Economic Development under Chávez

At first glance, the Chávez government's economic policies appear to be somewhat similar to the developmentalist policies of his predecessors, particularly of Carlos Andrés Perez's first presidency in 1974-1979. Indeed, the similarities are striking, in that both aimed or aim to control the exchange rate and capital flight, to industrialize the country via import substitution, to redistribute much wealth via generous social spending, and to maintain a high price of oil to pay for these policies. However, there is an important difference. The Chávez government, in contrast to that of Perez, places a strong emphasis on agricultural production, on citizen participation, and on workplace democracy. Also, the industrial policy of the Chávez government is less burdened by competing interest group politics and therefore potentially more coherent. Whether these additions to the developmentalist model are sufficient to overcome the typical problems of developmentalist economics remains to be seen, but so far the results have been fairly promising.

As others have pointed out,[25] the Chávez government's economic policy can be divided into three general phases, which roughly correspond to its economic and political fortunes. The first phase went from early 1999 to late 2001 and marked a period of consolidation, gradual growth, and moderate economic developmentalism. The second phase, which lasted from late 2001 until late 2003, was a period of heightened political conflict, economic decline, and austerity. Finally, the third period, which lasted from late 2003 until the present (late 2008) was a period of radicalization, strong economic growth, and an effort to create 21st century socialism. With the onset of a global economic recession and a dropping price of oil, though, it is quite likely that a new phase in economic policy is about to begin.

Following a very brief sketch of the first two phases, I will then present an in-depth analysis of the third phase, examining how this phase represents an approach to development that rejects neo-liberalism and goes beyond Keynesian developmentalism. This examination will be divided into a closer examination of policies related to oil production, non-oil production, social policy, fiscal policy, and economic democracy. Finally, I will conclude with an assessment of where these policies might lead in the near future, in light of the global economic crisis of late 2008.

Brief History of Economic Policy under Chávez

As stated earlier, Chávez's first three years in office were ones of economic moderation, compared to Venezuela's and Latin America's developmentalist past. However, compared to the country's and the region's more recent economic history, in which neo-liberalism had come to dominate the policy-making agenda, especially by the late 1990's, when Chávez was elected, his economic policy did represent a decisive break from the past. Chávez vehemently rejected the Caldera government's policies of gradually privatizing the oil industry by allowing more and more transnational oil companies into the country. Also, he rejected Venezuela's flouting of OPEC oil production quotas, which had contributed to the collapse of the price of oil by ruining OPEC countries production discipline more generally. And, he supported a much stronger role for the state in the direction of the country's economy. The lack of state revenues, though, meant that the government could not do all that much in terms of subsidizing strategic industries, let alone nationalize them.

Instead, Chávez first focused on reforming the constitution, which gave the state a substantial role in the economy, but which did not alter capitalist relations in Venezuela. The new constitution even enshrined some of neoliberalism's favorite prescriptions, of maintaining an autonomous central bank and of guaranteeing the right to private property. Still, the new constitution specified that the state is supposed to be in charge of oil production (outlawing its privatization), to guarantee "food sovereignty," and to defend other national industries. Also, the new constitution provides for a broad range of economic and social rights, such as the rights to work, health, food, and shelter, and it considers housework to be economic activity that entitles those who perform it (mostly women) to social security benefits.

In practical terms, though, the first three years were characterized mostly by a departure from previous governments' oil policy by making sure that the price of oil reached a fairer level. To do this, Chávez focused on bringing OPEC back together as a coherent organization. In his first year in office he thus visited all major oil exporting countries and then organized the second-ever summit of OPEC countries in Caracas in October 2000. Oil prices rebounded almost immediately, tripling from $8 per barrel in late 1998 to $24 per barrel by late 1999. In the process, the autonomy of the state oil company, PDVSA, was curtailed, and it was brought back under the auspices of the Ministry of Energy and Mines, as it was forced to abide by the new OPEC production quotas. As Venezuela's oil revenues rose for the first time in nearly a decade, the Chávez government was able to keep to its debt payment schedule and could afford to keep the IMF from imposing policy restrictions.

The economic consequences of these policies were a significant rebound after the 1999 recession, for which Chávez cannot be blamed because he just took office, in which Venezuela's economy shrank by 6 percent in 1999. The economy then recovered and grew by 3.7 percent in 2000 and by 3.4 percent in 2001. Unemployment took a similar turn, going from 11.2 percent in 1998, to 14.8 percent in 1999, and then recovering again in 2000 and 2001, by dropping slightly, to 13.9 percent and 13.3 percent respectively. The prudent fiscal policies of the time also meant that the government was able to get a handle on inflation, which had averaged around 50 percent per year during the previous two presidents. In 1999 inflation was brought down to 20 percent and then to 13.4 percent in 2000 and to 12.3 percent in 2001.

It was not until November 2001 that sharper contours of the Chávez government's economic policy became visible, with the introduction of 49 law-decrees that Chávez was authorized to pass with the help of a temporary enabling law. These laws included many economic aspects, such as mandates for banks to maintain loan portfolios that included at least 3 percent for micro-enterprises and 16 percent for agriculture. Also, one of the laws actively promoted the creation of cooperatives as a means of moving informal sector workers into the formal sector. However, the three most controversial laws were the Land Law, the Hydrocarbons Law, and the Fishing Law.

The main objective of the Land Law was to redistribute Venezuela's agriculturally viable land to small farmers and to eliminate "latifundios" (large and idle landed estates). The main objective of the Hydrocarbons law was to improve revenues and state control over the oil industry. It did this mainly by increasing the royalties both national and transnational oil companies paid to the government for extracting oil, by limiting foreign participation in oil production to minority stakes in joint ventures with the state oil company, and by reaffirming the oil industry's subordination to the Ministry of Energy and Mines. Finally, the main objective of the Fishing Law was to promote "artisanal" (as opposed to industrial) fishing by prohibiting large fishing boats from fishing near the coast. As such, these laws democratized ownership and revenues of key sectors of the country's economy.

The 49 law-decrees ushered in the second phase of the Chávez government's economic policies, in that they marked a radicalization of the government program towards a greater state intervention, social justice, and anti-neoliberalism. The laws also marked the start of a period of intense resistance from Venezuela's old political and economic élite. The opposition used the law-decrees as its touchstone for organizing against Chávez. In the process, it had the good fortune that the passage of the law-decrees coincided with the September 11, 2001 terrorist attack in the U.S., which caused a sudden decrease in Venezuela's economic fortunes, whereby the national budget had to be trimmed by about five percent, which had an immediate negative impact on economic growth figures and unemployment, leading, combined with the opposition-orchestrated media onslaught, to a gradual decline in Chávez's popularity.

The opposition took advantage of Chávez's weakened position by organizing a series of strikes and protests, which culminated in the April 11, 2002 coup attempt. Even though the coup was unsuccessful, it led to a severe economic crisis, whereby capital flight, currency devaluation, and inflation reached unprecedented highs. While the economy shrank by 8.9 percent in 2002 and capital flight caused currency devaluation, which led to an inflation of 31.2 percent because Venezuela imports about 60 percent of its food. The worst was yet to come, though, with the two-month shutdown of Venezuela's all-important oil industry, which began in early December 2002. The effect was massive, so that the economy shrunk by 26.7 percent in the first quarter of 2003, relative to the same quarter of the previous year. Unemployment jumped from 15 percent in January 2002 to 22 percent in March 2003 and poverty jumped from 44 percent to 54 percent in that period.

The one silver lining of the oil industry shutdown was that once the industry started to recover, the Chávez government was finally able to gain complete control over the industry. Prior to this, the opposition-oriented managers of PDVSA resisted each and every one of Chávez's attempts to reform the industry. However, after the shutdown, he was able to legally fire them all for having engaged in a political and thus illegal strike. Despite the firing of about half of PDVSA's workforce, of mostly administrative, managerial, and professional employees, the government managed to gain control over the oil industry in early 2003 and by May managed to bring production back up to pre-strike levels of three million barrels per day. Also, perhaps partly due to the shutdown, but mostly due to the start of the U.S. war in Iraq, oil prices started to climb gradually that year, which brought in new revenues for the government. Even though 2002 and 2003 were lost years, economically speaking, the economy fully recovered by 2004 and was set for an unprecedented four-year period of steady growth, averaging 10 percent per year until 2007.

It was this recovery that began in early 2004, which marked the beginning of the third phase in the Chávez government's economic policies, as Chávez started to pursue a more radical program of state-directed industrialization, nationalizations, and expansion of the "social economy," all in the name of creating 21st Century Socialism in Venezuela. Let us now turn to what, exactly, this most recent phase consists of with regard to the oil industry, non-oil industry and agriculture, social programs, fiscal and monetary policy, and the social economy.

Oil Industry Policy: State Direction

Oil policy during the Chávez presidency has been guided primarily by solidifying state control over oil production, maintaining price stability with the help of OPEC, and increasing oil revenues. These three policy priorities represent a sharp turnaround from the pre-Chávez years, when central government control over the oil industry was weak, OPEC was increasingly ineffective, and oil revenues were dropping not just because the price of oil was dropping, but also because the oil industry was being taxed less.

Ever since Venezuela nationalized its oil industry in the 1970's (1974-76), the industry was nominally under state control, but in practice the same management controlled it that had been in charge prior to nationalization. That is, while nationalization changed the ownership of the oil industry, it did not change the managers who maintained a strong orientation towards the goals and ideals of private transnational corporations. In practice this meant that the state oil company PDVSA was very suspicious and resistant towards its bosses in the Ministry of Energy and Mines and made every attempt to undermine ministry control. One way it did this was by purchasing assets abroad, such as refineries, with the argument that it needed to safeguard markets. However, with the use of transfer pricing, by selling oil to its own subsidiaries at below market rates, it in effect transferred profits to these subsidiaries, thereby avoiding taxation within Venezuela. This was one of the reasons why the share of oil revenues PDVSA paid to the government declined from 70 percent of its total revenues, to merely 30 percent between 1980 and 1998.[26]

The Chávez government tried to address this problem of lack of control over PDVSA by putting a new board of directors in place in late 2001. However, PDVSA management, with significant help from the opposition, succeeded in putting enough pressure on Chávez to reverse this decision (though not in time to avert the April 2002 coup attempt). It was not until after the oil industry shutdown of December 2002 to February 2003 that Chávez managed to gain control over the oil industry once all of the former opposition-minded management had been fired due to their participation in the illegal shutdown.

The second problem that oil policy had to address was that OPEC had become an increasingly ineffective cartel in the pre-Chávez years, largely thanks to the Venezuelan governments of the 1990s, which regularly ignored its OPEC production quotas and aimed to produce as much oil as it could. The result was that other OPEC countries began to ignore their quotas too and the price of oil declined rapidly to unprecedented lows, reaching as little as $8 per barrel in late 1998.

One of Chávez's first international initiatives once in office was to tour all OPEC member countries, to convince them to stick to production quotas. Chávez also visited some non-OPEC countries, such as Mexico and Russia, to convince these too that a reduction in oil production would be in their interest. The tour and subsequent second-ever OPEC summit in Caracas in October 2000 were quite successful if one considers that oil prices began to rise steadily shortly after these events, going from $12.28 per barrel in 1998 to $27.60 in 2000.[27]

Finally, the Chávez government had to reverse its predecessor's policy of gradual privatization and low taxes on the oil industry. The government of Rafael Caldera, for example, allowed transnational oil companies such as ExxonMobil and ChevronTexaco to produce oil in the extra-heavy oil rich Orinoco Oil Belt region under a mere 1 percent royalty agreement. Such unprecedentedly low royalties were justified according to the managers because it is expensive to extract extra-heavy oil, which is almost as viscous as tar. However, since oil prices were rising steadily from 1999 on, the government argued that it was time to change these agreements and with the passage of the 2001 hydrocarbons law implemented a new minimum royalty of 30 percent. Taxes, though, were lowered from 59 percent to 50 percent, with the argument that it is much easier for the Venezuelan state to control royalty payments than taxes, as these could be evaded by inflating costs. Also, placing a stronger emphasis on royalties than on taxes gives companies a greater incentive to be more efficient.

In mid April 2008 then, when the price of oil began rising incessantly, Venezuela instituted an "excess oil profit tax," whereby oil companies had to pay an additional tax on every dollar of the oil price above $70 per barrel. The tax rose again when the price rose above $100 per barrel.[28]

Another aspect of regaining control over and revenues from the oil industry was the partial nationalization of so-called "operating agreements" and of joint ventures. Since the early 1990s, when Venezuela's oil industry was opened to private investment, transnational oil companies were allowed to produce oil in older oil fields, which had become less profitable for PDVSA. The private companies did so under contract, meaning that PDVSA paid them to extract the oil. The consequence was that the transnationals had no incentive to produce efficiently. According to a PDVSA reports in 2002,[29] private companies were charging more for the oil extraction than the oil was worth, meaning that PDVSA was incurring heavy losses in many cases. This changed, though, when the Chávez government required foreign companies to migrate their operating agreements to joint ventures, whereby PDVSA would maintain a minimum 60 percent share. Also, in cases where foreign companies were already engaged in joint ventures, in the Orinoco Oil Belt, the government required them to sell a portion of their investment, so that PDVSA would become a 60 percent majority partner in all of these projects.

The Chávez government's policy of gaining control over the oil industry, of increasing its revenue contributions to the government, and of reconsolidating OPEC, represent a clear and dramatic break from Venezuela's recent neoliberal past. While this oil policy does not seem to be much of a break from the statist development policies of the 1950s and 1960s, it is different in that the Chávez government is following a non-dogmatic approach in that it still wants to involve the private sector, but only to the extent that is useful for the government and the economy. Also, the positive impact these changes had on government revenues was substantial. According to the Minister of Energy and Mines, Venezuela increased its revenues by $26.3 billion between 2000 and 2006, relative to what it would have earned had it not raised royalties, taxes, and taken a majority share in joint ventures.[30]

Non-Oil Policy: Diversification

Perhaps the most important policy for overcoming Venezuela's "Dutch Disease" is the effort to diversify the economy. One way the government has tried to do this is by encouraging the integration of the Latin American economies and by protecting itself from other economies. The idea is that Venezuela competes against economies that are more similar to its own, while keeping at bay economies that could dominate Venezuela, such as the U.S. In other words, Venezuela would initiate a "rational and not generalized opening to international competition."[31]

One of the main areas where the Venezuelan state can directly intervene in the diversification of production is the state-owned oil industry. Here, for example, the government's goal is to strengthen the vertical integration of oil production and commerce by focusing on producing more in the oil sector's downstream products, such as petrochemical products. As a result, in mid 2005, the government spun off the state oil company's petrochemical subsidiary, Pequiven, into an independent state-owned enterprise. Its specific mission is to double petrochemical production by 2012, from 11.5 million tons per year to 25 million tons. Also, it would prioritize the production of petrochemical products for national consumption, instead of for export, as had previously been the case. When Chavez signed the decree for creating the new company, he bemoaned the insanity that Venezuela exports the fertilizer it produces and imports fertilizer from other countries.[32]

Another example of greater diversification via the vertical integration of the oil industry is the effort the Chavez government has made to produce its own refinery pipes, which it has traditionally always imported from first world countries, but which it could just as well produce itself, given Venezuela's large iron and steel production. Similarly, in 2004 Chavez announced that PDVSA would repair and even build tankers in Argentina instead of the U.S. or other countries of the North. This represents a tremendous boost to Argentina's shipbuilding industry and makes regional economic integration more of a reality. Later, in mid 2006 the government announced that it would build its own shipbuilding industry, mostly to service the many tankers it is purchasing from Brazil, Argentina, and China (62 new tankers in total).[33]

Other important areas where the government is focusing its economic diversification efforts are the agricultural sector, the support of small and medium businesses, and the expansion and improvement of basic infrastructure. As mentioned in the beginning of this chapter, the focus on infrastructure is nothing new in Venezuelan economic policy, but will be examined more closely below. With regard to the support of small and medium businesses, the Chavez government has issued several decrees, which order all state institutions to prioritize purchasing with small and medium sized businesses and especially with cooperatives and with Latin American businesses. The government spends billions of dollars every year in state purchases, which represents an important boost to the private economy. The small and medium industrial business chamber of commerce, Fedeindustria, has repaid the favor by actively supporting Chavez quite loyally, even through the worst of the opposition offensives, such as during the April 2002 coup and the December to January 2003 oil industry shut-down.

Finally, the government has tackled the diversification of agriculture largely via its land reform program, which has benefited hundreds of thousands of small farmers. This program is being complemented with training, credits, equipment, and commercialization programs. The government's goal thus is to raise agriculture's percentage of GNP from 6 percent to 12 percent by 2007.[34] This target has been completely missed, though, in that agriculture made up less than 6 percent of GNP in 2008.[35] This gives rise to the suspicion that the Dutch Disease has not been overcome in the least, despite the government's efforts to diversify the economy.

Part of the problem is that while agricultural production has indeed increased by 33.9 percent between 1998 and 2007, sectors that are not affected by the Dutch disease, such as commerce, increased twice as rapidly, by 77.1 percent,[36] thereby drowning out agriculture relative to the rest of the economy. The other problem is that the government's main strategy for overcoming the Dutch Disease is to keep sectors such as agriculture and industrial production afloat; it relies mostly on subsidizing them, which accounts for their growth, but was not enough to make them grow more than other sectors.

Another important element in creating sustainable economic growth has been the prevention of capital flight and maintaining the stability of the country's currency. Until the banking crisis of 1984, Venezuela kept a fixed exchange rate with the dollar. However, once the banking crisis hit and the banks were bailed out with newly minted money, this fixed exchange rate could no longer be maintained and the reins were gradually let go, at first with different types of exchange rates, depending on the type of economic activity for which the dollars were to be used. By the late 1990s the currency was fluctuating quite wildly and devaluing almost constantly, especially every time a crisis hit and then the government would impose currency controls. When Chavez came into office the currency was floating against the dollar, but the central bank tried to keep fluctuations under control by purchasing the national currency, the Bolivar. In the lead-up to the 2002 coup, though, this was no longer possible because the central bank was losing too much of its foreign currency reserves, due to massive capital flight. The government thus had to let the currency float completely and the currency devalued by nearly 40 percent from January to February 2002. It then held steady for a while, until the oil industry shutdown, when it dropped precipitously again, in January 2003, and the government decided to impose a strict currency control, for the first time during the Chavez presidency.

This currency control made it relatively difficult for Venezuelans to exchange the local currency into dollars and thus kept a lid on capital flight. Only those who could prove that their business taxes had been paid in full and who needed to import goods for their business were allowed access to dollars. This had several beneficial consequences for the economy, such as steadily increasing foreign currency reserves, which by 2008 had reached $40 billion, which is as high as Canada's (and which has only a slightly larger population) and on a per capita basis is far larger than Germany's ($55 billion). Also, the control prevented capital flight and thus forced Venezuelans to seek domestic investment opportunities, instead of foreign investment opportunities, as was common. As a result, Venezuela's stock market experienced a major boom, whose index tripled between 2002 and 2005. High stock prices mean that more capital is available for Venezuelan businesses to invest, which, in turn, can mean a greater incentive for diversifying the economy.

Ultimately, the diversification of the economy is supposed to counter Venezuela's "Dutch Disease" problem by creating a greater degree of balance in the sources of the nation's wealth. Also, should Venezuela's oil revenues decline it would be in a better position to manage the decline with an economy that is not based purely on oil production. The success of this strategy has been thwarted, though, in the more recent years of Chavez's Presidency (2004-2008), due to the extraordinarily high oil revenues, which intensify the problems of the Dutch Disease and reduce incentives for economic diversification.

Fiscal Policy

Fiscal sustainability, according to both the government plan of 2001-2007 and of 2007-2013 is a key goal of the government's development plans. Ironically, ever since the oil boom of the late 1970's, Venezuela has been struggling with large state deficits and a large public debt. Part of the reason for this is that policymakers generally felt that they could count on oil income that was as high, at least, as it had been in the previous year. However, with the constantly declining oil prices of the 1980s and 1990s, this was rarely the case and so governments got in the habit of borrowing and running a budget deficit, thinking it could pay the debt off the next time oil prices rose again. Eventually it became clear that this was not going to happen and governments were forced to cut back, which they did, and which led to the gradual dismantling of Venezuela's welfare state between 1980 and 1998.

For the Chavez government, one of the most important elements in achieving fiscal sustainability was to increase government revenues. This, according to the government's plan, was to be done by increasing both the oil revenues and the non-oil revenues. Oil revenues were increased via higher oil prices and higher oil industry taxes. Non-oil revenues increased by enforcing the existing tax laws more strictly: In effect, the Chavez government has been able to increase both its oil revenues and its non-oil revenues, except for during the two crisis years. From the time that Chavez first came into office in 1999 until 2001, oil revenues increased from $6 billion to $11 billion. But these revenues dropped back to $8 billion in 2002 and $9.7 billion in 2003. Then, with the price of oil climbing steadily, oil revenues were significantly up again, at $13.5 billion for 2004 and $18.9 billion for 2005. Similarly, non-oil revenues increased from 1999 to 2001, from $14 billion to $19.5 billion, dropped in the crisis years to $10 billion and $14 billion, only to rise to $17 billion for 2004 and $20.0 billion in 2005.[37] Venezuela used to see such wild fluctuations in its revenues in the past, due to fluctuations in the price of oil. During the Chavez presidency, though, the oil price fluctuations were overshadowed by the economic effects of the political conflict, such as the coup and the oil industry shutdown, which provoked major recessions.

With regard to controlling Venezuela's debt, the Chavez government has been less successful than it was with augmenting its revenues. In some senses Venezuelan history is thus repeating itself, as its earlier period of greatest indebtedness, the late 1970s and early 1980s, corresponded with its period of greatest state revenues. More recently, though, Venezuela managed to pay down some of its debt during the 1990s, so that by 2006 its foreign debt is lower relative to other Latin American countries, at $26.7 billion and 22.3 percent of GDP.[38] Still, it is about $3.5 billion higher than when Chavez first came into office.

During the first three years of his term Chavez pursued a relatively fiscally conservative strategy and also transferred a significant amount of the public debt from foreign to domestic.[39] His fourth and fifth years in office (2003-2004), however, were characterized by deficits, mainly because revenues dropped dramatically due to the opposition's coup and oil industry shutdown. Total public indebtedness (foreign and domestic) thus rose from 27 percent of GDP in 2000 (the lowest level in 18 years)[40] to 39 percent in 2004. In absolute terms, the foreign debt was lowered from $23.4 billion in 1998 to $22 billion in 2001. But it rose again in the subsequent years, to $31 billion in 2005 and dropping in 2006 to $26.8 billion. Total debt, as a percentage of GDP, however, decreased significantly from 29.6 percent to 19.3 percent in the first nine years Chavez was in office (1999-2007).[41]

Social Economy

This aspect of Chavez's program has undergone an important evolution in the six years that Chavez has been in office. Originally Chávez emphasized creating a social economy in the sense of strengthening micro-enterprises and cooperatives and by democratizing ownership of rural and urban land. As Chavez and his movement radicalized, though, Chavez moved towards a much more anti-capitalist position. The role of the social economy and of endogenous development thus came to occupy center stage in the construction of an alternative to capitalism.

According to the government's Economic and Social Development Plan for 2001-2007, the social economy, is an alternative and complementary way to that which is known as the private economy and the public economy. Put another way, the concept serves to designate the production sector of goods and services that arrange economic and common social interests, supported by the dynamism of local communities and in an important participation of citizens and workers of the so-called alternative enterprises, such as the associative enterprises and self-managed micro-enterprises.

Other terms that the government has used for the social economy are the "solidaristic economy" and the "popular economy." In other words, within this economic sector economic activity is organized on the basis of solidarity and the common good, rather than on the basis of self-interest.

Altogether, the social economy encompasses at least five closely inter-related programs: redistribution of wealth (via land reform programs and social policies), promotion of cooperatives, creation of nuclei of endogenous development, industrial co-management, and social production enterprises.

Redistribution of Wealth and Micro-Credit

One of the main ways the government is attempting to correct for problems of unequal market allocation is via redistribution, mostly in the form of urban and rural land reform programs and numerous social programs. Another important form of redistribution is occurring via the extensive micro-credit program for the country's poor, so that these may create their own micro-enterprises (usually of one person or one family). In order to do this, the government has created numerous micro-credit banks, such as the Banco del Pueblo (People's Bank), Banco de la Mujer (Women's Bank), and Fondo de Desarrollo Microfinanciero (Fondemi—Fund for Micro-Finance Development). In addition to these, the 2001 banking law stipulates that all banks have to set aside at least 3 percent of their credit portfolio for micro-finance projects.[42] The increase in micro-credits has been dramatic, so that between 2004 and 2005 private banks alone gave out 140 percent more micro-credits, for a total value of $500 million in 2005:[43] This figure is in addition to the micro-credits that come from state banks, such as the ones named above.

Promoting Cooperatives

A second measure for facilitating the growth of a social economy is the government's support for cooperatives, which is often combined with the micro-credit program. State promotion of the cooperative movement occurs largely via Sunacoop, the National Superintendancy of Cooperatives, which is supposed to promote, supervise, and legalize cooperatives in Venezuela. In the first seven years of the Chavez government, cooperatives have mushroomed throughout Venezuela, with the help of training programs, logistical support, and credits. Their numbers increased from 762 in 1998 to over 100,000 by 2008.[44] The number of people involved in cooperatives increased similarly, from about 200,000 in 1998 to well over one million in 2005. This means that about 16 percent of formally employed Venezuelans are employed in cooperatives.

Part of the reason that cooperatives are flourishing in Venezuela is that the government is giving preferential treatment to cooperatives in all of its state purchasing of goods and services, including purchasing from state owned enterprises, such as PDVSA. Also, one of the government's main social programs, *Misión Vuelvan Caras* (Mission About Face),[45] provides work training and prepares participants for creating cooperatives once they complete the program. In September 2004 the government even created an entire Ministry devoted to the promotion of the social (or popular) economy (*Ministerio de la Economia Popular*—MinEP).[46]

Worker/State Industrial Co-Management

The third dimension of the social economy developed only once Chavez had already been in office for three years: worker managed factories.[47] That is, in 2002, shortly after the April 2002 coup attempt, the Chavez government embarked on an experiment in worker-state co-management of Venezuela's main electricity company, CADAFE. The experiment is still relatively small, though, as only two worker representatives are on the five-member company coordinating committee, which is an advisory body to the management. Another electricity company, CADELA, was also turned over to worker co-management, where worker participation is much more substantial and meaningful.

In late 2004 the government embarked on another experiment when it nationalized a paper production plant, Venepal, and allowed workers to co-manage the plant with the state (renamed as Invepal—*Industria Venezolana Endógena del Papel*). A little later, a similar move was made with a valve manufacturer, CNV (renamed to Inveval). Both of these companies had entered into bankruptcy largely due to their participation in the ruinous oil industry shutdown. The fifth and perhaps most important experiment in worker co-management is the state-owned aluminum company, Alcasa, which was turned over to workers in also in early 2005. These are relatively small efforts compared to the overall dimensions of Venezuela's state-owned industrial sector, but are a sign of probable future developments, especially considering that the government announced in 2005 that it was investigating over 800 other recently bankrupt businesses for possible worker takeovers. Between 2003 and 2008 workers have taken control over approximately 18 factories, which is an extremely small proportion of those said to be candidates for such takeovers.[48]

The reason these enterprises are co-managed between workers and the government, instead of completely self-managed, the way cooperatives are, is that large enterprises touch on interests that go far beyond those of the workers within these industries. As such, according to the government, the interests of society at large ought to be represented in the running of these enterprises, via the participation of society's representatives, in the form of the state. Left to their own devices, especially in the context of a competitive market economy, large self-managed enterprises would have little to no incentive to internalize social costs, such as pollution, or to pursue larger social interests of the common good. In some cases this model seems to be working, such as at ALCASA, where the state is giving the workers a large amount of say. Unfortunately, in other cases, such as INVEPAL, the state ends up with a majority vote on the governing boards of these enterprises and, as a result, workers end up being marginalized.[49]

Nuclei for Endogenous Development (NUDE)

Before we can examine the Endogenous Development Nuclei, we have to first clarify what endogenous development is supposed to mean. This is a relatively new concept within the development literature, which emerged largely as a complement to the concept of sustainable development. While sustainable development is meant to focus on making sure that development does not destroy the resource base of the area that is being "developed," it was still an open question as to how this development would come about. Often, especially in the context of neoliberal theory, development comes about when countries or communities open themselves up to outside investors, thus implying an exogenous development. The concept of endogenous development, though, implies that the resources, in terms of skills and materials, come from within the country or community that is being developed.

Endogenous development as the Chavez government defines it, is:[50]

1. based in existing capacities and necessities
2. motivates community participation in the planning of the economy, via new forms of organization, such as cooperatives and social networks
3. is organized from below towards above
4. is based on the values of cooperation and solidarity
5. uses appropriate technologies of the region without compromising the ecological equilibrium

Endogenous development, as the Chavez government intends to practice it, is supposed to be applicable to both the nation as a whole and to individual communities. On the community level it is mostly being applied in the Nuclei of Endogenous Sustainable Development (Nudes), which are specific communities that have been chosen for special government attention. These communities are thus supposed to become places where the endogenous development of the country as a whole is moved forward. However, unlike the general theory of endogenous development, which proposes that development should only come from within the community, governmental support for the Nuclei takes the form not only of educational programs, but also of financial start-up support for projects. The individual projects within the different nuclei are supposed to fit within one of five priorities for national development: agriculture, tourism, industrial production, infrastructure (transport, communication, education, health, etc.), and services. The emphasis, though, is on agriculture (50 percent) and industrial production (30 percent), paying a particular attention on achieving self-sufficiency with regard to the production of food, clothes, and shoes. By March 2005 there were 149 nuclei of endogenous development throughout the country.[51]

Mission about Face (Vuelvan Caras)/Mission Ché Guevara

The Nuclei for Endogenous Sustainable Development were created relatively early in the Chavez administration. Two or three years later, in early 2004, the government added the *Misión Vuelvan Caras* (Mission About Face, later renamed Mission Ché Guevara, MCG), which has been designed to provide support to the nuclei. Actually, this mission has become one of the most important missions, according to government officials, because it represents the most tangible and practical effort to transform Venezuela's capitalist economy into a socialist economy. According to the government's literature, MCG is "the government's strategy to transform the existing economic model into one of endogenous and sustainable development."[52] As such, one of its main tasks is to integrate all of the other missions in the service of MCG. The primary function of the MCG is to provide skills training and logistical help for unemployed Venezuelans to start cooperatives, if possible, in the context of a Nucleus of Endogenous Sustainable Development.

Elias Jaua, who was the first Minister of Popular Economy, which is in charge of MCG, says that 300,000 Venezuelans will have found work through the mission by May 2005. One million more Venezuelans will have passed through the MCG program and found work, according to Jaua, by mid 2006. Jaua insists, though, that the mission is much more than an employment program. One of its key tasks, he says, is "the cultural transformation of the way in which society produces."[53]

Social Production Enterprise (EPS)

Increasingly, while Chavez was publicly advocating 21st century socialism, he was also placing greater emphasis on the need for communities to be involved in the creation of this socialism. Chavez argued that workers needed to develop a new socialist ethic, which would be in solidarity not just with their fellow workers, but also with the larger community.[54] Chavez's recognition of the importance of community appears to have come from his reading of a book by the Marxist theorist, Istvan Mészáros which talks about the need to base exchange on a "communal system of production and consumption."[55] That is, Chavez began to recognize and talk about how in capitalism consumption and production occur on the basis of the individual self-interest of buyer and seller and thus exclude concerns of those outside of the immediate exchange process. Production and consumption, thus, should be communally based, so that the concerns of the entire community are taken into account.

The primary means for making sure that social and communal concerns are included in the production and consumption process would thus be the newly formulated concept of Social Production Enterprises (EPS). Officially the concept of an EPS was first introduced with a decree in September 2005, which stated that enterprises organized as an EPS had to fulfill a list of requirements, such as to "privilege the values of solidarity, cooperation, complementarity, reciprocity, equity, and sustainability, ahead of the value of profitability."[56] Furthermore, they had to invest at least 10 percent of their profits in the communities in which they operate and produce "goods or services in which work has its own meaning, without social discrimination nor privileges associated with one's position in a hierarchy, in which there is substantive equality between its members, planning is participatory, and operate under either state, collective, or mixed ownership."[57] In other words, purely private companies cannot qualify as EPS. Companies that do fulfill these requirements are then eligible for special financing, state purchasing, and other preferential benefits from the state. As of mid 2006, 500 EPS had registered, with another 7,000 in the process of doing so.[58]

Social Economy Conclusion

Taken together, the policies of promoting micro-credits, cooperatives, worker co-management, nuclei of endogenous and sustainable development, Mission Ché Guevara, and the EPS all are supposed to create and expand the social economy in Venezuela. To what extent this program will succeed is still too early to tell. The plans are ambitious, though. However, the compatibility and therefore durability of this social economy with the larger capitalist economy still needs to be proved. If the social economy only survives by virtue of government subsidies then any downturn in Venezuela's volatile oil revenues could cause these jobs to evaporate relatively quickly. It is thus still an open and crucial question as to whether this social economy can compete with the regular economy, with other Latin American economies, and with the world economy (if exposed to these).

Another issue the social economy faces is in the cultural dimension. Government representatives such as President Chavez and former Popular Economy Minister Elias Jaua repeatedly emphasize that these new forms of organization of production are meant to not only increase democracy and equality, but they must also create a new culture that values solidarity and cooperation above individualism and competition. Experiments in other places, most notably in the Basque region of Spain known as Mondragon,[59] have shown that it is possible to successfully foster a new culture of solidarity and cooperation that also enjoys economic success. However, they have also shown that the economic success of such experiments suffer setbacks when that very success increases exposure to global market forces, which then causes the experiment's adaptation to the global market, which in turn means the adoption of competitive market values in the place of cooperative and solidarity values.

The government's plans for the future do, though, indicate that no matter the obstacles for a social economy, it intends to expand this social economy significantly during Chavez's 2007-2013 term. The government's program for this term states that while the coexistence of social economy, state enterprises, and capitalist enterprises is expected to continue, the enterprises of the social economy are to grow in number and size to such an extent that sometime, in an unspecified future, this sector is equal in size to that of the other two more or less equally sized sectors. Exactly how this is to happen, whether via nationalizations of private enterprises, by increasing government support for the social economy, or some other means, is not entirely clear. The program does suggest, though, that this transformation is to happen gradually and at least partly by converting some private enterprises into social economy enterprises. The draft program also states that state enterprises will be transformed into social production enterprises (EPS).

Social Policies

Beginning in late 2003, when Venezuela's oil industry was recovering from the economically debilitating politically motivated shutdown of earlier that year, the Chávez government launched the first in what would later become a plethora of new social programs known as "missions." In the five years since their nation-wide implementation, these missions have significantly helped alleviate the country's massive poverty. The programs include free community health care, free education programs, discount super markets, and employment programs.

At first, the missions were all organized outside of the regular public administration, in a somewhat ad-hoc basis, often either with the help of the military or of the state oil industry, PDVSA. Part of the reason for this was that the existing public administration was too ossified and slow to allow the rapid implementation of social programs. In a sense, the government set up parallel state structures through which the missions were implemented.

By late 2006 the Chavez government had created 18 missions, dealing with such a wide variety of issues as small scale mining, military reserves, promotion of science research, promotion of Venezuelan culture, indigenous rights, land reform, housing, helping the homeless, stipends for single mothers, and reforestation, in addition to the previously mentioned ones in health, education, and food distribution. Each of these received a creative name, often based in the country's history. Together, Chavez called these missions, "Mission Christ," whose overall purpose was to completely eliminate poverty in Venezuela by the year 2030.

The first such mission, "Inside the Barrio" (Barrio Adentro) is based on bringing nearly 30,000 Cuban doctors, nurses, dentists, and other health professionals to Venezuela, to work directly in the country's poorest communities, providing primary care directly in the neighborhoods. Other missions that were set up with significant help from the Cubans were the literacy training program, Mission Robinson, and the high school completion program, Mission Ribas (both named after Venezuelan independence heroes). The perhaps most important mission for helping poor Venezuelans find employment is the previously mentioned Mission Che Guevara (originally called "Mission About Face"), which provides vocational training and prepares its participants to set up worker cooperatives.

A very important innovative feature of almost all of the missions is that they work very closely with the communities, often requiring community members to set up committees of volunteers who would help coordinate and implement the various missions. As such, the missions represent an important aspect of the government's effort to create a participatory democracy.

Beyond Neoliberalism: but not beyond Developmentalism?

Clearly, the Chávez government's economic policies represent a significant move away from neoliberalism, particularly in its efforts to reverse privatization, maintain control over the currency and over capital flight, and its subsidies for diversifying economic production. What still needs to be examined is, first, whether these policies have been successful so far in developing the country along the lines of the capabilities approach to development and, second, whether these policies are viable in the long-term. A third issue, to be examined in the conclusion, is whether the policies represent a move beyond the typical developmentalist policies of a previous era.

With regard to the first question, it makes sense to briefly review Venezuela's progress towards achieving the UN's Millennium Development Goals, since these in essence deal with some of the main indicators that the capabilities approach is interested in, such as eradication of extreme poverty, universalization of education, gender equality, lowering of infant mortality, and environmental sustainability.

Regarding Venezuela's official poverty rate, the Chávez government has been able to lower this by about one third, from 41.6 percent of households in 2000 to 28.5 percent in 2007 and extreme poverty by half, from 16.7 percent to 7.9 percent.[60] While this might not seem as a particularly large reduction in a time of steadily increasing oil revenues, one has to keep in mind that in 2003 the household poverty rate shot up to 55.1 percent (and the extreme poverty rate to 25 percent) due to the oil industry shutdown, thus forcing the government to make up for lost ground between 2003 and 2005.

With regard to education, the government has managed to significantly increase the percentage of the population receiving education at all levels. Enrollment in preschool education has increased from 45 percent in 1998/99 to 60.6 percent in 2005/6, in elementary school from 89.7 percent to 99.5 percent, in high school from 27.3 percent to 41.0 percent, and higher education from 21.8 percent to 30.2 percent. This represents an increase in all levels (except elementary, which is now nearly universal) by about one third of the population.

The millennium development goal (MDG) with regard to gender equality refers primarily to educational equality. Here the gap between boys and girls in elementary school education was never much of an issue in Venezuela in the first place, with boys actually having a slightly lower level of elementary and high school enrollment than girls.[61]

Another millennium goal, infant mortality, though, was reduced significantly, between 1998 and 2006, from 21.4 deaths per thousand live births, to 14.2 per thousand. In contrast, the maternal mortality rate, which is another MDG, has not changed at all during Chávez's presidency. This is probably due, though, to the fact that Venezuela's maternal mortality rate is already one of the lowest in Latin America, at 60 deaths per 100,000 live births (Latin American countries have an average rate of 130 per 100,000 live births).[62]

Finally, with regard to access to drinking water, the Venezuelan government has managed to increase this from 80.5 percent of the population in 1998 to 91.5 percent in 2005. The MDG of halving the number of people who do not have access to drinking water has thus been halved well before the target year 2015.[63] A large part of the success in achieving this goal is directly relatable to the government's participatory approach to solving social problems. That is, access to drinking water was improved through an intense cooperation process between the water company and the affected communities, which had to form "technical water committees" that would work with the utility company.

Therefore, in terms of improving Venezuelans', particularly poor Venezuelans' capabilities for creating a better life for themselves, significant progress has been made in the nine years since Chávez was first elected president, at least as measured by the MDG statistics. Another factor in this approach, though, would be to examine the political freedoms Venezuelans enjoy, to see how these have changed. However, since this paper is focusing on the material aspects of development, there is insufficient space to enter into such an evaluation here.[64]

Long-Term Economic Viability

With regard to the question of whether the government's policies are viable in the long-term, the picture is a bit more complicated. First, there are policies that depend on the high oil revenues, such as the state subsidies and investment in state-owned industries and the social welfare programs, which are likely to suffer if the price of oil declines as it has in late 2008. Policies that do not depend on oil revenues, such as the implementation of a participatory democracy, increasing and improving tax collection, and land reform, are likely to continue and deepen.

However, from an economic development perspective, there is a more serious viability issue with regard to the government's efforts to control inflation and capital flight via control of the exchange rate. That is, in order to stem capital flight, the government has imposed strict currency exchange controls, where only those who can document that they need hard currency for the import of domestically needed products are allowed to change bolivars into dollars. Some other exceptions also apply, such as for people who travel abroad or need to pay debts or education expenses in dollars. While people still can get around these rules by exchanging their local currency into dollars on the black market, doing so incurs a significant cost to them because the black market exchange rate hovers around double the official exchange rate.

The main problem with the currency control is that although inflation in Venezuela has averaged 20 percent over the past four years the official exchange rate has remained the same, at 2.15 bolivars to the dollar, over the same period. In other words, while the currency lost about 50 percent of its value due to inflation, the exchange rate has remained the same, allowing businesses to import products that can cost half as much as the same product would have cost four years earlier, after adjusting for inflation. In effect, imports end up having an unfair advantage in the Venezuelan market relative to domestic products. The consequence is a significant heating up of the effects of the "Dutch Disease," where domestic industry and agriculture (importable goods) can only survive with government help.

The reason the government does not want to adjust the exchange rate in order to keep up with the currency's loss in value is because doing so would further accelerate inflation, as over 70 percent of the country's consumer needs are imported. The government thus appears to be stuck between a rock and a hard place with regard to the exchange rate. On the one hand the currency keeps losing value because high oil revenues tempt the government to bring more currency into the country than there are corresponding products or increase in domestic production. On the other hand, the government tries to control inflation by increasing imports, to meet increasing domestic demand, but in effect subsidizes imports via an unchanging exchange rate, so that the inflation that has already taken place does not cause even more inflation.

A second long-term development problem has to do with the instability of the price of oil. Before the 2008 global recession kicked in, the Chávez government was quite certain, just as many oil analysts, that the price of oil would remain high for the foreseeable future. As a result, Chávez proceeded to dismantle a rainy day savings fund, the Macro-Economic Stabilization Fund (FEM), which was supposed to automatically gather oil revenues whenever the price of oil rose above the average price of the previous five years and could only be withdrawn when the price dropped below the five-year average. This fund was introduced shortly before Chávez was elected and was originally supported by him. However, once the price of oil started to rise continuously and oil analysts said that it would continue to do so indefinitely, the government began to modify the law, making contributions to the fund mostly discretional, rather than mandatory. As a result, the FEM received practically no contributions between 2003 and 2008.

This decision to dismantle the FEM, combined with the collapse in the world price for oil, which dropped 70 percent in the last five months of

2008, is threatening to wreck havoc on Venezuela's 2009 budget. This would endanger not only countless social programs and investment projects to diversify the economy, but also places at risk Venezuela's entire production of extra-heavy oil, which makes up about one quarter of its oil production and which is not profitable at an oil price of $30 per barrel. Of course, it is unlikely that the price of oil will remain for long as low as it has dropped in December 2008, especially since the lack of revenues for future investment could mean less supply once the world economy gets going again. In the meantime, though, the Chávez government and Venezuelans (just as the rest of the world) face a very uncertain economic future.

Conclusion

There is little doubt that most of the Chávez government's economic policies closely resemble the development policies of the pre-neoliberal era. However, it would be a mistake to believe that this is all there is to Venezuela's current development path. An important aspect that most observers tend to forget is that hand in hand with the renewed emphasis on direct state support for industry and agriculture is a policy of involving the general population in its own development. While it is difficult to quantify the impact this participatory aspect has had on the country's development, it is distinctly possible that one of the reasons why Venezuelan development has been more successful than that of other oil producing countries is traceable to citizen participation.

This participation takes on a wide variety of forms, such as in the involvement of Venezuelans of all walks of life in constructing and even controlling their workplaces through cooperatives, worker-controlled factories, and social production enterprises; their active participation in the social programs known as missions; the direct democratic control over the development of their neighborhoods via their communal councils; and the increasing role of nuclei for endogenous development (NUDE) in fostering "communities of production and consumption."

In short, even though these realms of participatory development and democracy are still in their infancy in Venezuela and even though many macro-economic problems have not been resolved, they do sow seeds of hope that a different kind of development is possible—one that not only places an emphasis on the development of people's capacities, but one that is directed by citizen participation and not just by state activism. The Chávez government has repeatedly stated that it plans to expand this realm of the participatory or "social" economy. The extent to which it succeeds in doing so will be the real test of whether a true and radical alternative to neoliberalism and even capitalism is possible in the 21st century.

Chapter 6

AFRICAN RESISTANCE TO GLOBAL FINANCE, FREE TRADE AND CORPORATE PROFIT-TAKING

Patrick Bond

The 2008 crash of world financial markets, followed by the onset of industrial-economy recession—and possibly world depression—confirmed warnings that so many progressive activists and researchers have offered African elites over the past three and a half decades, namely that they should *protect national economies from vulnerabilities associated with global financial system volatility and multinational corporate abuse.* Such abuse is of both a macro and microeconomic character. Although such warnings were rarely heeded, nevertheless counter-hegemonic processes have recently emerged in the spheres of finance, trade and investment that offer grounds for optimism:

- ongoing financial chaos offers new ideological space and material justifications for African finance ministries to re-impose exchange controls and reregulate finance, and to find sources of hard currency not connected to the Bretton Woods Institutions or Western donors;
- after pressure by the Africa Trade Network and allied radical intellectuals, rising resistance to European Union Economic Partnership Agreements by African states appears to have foiled the most dangerous neoliberal trade strategy, at a time the World Trade Organization's Doha Agenda has been declared dead, in no small part thanks to persistent African opposition (first in Seattle in 1999 and then in Cancun in 2003); and
- opposition to objectionable multinational extractive investments is reflected in ferocious anti-corporate activism in venues ranging from communities (keeping resources in the ground) to the world's courts (demanding apartheid reparations), in turn challenging national states

to take a stand on the choice of eco-social welfare or corporate profits.

The possibilities for radical change are countered by the likelihood of ongoing elite compradorism, of course. But from the bottom up, more activists are pointing out the self-destructive nature of African elites' collaborationist strategies, and as an alternative approach, offer pilot breakthroughs in "deglobalized" production of AIDS medicines and water (as US pharmacorps and French/British water companies are repelled from many capital cities). These are only the most visible outcomes of movements for decommodification and deglobalization. Moreover, Latin American leadership offers concrete strategies to delink from global financial, trade and investment circuitries, particularly as long-term depressionary tendencies make obvious the limits of neoliberal globalization.

However, there remains a residual group of African leaders (and their economic advisors) convinced that their future lies in further integration into the world economy. Such elites had a hard time explaining to their subjects the implications of this disastrous strategy as the crisis intensified: these included the decline in financial activity associated with trade (the Baltic Dry Index fell to an all-time low); lower prices for African exports (especially petroleum, minerals and crops); fewer portfolio investments; less credit for real investment or for financing state securities; a decline in remittances by overseas workers; and less overseas development aid. Various estimates of the sharp fall in Africa's GDP growth rate put it at roughly half the 5.8 percent recorded in 2008.

One result of the global crisis is the set of human costs, such as 700 000 African babies who will die needlessly in 2009 because of the world financial crisis, as the World Bank chief economist (Shanta Devarajan) estimates. Bank records of Sub-Saharan African child and infant mortality, aid flows and consumer price inflation are all extremely high during periods of 'growth deceleration' such as Africa is anticipated to suffer during 2009-10, as shown in Table 1. Consider the manifestations of the crisis especially in the spheres of finance, trade and investment.

Finance

The world financial meltdown that began in 2007 and gathered pace in late 2008 had its roots in the neoliberal export-model (dominant in Africa since the Berg Report and onset of structural adjustment during the early 1980s) and even more deeply, in thirty-five years of world capitalist stagnation/volatility.[1] As South Centre director (and Ugandan political economist) Yash Tandon put it, "The first lesson, surely, is that contrary to mainstream thinking, the market does not have a self-corrective mechanism."[2] This is particularly important in relation to financial markets, as critical Africans have long known.

Systematic financial disequilibration means that Africa receives sometimes too much and often too little in the way of financial flows, and

Table 1: SubSaharan Africa in social crisis

Differences between sample averages, selected variables, SSA 1975-2005

	Growth acceleration		Growth deceleration	
	During	Otherwise	During	Otherwise
Life expectancy (years)	51.3	50.1	48.1	51.0
Dependency ratio	.91	.93	.93	.92
Under 5 mortality (per 1,000)	145.8	161.9	187.1	148.8
Infant mortality (per 1,000 live births)	84.3	93.9	113.2	85.5
Primary completion rate (percent of relevant age group)	52.5	49.9	41.4	52.9
ODA (percent GDP)	13.6	13.6	11.9	14.11
ODA per capita (US$)	68.3	53.2	41.5	61.2
Consumer price index (percent)	15.1	75.2	177	23.2

Source: http://africacan.worldbank.org/a-sub-prime-crisis-in-the-us-and-infant-deaths-in-africa the inexorable result during periods of turbulence is intensely amplified uneven development.[3] Africa has long suffered a disproportionate share of pressure from the world economy, especially in the sphere of debt and financial outflows.[4] But for those African countries which made themselves excessively vulnerable to global financial flows during the neoliberal era, the meltdown had a severe, adverse impact.

In Africa's largest national economy, for example, South African finance minister Trevor Manuel had presided over steady erosion of exchange controls (with 26 consecutive relaxations from 1995-2008, according to the Reserve Bank)[5] and the emergence of a massive current account deficit—9 percent in 2008, the second worst in the world. The latter was in large part due to a steady outflow of profits and dividends to corporations formerly based at the Johannesburg Stock Exchange but relisted in Britain, the US or Australia during the 1990s (Anglo American, DeBeers, Old Mutual, Didata, Mondi, Liberty Life, BHP Billiton). In the second week of October 2008, South Africa's stock market crashed 10 percent (on the worst day, shares worth $35 billion went up in smoke) and the currency declined by 9 percent, while the second week witnessed a further 10 percent crash. The speculative real estate market had already begun a decline that might yet match those of other hard-hit property sectors like the US, Denmark and Ireland, because South Africa's early 2000s housing price rise far outstripped even these casino markets (200 percent from 1997-2004, compared to 60 percent in the US).

The result was that by February 2009, South Africa was listed by *The Economist* as the 'riskiest' of 17 emerging market economies. The main troubles were that it held the highest current account deficit, and also had low reserves and high short-term foreign debt repayments (third worst after Korea and Indonesia). Moreover, South Africa's "banks depend on borrowing, often from abroad, to finance domestic lending and so will be squeezed by the global credit crunch... The rand, which has already fallen sharply, remains one of the most vulnerable emerging-market currencies."[6]

On the other hand, the cost of market failure could at least be offset somewhat by ideological advance. The main gains so far were in delegitimizing the economic liberalization philosophy adopted during the 1994-2008 governments of Nelson Mandela and Thabo Mbeki. Indeed Mbeki's dramatic September 2008 departure from office occurred partly because of substantially worsened inequality and unemployment since 1994, which in turn was partly responsible for tens of thousands of protests during the late 2000s.[7] To illustrate the vulnerability: when a solidarity letter Manuel wrote to Mbeki, resigning from his government on its second-last day was released to the press (by Mbeki) on 23 September 2008, the stock and currency markets imposed a $6 billion punishment within an hour. The crash required incoming caretaker president Kgalema Motlanthe to immediately reappoint Manuel with great fanfare. In the same spirit, Mbeki's replacement as ruling party president, Jacob Zuma, had visited Davos and paid tribute to Merrill Lynch and Citibank in 2007-08 (ironically in light of the impact of the latter two institutions' contribution to the global financial crisis, they were insisting on having *their* "jitters" calmed). Zuma had already assured international financiers (e.g. in Los Angeles in late 2007) that Manuel's economic policy would not change:

> Some have said that if Zuma is in charge of the administration, it will move left because of his support from the trade unions, which are very left, and those from SA Communist Party . . . and therefore that the economic policies of the government will change. I had thought this was not a big issue but I am grateful that I have an opportunity to explain and would love to tell you, brothers and sisters, that nothing is going to change.[8]

Hence the opening of ideological space to contest neoliberalism in practice became a crucial struggle for the trade unions and SA Communist Party. As the Party's leading intellectual, Jeremy Cronin, put it, "The inability to appreciate the dialectical character of world capitalism's trajectory, was to lead Mbeki... to gravely misread the global situation, to imagine an 'African renaissance" based on catching-up and aligning ourselves to the 'West', with the promise of an ineluctable, evolutionary way forward—'today is better than yesterday, and tomorrow will be better than today.'"[9] That strategy obviously failed, as global integration failed to generate the promised growth, or trickle-down the wealth earned in the commodity boom.

In contrast, as the financial meltdown unfolded in the US and Europe, the merits of South Africa's residual capital controls became clearer. According to one business newspaper, thanks to exchange controls, "There is a healthy degree of trapped liquidity within the financial system." [10] Another factor was that many exotic financial products had been banned. As a leading official of the central bank, Brian Kahn, explained,

> The interbank market is functioning normally and the Reserve Bank has not had to make any special liquidity provision. We have a relatively sophisticated and well-developed banking sector, and the question then is, what has saved us? (This may be tempting fate, so perhaps I should say what has saved us so far?) This all raises the old question whether or not exchange controls work. The conventional wisdom is that they do not, particularly when you need them to work. We seem to have been exception to this rule. It turns out that we were protected to some extent by prudent regulation by the Bank regulators, but more importantly, and perhaps ironically, from controls on capital movements of banks. Despite strong pressure to liberalize exchange controls completely, the Treasury has adopted a policy of gradual relaxation over the years. Controls on non-residents were lifted completely

in 1996, but controls on residents, including banks and other institutions, were lifted gradually, mainly through raising limits over time. With respect to banks, there are restrictions in terms of the exchange control act, on the types of assets or asset classes they may get involved in (cross-border). These include leveraged products and certain hedging and derivative instruments. For example banks cannot hedge transactions that are not SA linked. Effectively it meant that our banks could not get involved in the toxic assets floating that others were scrambling into. They would have needed exchange control approval which would not have been granted, as they did not satisfy certain criteria. The regulators were often criticized for being behind the times, while others have argued that they don't understand the products, but it seems there may be advantages to that! Our banks are finding it more difficult to access foreign funds and we have seen some spikes in overnight foreign exchange rates at times. But generally everything seems 'normal' on the banking front. Our insurance companies and institutional investors were also protected to some extent, in that there is a prudential limit on how much they can invest abroad (15 per cent of assets), and the regulator in this instance (the Financial Services Board) places constraints on the types of finds or products they can invest in. (Generally it appears that exotics are excluded). One large South Africa institution, Old Mutual, moved its primary listing to the UK a few years back (when controls were relaxed), and the plc has had fairly significant exposure in the US.[11]

Demands for deeper exchange controls were made by the SACP in South Africa. As for the rest of Africa, similar opportunities to contest financial system orthodoxy now arise. At this stage, it is practically impossible for staff from the most powerful external force in African economic policy, the International Monetary Fund (IMF), to advise elites with any credibility. The IMF's October 2006 *Global Financial Stability Report*, after all, claimed that global bankers had shown "resilience through several market corrections, with exceptionally low market volatility." Moreover, global economic growth "continued to become more balanced, providing a broad underpinning for financial markets." Because financial markets always price risk correctly, according to IMF dogma, investors could relax: "[D]efault risk in the financial and insurance sectors remains relatively low, and credit derivatives markets do not indicate any particular financial stability concerns." The derivatives and in particular mortgage-backed securities "have been developed and successfully implemented in U.S. and U.K. markets. They allow global investors to obtain broader credit exposures, while targeting their desired risk-reward trade-off." As for the rise of credit default swaps (the $56 trillion house of cards bringing down one bank after the other), the IMF was not worried, because "the widening of the credit default swaps spreads [i.e. the pricing in of higher risk] across mature markets was gradual and mild, and spreads remain near historic lows." [12]

Fast forward to the April 2008 launch of the IMF's "Regional Economic Outlook for Sub-Saharan Africa" study: IMF Africa staffer John Wakeman-Linn's slideshow, 'Private Capital Flows to Sub-Saharan Africa: Financial Globalization's Final Frontier?', concluded that the vast rush of finance is generally good for Africa, but policies would have to be changed—making Africa more vulnerable to the international financial system—in order to take full advantage:

- More transparency and consistency: exchange controls in SubSaharan Africa are complex and difficult to implement.
- Gradual and well-sequenced liberalization strategy can help limit risks associated with capital inflows.
- Accelerated liberalization in the face of large inflows may help their monitoring (e.g. Tanzania); selective liberalization of outflows may help relieve inflation and appreciation pressures, but further work needed on modalities. [13]

The IMF proclaimed the merits of liberalization and rising financial flows to Africa, especially portfolio funding (i.e., short-term hot money in the forms of stocks, shares and securities issued by companies and government in local currencies but readily convertible). Such 'hot money' - speculative positions by private-sector investors – flowed especially into South Africa's stock exchange, and also to a lesser extent into share markets in Ghana, Kenya, Gabon, Togo, and Seychelles.

However, financial outflows continue apace. An updated report on capital flight by Leonce Ndikumana of the Economic Commission for Africa and James Boyce of the University of Massachusetts shows that thanks to corruption and the demise of most African countries' exchange controls, the estimated capital flight from 40 Sub-Saharan African countries from 1970-2004 was at least $420 billion (in 2004 dollars). The external debt owed by the same countries in 2004 was $227 billion. Using an imputed interest rate to calculate the real impact of flight capital, the accumulated stock rises to $607 billion. According to Ndikumana and Boyce,

> Adding to the irony of SSA's position as net creditor is the fact that a substantial fraction of the money that flowed out of the country as capital flight appears to have come to the subcontinent via external borrowing. Part of the proceeds of loans to African governments from official creditors and private banks has been diverted into private pockets—and foreign bank accounts—via bribes, kickbacks, contracts

awarded to political cronies at inflated prices, and outright theft. Some African rulers, like Congo's Mobutu and Nigeria's Sani Abacha, became famous for such abuses. This phenomenon was not limited to a few rogue regimes. Statistical analysis suggests that across the subcontinent the sheer scale of debt-fueled capital flight has been staggering. For every dollar in external loans to Africa in the 1970-2004 period, roughly 60 cents left as capital flight in the same year. The close year-to-year correlation between flows of borrowing and capital flight suggests that large sums of money entered and exited the region through a financial 'revolving door'. [14]

Where did this leave African debtors in 2008? According to the IMF, the "debt sustainability outlook" of low-income African countries "has improved substantially, with 21 out of 34 countries classified on the basis of the Debt Sustainability Framework at a low or moderate risk of debt distress at end-2007."[15] Yet the major lesson from the prior quarter-century of debt distress was not the abstract ratios, but instead, the ability to pay the debt in context of pressing human needs. It was here, according to London-based Jubilee Research, that the Bretton Woods institutions had not accurately assessed the damage done by debt, or the injustice associated with repaying debt inherited from prior undemocratic governments:

> Current [mid-2008] approaches to debt relief (HIPC and MDRI for poor countries, and Paris and London Club renegotiations for middle income countries) are not solving the problems of Third World indebtedness. HIPC and MDRI are reducing debt burdens but only for a small range of countries and after long delays, and at a high cost in terms of loss of policy space. While non-HIPC poor countries continue to have major debt problems and middle-income country indebtedness continues to grow. [sic] The present approach is marred by the involvement of creditors as judge, prosecution and jury in direct conflict with natural justice and by the failure to take into account either the human rights of the people of debtor nations or the moral obscenity of odious debt. It is all too little and too late... Even after the debt relief already granted under HIPC and MDRI, 47 countries need 100% debt cancellation on this basis and a further 34 to 58 need partial cancellation, amounting to $334 to $501 billion in net present value terms, if they are to get to a point where debt service does not seriously affect basic human rights. [16]

Hence the system of debt peonage remains, and the only prospect for its relief is the weakening of Washington's power, along with the overhauling of the aid system which is so closely connected to debt.[17] The Accra Agenda for Action (AAA) conference in September 2008 provided an opportunity to address the problems of donor/financier cross-conditionality, 'phantom aid' (including tied aid), corruption, waste, economic distortions and political manipulation, as well as to add the South's demand for repayment of the North's ecological debt to the south. But the opportunity was lost, and even mild-mannered NGOs realized they were wasting their time, as a staffer at Civicus, Nastasya Tay, revealed:

> A colleague from a major international NGO gave an excellent summary of the whole High Level Forum process: 'Why should I attend interminably long meetings, to passionately lobby for reform, when countries like the US and Japan are refusing to sign on because of some 'language issues' with the AAA? In the end, we will have worked incredibly hard to, if we're lucky, change a few words. And it's just another document.' [18]

Hence, for some African countries, the solution lies in an alternative source of hard currency finance. Not only does China provide condition-free loans to several of Africa's most authoritarian regimes. More hopefully, Venezuela is considering a proposal from the Center for Economic and Policy Research in Washington to replace and displace the IMF, as happened in Argentina in 2006, in which case repaying the IMF early or even defaulting would be feasible. (Whether Venezuela maintains a petrodollar inflow to raise such resources for on-lending is another matter.) In other African countries, progressive social movements have argued for debt repudiation and are concerned about any further financial inflows beyond those required for trade financing of essential inputs. This would also entail inward-oriented light industrialization oriented to basic needs (and not to luxury goods, a major problem that emerged in Africa's settler colonial economies during the 1960s-70s).

The crucial ingredient for establishing an alternative African financing strategy from the left is pressure from below. This means the strengthening, coordination and increased militancy of two kinds of civil society: those forces devoted to the debt relief cause, which have often come from what might be termed an excessively polite, civilized society based in internationally-linked NGOs which rarely if ever used "tree shaking" in order to do "jam making"; and those forces which react via short-term 'IMF Riots' against the system, in a manner best understood as *un*civilized society. The IMF Riots that shook African countries during the 1980s-90s often, unfortunately, rose up in fury and even shook loose some governments' hold on power. However, when these, contributed to the fall of Kenneth Kaunda in Zambia (one of many examples), the man who replaced him as president in 1991, former trade unionist Frederick Chiluba, imposed even more decisive IMF policies. Most anti-IMF protest simply could not be sustained.

In contrast, the former organizations are increasingly networked, especially in the wake of 2005 activities associated with the Global Call to Action Against Poverty (GCAP), which generated (failed) strategies to support the Millennium Developmental Goals partly through white-headband consciousness raising, through appealing to national African elites and through joining a naïve appeal to the G8 Gleneagles meeting.[19] Since then, networks tightened and became more substantive through two Nairobi events: the January 2007 World Social Forum and August 2008 launch of Jubilee South's Africa network. These networks could return to the cul-de-sac of GCAP's "reformist reforms"—i.e., to recall Andre Gorz's phrase, making demands squarely within the logic of the existing neoliberal system and its geopolitical power relations, in a manner that disempowers activists if they gain slight marginal changes. [20]

Or they could embark upon "non-reformist reform" challenges, by identifying sites where the logic of finance can be turned upside down. The most striking case might have been the South African 'bond boycott' campaign of the early 1990s, wherein activists in dozens of townships offered each other solidarity when collective refusal to repay housing mortgage bonds was the only logical reaction. This forewarned the 1995-96 "El Barzon" ("the yoke") strategy of more than a million Mexicans who were in debt when interest rates soared from 14 to 120 percent over a few days in early 1995: they simply said, "can't pay, won't pay". That slogan was also heard in Argentina in early 2002, following the evictions of four presidents in a single week due to popular protest. The ongoing pressure from below compelled the government to default on $140 billion in foreign debt so as to maintain some of the social wage, the largest such default in history. In Ecuador in early 2009, following a "debt audit" initiated by the Jubilee South movement, President Rafael Correa announced a default on foreign debt in part because of the "odious" character of loans made to dictators in prior decadesThe global failure to reform financial markets is one reason for the need to strike more decisively from the grassroots and national scales of politics. In early 2009, the World Economic Forum's *Global Risks 2009* report confirmed, "The degree to which the world has lost confidence in its institutions and systems is serious. Without confidence, we could face a protracted and potentially calamitous downward spiral." [21] Not only is the financial system still at risk. The calamitous spiral of recession and depression fed by crashing asset prices could forever end civil society's confidence in the soaring Millennium Development Goal rhetoric of UN officials. Such rhetoric was meant to be backed by hard cash, and in October 2008, General Assembly president Miguel d'Escoto Brockmann (a former Nicaraguan Sandinista foreign minister) asked for help from an impressive group of economists, led by Columbia University professor Joseph Stiglitz. But the context for the commission's work is extremely unfavourable, as signified by the refusal by IMF and World Bank leaders to bother attending the UN Financing for Development conference in Doha in November 2008. In January 2009, the UN Commission of Experts on Reforms of the International Monetary and Financial System, led by Stiglitz, passed eleven

"Recommendations for Immediate Action", including unrealistic development aid increases of 20 percent.

However, instead of advocating the replacement of the IMF with a more democratic and growth-oriented institution, as Stiglitz did in August 2002 on the Left Business Observer radio program, the commission suggests the Fund be re-legitimized and re-capitalized. Stiglitz's group also declined to express support for capital controls to protect developing countries from global financial turmoil, contrary to his earlier pronouncements. And the commission neglected to consider how to convert the recent wave of bank nationalizations from what might be termed 'lemon socialism' (bailing out failed capitalists) into genuine public development finance utilities. Nor was there mention of Odious Debt and reparations, in spite of South African anti-apartheid activists' US 'Alien Tort Claims Act' court strategy (with Stiglitz as *amicus curiae*), aimed at recovering $400 billion in pre-1994 debt repayments and profit outflows. Environmentalists hoping for detailed strategies to address the North's ecological debt to the South and the financing implications of climate crisis were distressed. Those desiring a Tobin Tax, arms tax or the abolition of unregulated hot money centers did not find a mention. Neither was commodity price regulation on the commission's immediate agenda, notwithstanding extreme volatility. Stiglitz and colleagues also revived the tired old Doha Agenda of trade liberalization, and they attempted to restore faith in a mildly reformed market ideology. [22] All of these suggest that the longstanding problem of global economic governance is nowhere near to being resolved; elites are simply not capable of putting together the appropriate ideas and the political forces required to share sacrifices and coordinate economic recovery.[23]

Figure 1: Private capital inflows to Africa (US$billions)

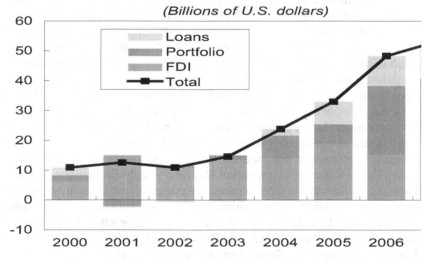

Source: International Monetary Fund (2008), *Africa Economic Outlook,* Washington, DC, April

Figure 2: Portfolio inflows to Africa (percent of GDP)

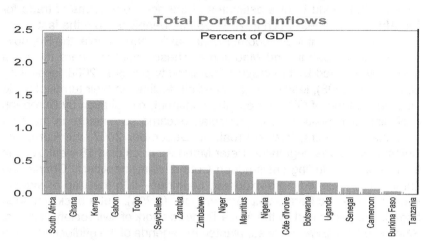

Source: International Monetary Fund (2008), *Africa Economic Outlook,* Washington, DC, April

Trade

As in the case of finance, a tumultuous and highly politicized process exists in relation to trade. As one reflection of the adverse

Table 1: Africa in economic crisis

Terms of trade shocks (percent of 2006 GDP)

	2008/2007		2009/2008
Top five			
Equatorial Guinea	32.5	Seychelles	5.4
Angola	21.9	Eritrea	3.8
Congo, Rep.	19.3	Togo	3.6
Gabon	17.9	Comoros	2.2
Mauritania	16.3	Senegal	2.2
Bottom five			
Togo	-6.1	Nigeria	-10.2
Senegal	-6.2	Gabon	-12.5
Cape Verde	-6.8	Congo,Rep.	-13.6
Eritrea	-9.8	Angola	-15.1
Seychelles	-10.5	Equatorial Guinea	-20.9

Source: http://africacan.worldbank.org/commodity-price-shocks

consequences for specific, highly export-dependent African economies, consider the World Bank's estimates of the decline in terms of trade for five African countries which in 2007-08 had benefited from the last stage of the 2002-08 commodity boom: Equatorial Guinea, Angola, the Republic of the Congo, Gabon and Mauritania. These countries were the most adversely affected by the crash of commodity prices in 2008 (especially oil from mid-2008), leading to double-digit declines in their terms of trade as a percentage of GDP. Across the continent, exploitation by European capitalists and politicians, in particular, became so extreme in the past year that something had to break. In December 2007, the European Union's then trade negotiator, Peter Mandelson, cajoled 18 weak African leaderships—including crisis-ridden Cote d'Ivoire, neoliberal Ghana and numerous frightened agro-exporting countries—into the trap of signing interim 'Economic Partnership Agreements' (EPAs). But a backlash soon began, fostered in part by the Africa Trade Network of civil society activists. Since 2002, the EPAs have supplanted the agenda of the gridlocked World Trade Organization (WTO), just as bilateral trade deals with the US, China and Brazil are also now commonplace. A united Europe deals with individual African countries in an especially pernicious way, because aside from free trade in goods, Mandelson hinted in October 2007 at other invasive EPA conditions that will decimate national sovereignty: "Our objective remains to conclude comprehensive, full economic partnership agreements. These agreements have a WTO-compatible goods agreement at their core, but also cover other issues."[24] Such 'Singapore' issues (named after the site of a 1996 WTO summit) include investment protection (so future policies don't hamper corporate profits), competition policy (to break up local large firms) and government procurement (to end program like South Africa's affirmative action). These were removed from the WTO by African negotiators during the Cancun summit in 2003, but have reemerged through EPA bilaterals.

Europeans' regular abuses of donor power include threats of trade preference withdrawal if EPAs are not signed. European capital has made its own needs clear: not only access to cheap commodities, as was enjoyed under the Lomé Convention, but also unrestricted African market access, protection from potential restrictive public policies, and a buffer from Chinese competition. There are other problems, and corresponding resistance. For example, African farmers' ability to sell on the local market will be undercut by rapid trade liberalization that opens the way to surges of cheap, often subsidized imports. Women are most adversely affected. Earlier allegedly 'developmental trade' strategies, such as the EU's "Everything But Arms" deal, haven't worked, because of strict rules of origin and serious supply-side constraints. There is simply no capacity in African firms to penetrate Europe given the continent's small production runs and high transport costs. Moreover, climate change will soon invoke hefty taxes on ships (whose dirty bunker oil sends vast amounts of CO_2 into the atmosphere). Yet EPAs will require an even greater African investment in port infrastructure and other management costs necessary to facilitate trade.

From early on, African progressives—especially within the African Trade Network—called on elites to halt the negotiations. A conference of the Council for the Development of Social Science Research in Africa (Codesria) in June 2008 generated tough commentary from academics and civil society experts:

- Zimbabwean anti-EPA campaigner Nancy Kachingwe, "These are not trade agreements, they're structural adjustment program. It's about policy and all sorts of other controls, and the impacts are the same."
- Bernard Founou-Tchuigoua of the World Forum for Alternatives in Dakar, "In these agreements there is inherent corruption, in their very substance."
- Gyekye Tanoh of Third World Network in Accra: "The key thing for Mandelson is to gain exclusive preferential market access. Europe is gaining 80% of our markets in exchange for what is effectively just 2% of theirs. The effect of trade liberalization on African agriculture is a disaster, with only one sector anticipated to grow: agro-processing. That's the one that most easily invites European capital to scale up investments in joint ventures. Agricultural output would only increase by 1 percent, our studies show. But the big contradiction is in the export of cash crops, at a time of severe pressure on food products."
- Senegalese scholar Cherif Salif Sy: "Most of Africa has an electricity crisis, and yet to get economies of scale for European agro-processing companies if they locate in Dakar, they require vast amounts of electricity. And they come with the power to demand a lower price, which puts much more stress on our grid and causes the price to go up for local buyers, and the supply to be redirected."
- Third World Network director Yao Graham concedes: "Unions have been too syndicalist, while our justice movements have been exhausted fighting structural adjustment. The local private sector has been absent. But in some regions, like West Africa, agricultural producers have been well organized and opposed to EPAs. Links to the Caribbean are weak. But we are working behind enemy lines with progressive allies in Europe, including within the Brussels parliament. It should be possible to shrink the EPA agenda to nonreciprocal market access to goods, and no more. This we can win in coming months." [25]

Surprisingly, the activists were joined by the South African government (especially deputy trade minister Davies)—in the wake of the 2004 departure (for the public enterprises ministry) by former trade minister Alec Erwin. Erwin had been so effective in alliance with northern interests that he was once endorsed for WTO director in the *New York Times* and *Foreign Policy*. But because Mandelson squeezed so hard prior to his September 2008 return to the British government as business minister, he helped break crucial links between elites. Led by Senegalese and Malian politicians, most African officials at the Codesria conference agreed with the left intelligentsia that dangers now arise of:

- regional disintegration (due to EU bilateral negotiations and subregional blocs) and internecine race-to-the-bottom competition;
- threats of not only deindustrialization but further EU penetration of the African services sector;
- increasing social polarization (including along gender lines), and the rise of parasitical classes; and
- much greater gains for some sectors of the capitalist class: owners of plantations, mines and oil fields; commercial circuits of capital; and financial institutions.

If African elites seem to be awakening to how much damage North-dominated trade is doing, two other processes will amplify the concern about overreliance upon trade. First is the rise of commodity prices from 2002-07, and their subsequent crash, in a manner that recalls traditional primary export price volatility. Moreover, with global growth slowing, the very high trade growth rates of the 2005-07 period will nearly certainly decline, possibly into negative territory, with African raw materials exports most adversely affected. Moreover, the partial freezing of credit markets in October 2008 threatened interbank transfers, and in turn trade finance.

Finally, from the 2009 Copenhagen climate conference, there will very likely emerge trade-related carbon taxes, especially on ships that utilize bunker fuels. Africa's long distance from wealthier markets is already a concern for what are entirely appropriate 'buy-local' campaigns, but for which more analysis is needed regarding adverse impacts on African small-scale farming (given that a great deal of the agricultural produce, especially horticulture, is produced in plantations and by multinational corporations). Even more rigorous civil society campaigning is required to halt climate change, and to generate ecological debt repayment for Northern overconsumption of environmental space. After all, according to the United Nations Intergovernmental Panel on Climate Change, "It is projected that there could be a possible reduction in yields in agriculture of 50 percent by 2020 in some African countries... Crop net revenues could fall by as much as 90 percent by 2100, with small-scale farmers being the most affected." [26]

Investment

There are signs that the kind of free reign enjoyed by the forces of Foreign Direct Investment, especially in the extractive industries, is under substantial attack. [27] For example, in mid 2008, Ogoniland opponents of Shell evicted the firm from a part of the Delta, with other groups taking the baton; the water corporatization, prepaid meters and predatory pricing by Suez in Johannesburg was rejected in the courts; and opponents of corporations that financed and profited from apartheid were challenged in the US courts. Each deserves a short briefing.

First, in early June 2008, the British-Dutch firm Shell Oil was instructed to depart from the Ogoniland region within the Niger Delta, where in 1995 Shell officials were responsible for the execution of Ken Saro-Wiwa by Nigerian dictator Sani Abacha. After decades of abuse, women protesters, local NGOs and the Movement for the Survival of the Ogoni People (MOSOP) had achieved sufficient pressure to evict Shell. As Nigerian president Umaru Musa Yar'Adua remarked 'There is a total loss of confidence between Shell and the Ogoni people. So, another operator acceptable to the Ogonis will take over.' Shell was also attacked on several occasions in subsequent months by the Movement for the Emancipation of the Niger Delta, crippling several oil facilities. In Paris, Total's Christophe de Margerie hinted at a "withdrawal" for similar reasons: "We have people who work over there...who are unfortunately more and more often subjected to major aggressions (or being) kidnapped. We are asking ourselves the question (about whether to follow Shell)."[28]

The expansion of the Oil Watch campaign to "'Keep the oil in the soil!" made great progress in Durban in September 2008, when the NGO groundwork invited dozens of community activists from oil and gas-rich sites across the continent for consultation with the Nigerians. As one example, the South Durban Community and Environmental Alliance launched a campaign—and formal Environmental Impact Assessment intervention—to prevent construction of a $1.2 oil pipeline from the refineries in Durban's black residential areas, through low-income communities, to Johannesburg, in part by invoking climate considerations. In October 2008, Niger Delta activists began a series of lawsuits, first in San Francisco to sue Chevron for billions of dollars of damages to communities and the environment, and later in New York to sue Shell under the terms of the Alien Tort Claims Act. They are partly inspired by the Ecuadoran example, where pressure by Accion Ecologia compelled a hesitant president Rafael Correa to announce in August 2007 that he would leave untouched $12 billion in oil reserves under the Yasuni National Park, an Amazonian park with strong indigenous peoples' traditions and livelihoods at stake. What Correa requested in return was $5 billion in payments from the North by way of ecological debt repayment; only Norway has begun the discussion at this writing. In December 2008, Correa defaulted on Ecuador's foreign debt, declaring it illegitimate.

Second, water is an issue where a recent partial victory can be declared. In Johannesburg, the Campaign Against Water Privatization and Anti-Privatization Forum were supported by two NGOs with legal and advocacy expertise, the Freedom of Expression Institute and Centre for Applied Legal Studies. Residents from Phiri township in Soweto took Suez's low level of free water provision (an average of 25 liters per person per day) and prepayment meters to the High Court in 2007. [29] Unlike conventional meters in rich suburbs which provide due warning of future disconnection (and an opportunity to make representation) in the form of notification in red writing at the bottom of the monthly bill, pre-paid meter disconnection occurs automatically and without warning following the exhaustion of the Free Basic Water supply. If the disconnection occurs during the night or over a weekend when water credit vendors are closed, the household has to go without water until the shops are open again, and if the household does not have money for additional water, it must borrow either money or water from neighbours in order to survive. This represents not only a threat to dignity and health, but also a direct risk to life in the event of a fire; two children's deaths in a Soweto shack fire resulting from pre-paid meters catalysed the lawsuit. On 30 April 2008, High Court judge Moroa Tsoka ruled that imposing credit control via prepayment meters "in the historically poor black areas and not the historically rich white areas" was racist, as installation apparently occurred "in terms of color or geographical area". Moreover, Johannesburg Water's community consultation process was "a publicity stunt" characterized by a "big brother approach". Tsoka ordered removal and prohibition of the prepayment meters and the provision of 50 liters per person per day free. (National and municipal governments announced an appeal, which will begin in the Supreme Court in March 2009.)

Third, the strategy to recover apartheid-era profits from transnational corporations is advancing in the US courts thanks to the breadth of the Alien Tort Claims Act (ATCA). In 1997, ATCA Holocaust Litigation cases against Swiss banks were settled out of court for $8 billion. A group of South African activists including Dennis Brutus and Lungisile Ntsebeza, as well as the Khulumani Support Group for apartheid victims and Jubilee South Africa, used the ATCA to sue dozens of multinational corporations, including Reinmetall Group, British Petroleum (BP), Shell, Chevron Texaco, Exxon Mobil, Fluor Corporation, Total Fina-Elf, Ford Motor Company, Daimler-Chrysler, General Motors, Fujitsu, IBM, Barclays Bank, Citibank, Commerzbank, Credit Suisse, Deutsche Bank, Dresdner Bank, J P Morgan Chase, UBS, Anglo American, Gold Fields and Sasol. Not long after the activists' cases were filed, in mid-2003, the South African government was requested by the Bush Administration to oppose Khulumani and other plaintiffs, and agreed to do so after a period of relative neutrality. Mbeki had initially offered "neither support nor condemnation," but soon reversed this tack, proclaiming that it was "completely unacceptable that matters that are central to the future of our country should be adjudicated in foreign courts which bear no responsibility for the well-being of our country, and the observance of the perspective contained in our constitution of the promotion of national reconciliation." In July 2003, following an intervention by Colin Powell, Mbeki and justice minister Penuell Maduna went to even greater lengths to defend apartheid-era profits, arguing in a nine-page brief to a US court hearing a reparations case, that by 'permitting the litigation', the New York judge would discourage "much-needed foreign investment and delay the achievement of the government's goals. Indeed, the litigation could have a destabilizing effect on the South African economy as investment is not only a driver of growth, but also of unemployment". This was ridiculed by the plaintiffs' friend of the court, Nobel economics laureate Joseph Stiglitz.[30]

But in November 2004, taking the most conservative approach possible, judge John Sprizzo of the Southern District of New York dismissed the apartheid-related lawsuits on grounds that Pretoria "indicated it did not support the lawsuits and that letting them proceed might injure the government's ability to handle domestic matters and discourage investment in its economy". [31] But three years later, on 12 October 2007, litigants won an appeal on grounds Sprizzo's logic was faulty. [32] Desperate to put the case behind them, the companies requested a Supreme Court hearing instead of a return to the lower levels. In February 2008, the US' highest court heard arguments from the Bush White House against the "unprecedented and sprawling" lawsuits. Bush was supported by the governments of Britain, Germany, Switzerland, and even South Africa. [33] In May 2008, the Supreme Court found that sufficient of their members were in conflict of interest due to personal investments in the apartheid-tainted companies, that they could not act on the case, and hence returned it to Sprizzo's court for 2009 consideration.

No matter the outcome and whether it can be extended to victims of slavery, colonialism and neocolonialism (as plaintiffs' strategists envisage), the main point of the strategy is to disincentivize future corporate involvement in repressive regimes. According to South Africa's *Times* newspaper:

> Millions of South Africans are eligible to join a class-action lawsuit against US-based multinational corporations accused of aiding and abetting the apartheid government... Nicole Fritz, the director of the SA Litigation Centre, said that companies that were not perpetrators of human rights violations but were complicit in such violations through their dealings with oppressive governments were now potentially liable in law for their actions. The Supreme Court ruling could open the way for similar cases, Fritz added. [34]

Similar cases would underscore how important it is to disincentivize profits generated through operations within dictatorial regimes. Burma and Zimbabwe are examples, since popular movements have discouraged financial support for the prevailing governments. In mid-2008, just as Robert Mugabe's Zanu(PF) committed torture and murder to ensure his reelection, AngloPlats announced a US$400 million investment in lucrative Zimbabwean mines. Prior to the very unstable deal between Mugabe and the Movement for Democratic Change in September 2008, the Zimbabwe Congress of Trade Unions had requested border blockades by the Congress of SA Trade Unions. The April 2008 refusal of Durban dockworkers to unload three million Chinese bullets was an exemplary case of such solidarity. [35]

Aside from situations in which oppressed peoples request sanctions as part of their pressure campaign, the more general case against multinational corporate investment in Africa includes the argument that extractive industry activity draws out more net wealth than is returned in royalties, reinvestment and backward/forward linkages. Most of Africa suffers dramatic declines in net wealth year on year, as non-renewable resources are taken forever, with most profits repatriated to mining and oil firms headquartered in North America, Europe, Australia and China. [36] The demand for "ecological debt" repayment is increasingly on the agenda of activist movements such as Jubilee Africa and

ActionAid, in order to begin to account for the damage done by such extraction.

As commodity prices plunge from their 2002-07 speculation-driven bubble prices, as trade deals with the North are unveiled as clearly disadvantageous, and as trade finance becomes difficult as a result of bank mistrust of counterparty debt, and as hot money portfolio flows dry up and new sources open for hard currency, the argument for "delinking" and "deglobalization" becomes all the more compelling. [37] For African national elites who would aim to shake off the power politics of aid and debt, there are now several important strategic options. Several have been pioneered in recent years by Latin Americans who have broken with the Western aid/debt establishment. Consider these examples:

1) Ecuador's government raised the call for the North's payment of "ecological debt" as a resource curse antidote, by proposing in August 2007 to "leave the oil in the soil" in the Yasuni National Park, demanding payment of roughly $5 bn in compensation.

2) Ecuador also hosted a "debt audit", and upon release of findings of extensive corruption associated with past debt, defaulted on payments due in January 2009 on foreign debt worth $10 billion, on grounds that the inherited debt was "obviously immoral and illegitimate".

3) Venezuela imposed capital controls in 2004 and thus solved a major capital flight problem associated with an unpatriotic bourgeoisie (following a lead by Malaysia in 1998 whose capital controls aimed to halt external speculative trading in the ringgit).

4) Venezuela called for the closure of the World Bank and International Monetary Fund in October 2008.

5) Venezuela provided dramatic funding increases for thousands of alternative communal banks whose purpose is providing credit 'for popular power'.

6) Ecuador had already expelled the World Bank resident representative in 2007 on grounds of the institution's interference with the country's oil reforms two years earlier.

7) Argentina made an early repayment of IMF debt in 2005, followed by many other middle-income borrowers so that by September 2008 the IMF was so unpopular it was called the "Turkish Monetary Fund" (in honor of its only major middle-income client).

8) Brazil provided financial support for the launch of the Bank of the South.

9) The presidents of Brazil, Venezuela, Paraguay, Ecuador and Bolivia met with the World Social Forum in January 2009 at Belem, which reflected a new development in alliance-formation that holds great potential for future linkages between the Left holding state power and the left applying popular pressure from below.

Most African countries, elites and civil societies have been slow to take advantage of the new context, which allows an aggressive posture towards both donors—who are cutting back in any case—as well as financiers. With the financial and commercial circuits of global capital in extreme retreat, it is time for African economies to fill in the gap.

Regrettably, a necessary prerequisite to make all the above strategies more feasible is the *re-delegitimization of US power.* Most obviously, a world addicted to the US dollar as the reserve currency will be at the mercy of the US state, as one example. The insane mutually-assured destructive system of US Treasury Bill purchases by East Asian investors—so as to ensure a market for their consumer goods—began running into the contradiction of huge declines in Chinese, Japanese, Taiwanese and Korean dollar reserves wealth, as the US currency fell substantially in recent years. A multi-currency exchange system is inevitable, and to the extent it is conjoined with national exchange controls and hence less extreme volatility in financial trading, will be advantageous for economic development, compared to the current currency anarchy. Something like Keynes' International Currency Union—which would penalize balance of trade surpluses—would be ideal, but given the neoliberal and neoconservative forces in multilateral institutions, is probably out of the question in our lifetimes.

The big problem remains the US state, because to counteract US economic and cultural decline, two strategies are now in play: political revitalization via Barack Obama's carefully-crafted image as a non-imperialist politician with roots in African-American, Kenyan and even Indonesian traditions; and the activism anticipated through his secretary of state, Hillary Clinton, a strong supporter of the US war against Iraq. Obama may not run as extreme a militarist regime as Bush/Cheney did or as McCain/Palin would have done. Yet as Jeremy Scahill points out, there is the awful precedent of Washington's imperialist habits during Bill Clinton's administration:

> The prospect of Obama's foreign policy being, at least in part, an extension of the Clinton Doctrine is real. Even more disturbing, several of the individuals at the center of Obama's transition and emerging foreign policy teams were top players in creating and implementing foreign policies that would pave the way for projects eventually carried out under the Bush/Cheney administration. With their assistance, Obama has already charted out several hawkish stances. Among them:

- his plan to escalate the war in Afghanistan;
- an Iraq plan that could turn into a downsized and rebranded occupation that keeps US forces in Iraq for the foreseeable future;
- his labeling of Iran's Revolutionary Guard as a "terrorist organization";
- his pledge to use unilateral force inside of Pakistan to defend US interests;
- his position, presented before the American Israel Public Affairs Committee that Jerusalem "must remain undivided"—a remark that infuriated Palestinian officials and which he later attempted to reframe;
- his plan to continue the War on Drugs, a backdoor US counterinsurgency campaign in Central and Latin America;
- his refusal to "rule out" using Blackwater and other armed private forces in US war zones, despite previously introducing legislation to regulate these companies and bring them under US law.[38]

In addition to Hillary Clinton and the reappointment of Bush's defense secretary Robert Gates, Scahill warns of the following imperialist influences: vice president Joe Biden, chief of staff Rahm Emanuel, former secretaries of state Madeleine Albright and Warren Christopher, former defense secretary William Perry, former UN ambassador Richard Holbrooke, and other key Clinton-era figures (Dennis Ross, Martin Indyk, Anthony Lake, Lee Hamilton, Susan Rice, John Brennan, Jami Miscik, John Kerry, Bill Richardson, Ivo H. Daalder, Sarah Sewall, Michele Flournoy, Wendy Sherman, Tom Donilon, Denis McDonough and Mark Lippert). As Scahill concludes,

> Barack Obama campaigned on a pledge to bring change to Washington. 'I don't want to just end the war,' he said early this year. 'I want to end the mindset that got us into war.' That is going to be very difficult if Obama employs a foreign policy team that was central to creating that mindset, before and during the presidency of George W. Bush.

What is most crucial, then, for a realistic post-neoliberal project, is ongoing delegitimization of the US in its political and military modes. One danger zone is Africa, where the Bush/Cheney/Gates geopolitical and military machinery ground to a halt in the form of the Africa Command. No state aside from Liberia would entertain the idea of hosting the headquarters (which remained in Stuttgart), notwithstanding an endorsement of AFRICOM from even Obama's main Africa advisor, Witney Schneidman.

More importantly, even if Obama restores a degree of US credibility at the level of international politics, US military decline will continue to be hastened by failed Pentagon strategies against urban Islamist guerilla movements in Baghdad, rural Islamist fighters in Afghanistan and Pakistan, and the belligerent nuclear-toting state of North Korea. None of these forces represent social progress, of course, but they probably are responsible for such despondency in Washington that other targets of US imperial hostility, such as the governments of Cuba, Venezuela, Bolivia and Ecuador, remain safe from blatant overthrow in the near term.

In turn, those four Latin American countries have the best opportunity in the world, today, to build post-neoliberal economic, social and environmental projects. The latter eco-socialist project is vitally important, because in addition to offering an alternative to the environmentally controversial policy of "petro-socialism" as practiced in Venezuela, there are some inspiring examples in Cuba's post-carbon innovations, in Bolivia's indigenous people's power and in Ecuador's official commitment—no matter how it wavers in practice—to a "keep the oil in the soil" policy in the Yasuni National Park. The social and economic advances in post-neoliberal Venezuela are important, as are Keynesian strategies being implemented in China (the world's most expansive public works project—albeit with ecological disasters) and Argentina, as key examples.

From South Africa, our window on this new world shows quite clear dangers of both Pretoria government officials and NGOs (for example, Civicus, headquartered in Johannesburg) being co-opted into renewed neoliberal (and even neoconservative) US imperial projects, especially if Obama draws upon his African roots for socio-political power. Antidotes remain, of course, and are expressed through anti-imperialist sentiments emerging in both the centre-left political actors (the trade unions and SA Communist Party) and the independent left social movements (especially those acting in solidarity with Zimbabweans, Swazis, Palestinians and Burmese).

But the most powerful South African example is not the negation of neoliberalism and imperialism, but rather the grassroots activist initiatives— such as acquiring generic AIDS medicines and free public water supplies— against the forces of micro-commodification and macro-neoliberalism. These are indeed the most useful signals that another world—realistically post-neoliberal—is not only possible, but is being constructed even now.

Part III

MIRACLES OR MIRAGES UNDER GLOBAL NEOLIBERALISM

Introduction

Part 3 examines development trajectories under global neoliberalism of a selection of states in Southeast and East Asia, North Africa and Latin America. What is important to keep in mind in these regional and case studies is the conceptual slippage which has occurred in development policy making across the neoliberal "Washington Consensus" decades where the operative word "development" has been displaced by the term "growth". While it is true that in its origination in the post-World War II period, the mainstream development field never clearly specified what "development" meant, there nevertheless existed a tacit "qualitative" understanding of development as mirroring economic and social welfare changes experienced by the advanced industrial Western world. Today, development is approached as a largely *quantitative* phenomenon with policy concerns narrowly directed toward macroeconomic indicators such as rates of growth and increasing gross domestic product.

In Chapter Seven, John Weeks tracks the growth indicators for Indonesia, South Korea, Malaysia and Thailand (designated by the acronym IKMT) with, to some extent, other states in the region as well, from the 1960s through the Asian Crisis into the early years of the 21st century. The attribution of "miracle" status to IKMT by the World Bank following from the astronomical growth rates these states posted to 1996, Weeks argues, had as much to do with their relative backwardness in connecting with the global economy as the Asian Crisis had little to do with any individual economic traits. Nevertheless, according to Weeks, the Asian Crisis did punctuate the end of an era. For while IKMT recovered rather swiftly, the high growth rates they manifested became a thing of the past. Chapter Seven suggests that that the pattern IKMT displayed is likely to be repeated by the next generation of potential growth economies including China, and that whatever miracle status is achieved is certain to be short lived.

Seongjin Jeong and Richard Westra look closer at the economic development of South Korea in the aftermath of the Asian Crisis and International Monetary Fund (IMF) restructuring. Concurring with Weeks, Chapter Eight recognizes that the period of posting astronomical growth rates ended with the Asian Crisis. Nevertheless, Korea began to display relatively high rates of growth within a few years of the crisis which continued well into the 21st century. The analysis of Jeong and Westra also supports the contention of Weeks that the 1997 Asian Crisis in Korea had little to do with individual economic propensities such as Enron/Worldcom style "crony capitalism". Chapter Eight indicates the clear affinities between capitalist development in Korea preceding the crisis and that existing in advanced Western economies. What the chapter exposes, however, are the debilitating social and economic dislocations festering beneath Korea's "miracle" of high growth rates. It concludes with discussion of how the recent Wall Street-induced economic meltdown has exacerbated these. Jeong and Westra also assess the progressive potential of the gathering alterglobalization movement in Korea.

In Chapter Nine, Ake Tangsupvattana provides a succinct summary of Thailand's nascent capitalist development and political transformation en route to an inside look at core elements of neoliberal restructuring of Thailand's economy following the Asian Crisis. Ake first reviews the impact of the crisis on the financial and banking structure of Thailand. His analysis shows how the crisis and subsequent devaluation of the Thai baht and business assets provided fertile ground for foreign capital to rapidly roll back into Thailand to purchase assets at fire sale prices. He then turns to two elements of the neoliberal restructuring of Thailand that have received far less attention in the mainstream press: One is the fallout from the Thai-China free trade agreement not only on the macro balance of payments but on local agriculture in the Northeastern part of Thailand. The other is the deregulation of the retail sector which allowed global hypermarket outlets to invade—the result being mass unemployment in the retail sector as traditional shopping venues in Thailand were destroyed.

In Chapter Ten Angela, Joya compares the trajectories of development in Egypt and Syria in the Post-World War II period with a focus on the economic shift towards neoliberalism. Her paper commences with an historical summary of the development process and policies of both countries and the changes that were spurred by the 1980s global third world "debt crisis". The chapter foci then shifts to a close examination of the neoliberal models embraced by both states through the 1990s and the indigenous factors that determined the pace of the neoliberal reform initiative. Joya notes the contradictions of the neoliberal model as well as its failures in meeting stated neoliberal development goals of both Egypt and Syria. She demonstrates how, rather than responding to the needs of citizens, the neoliberal economic model serves the interests of a globally oriented class of powerful interests that have dominated the state in both countries in the course of the 1990s. As a result, neoliberalism redistributed power within the ruling class away from the "statist" bureaucrats who had dominated the state in the 1970s and 1980s. She concludes with a balance sheet of attempts at political liberalization and identifies the factors that shape the pace and nature of such struggles under the neoliberal economic model.

In this volume's final chapter Cliff Durand succinctly addresses the mirage of neoliberal development in Mexico, the latter being originally touted as a miracle in mainstream development textbooks in the heady import substitution industrialization days, long before the rise of East Asia. With the integration of Mexico into the North American Free Trade Agreement it became a perfect test case for neoliberal development policies, argues Durand. Chapter Eleven then takes up both the quantitative and qualitative dimensions of the neoliberal morass in Mexico. Of particular significance are Durand's figures on the purported employment benefits of "free trade" and the facts of divestiture under neoliberalism of the form of landholding enshrined in Mexico's revolution. The chapter then concludes with some scenarios for Mexico's future in the context of the current global economic meltdown.

Chapter 7

MIRACLES AND CRISIS IN EAST AND SOUTHEAST ASIAN COUNTRIES

BOOM, COLLAPSE AND RECOVERY

John Weeks

Introduction

For over thirty years, four countries were among the fastest growing in the world, granted the title of "miracles" by the World Bank.[1] From the early 1960s to the mid-1990s Indonesia, the Republic of Korea, Malaysia and Thailand averaged GDP growth rates in excess of six percent.[2] In 1997 all four entered into a severe economic crisis, with Indonesia and Thailand suffering economic collapse, while Korea and Malaysia experienced sharp decline. While severe, these depressions were followed by recovery to moderate growth, though slower than during the thirty-year boom. This chapter analyzes that history of growth, crisis and recovery.

The following section reviews the long boom and considers some of its causes. The third section offers an analysis of the crisis years. The orthodox explanations are considered and rejected as improbable. More convincing is that to varying degrees, the governments of the countries adopted policies that made their economies increasingly vulnerable to the external "shocks" that occurred in the 1990s, which invited financial speculation. In this section the declines suffered by the previously rapidly growing four are compared to the much stronger performances of the Asian transition countries (especially China and Vietnam). In the fourth section the recovery during the 2000s is considered. The final section seeks to account for the high growth rates of the IKMT countries during their boom, and of other fast growing countries in the region. The paper will then be concluded.

The Long Boom, 1960-1996

The central problem in considering the remarkable performance over three decades of the IKMT countries is to separate ideology from economic analysis. During the 1970s, mid-way through the long boom, the analysis was straightforward: these countries had enjoyed relatively high investment rates that laid the basis for a potentially high growth rate, and industrial policies combining export promotion with subsidies and import substitution provided the medium term demand stimulus.[3] From the latter part of the 1970s through the 1980s and into the 1990s, economic ideology shifted towards an increasingly fundamentalist neoliberalism. This shift was manifested in a 1993 World Bank study called, inaccurately,[4] *The East Asian Miracle*, in which it was argued that the Asian boom countries represented examples of the policy application of free market principles, "market-friendly" policies. Part of this argument asserted that this alleged policy approach explained why the Asian "miracles" had performed so much better than the Latin American countries.

The unfavorable comparison to the Latin American countries has little validity. The orthodoxy attributes the difference in performance between the Latin American countries and the "miracles" to basic differences in policy orientation: that the high growth Asian countries pursued sound macro policies, while Latin American governments persisted with "closed economy", import substitution regimes characterized by heavy state intervention.[5] This interpretation has been the source of considerable mischief in policy advice from international organizations.

If the Latin American governments failed on macro basics, while the governments of the Asian "miracles" excelled prior to some crisis period, then this provides a superficial explanation for the Latin American debt crisis of the 1980s and, by implication, for the later Asian crisis which is treated in the next section. The Latin American crisis would be explained by unwise policy choices over several decades, and the Asian financial crisis[6] by deterioration in what had previously been sound policy fundamentals. However, inspection of the statistics yields unexpected conclusions. The oft-quoted "stylized facts" about Latin America prove invalid: on average, fiscal deficits were not higher in the Latin American countries, nor did government expenditure take a significantly larger share of national income.[7]

Whatever the explanation for the growth rates of Indonesia, Korea, Malaysia and Thailand, they were impressively high as Table 1 shows. Indonesia had slow and negative rates in the first half of the 1960s, but the other three countries grew in excess of six percent, and during the 1980s and into the 1990s this rate of growth was sustained and exceeded by all four countries. As impressive as these growth rates were, they were not unique to the market economies of East and Southeast Asia, because China grew even faster in the 1960s and almost as fast in the 1970s, well before the market reforms were introduced. The most obvious explanation for the growth rates for the four 'miracles' and China was high investment, as Table

2 demonstrates. During the 1970s the share of gross investment in GDP of the IKMT group was close, or above twenty-five percent, rising towards thirty percent in the 1980s, and well above thirty percent in the 1990s before the Asian crisis of 1997-1999. China, too, had high investment rates of over thirty percent of GDP from 1970s onwards.

The Philippines was no exception to the investment and growth rates link. While its growth rates in the 1960s and 1970s were below those for the IKMT group (except for Indonesia in the 1960s), they were high compared to developing countries as a whole. The dramatic fall in the 1980s can be explained by the same growth-depressing effect suffered by the Latin American countries: a rapidly growing and unsustainable external debt.[8] The growth depressing effect is demonstrated in Table 3, which calculated the observed investment-growth ratio by country.[9] For the ten countries in the table over four time periods, in only three cases did this ratio exceed five, the Philippines during the 1980s and 1990s, and Myanmar in the 1980s. For the other countries, higher ratios were typically associated with rapid growth rates, most notably for Thailand, whose highest value for the investment-growth ratio was associated with the country's most rapid growth rate for the four time periods.[10] The emphasis that some authors place on export growth as the explanation for the long boom may confuse cause and effect especially since the argument cannot be made for Indonesia and is dubious for Malaysia.[11] Section five considers these investment-growth ratios in detail.

In addition to high average rates of growth, the variation in growth for the IKMT group was relatively low, as Figure 1 shows. Korea had the highest average and also had the highest coefficient of variation, .39, which implies an annual average deviation of less than two percentage points in absolute value. The annual variation for the other three countries was in each case less than 1.5 percentage points. While the cyclical patterns of the countries do not coincide, one can observe clear patterns in the growth rates. As the Asia crisis approached, Indonesia and Malaysia were in an upswing, with growth rates well above the long term average, Korea was in the process of recovery to more rapid growth, and only Thailand was experiencing relative decline. The Philippines was also in a cyclical upswing (Figure 2), after a negative rate in 1991. Thus, with the possible exception of Thailand, the pre-crisis growth rates of the IKMT group and the Philippines did not suggest the growth collapse to come.

For the transition countries growth was strong in the 1990s (Figure 3), particularly robust for China at 10.5 percent a year and Vietnam at 7.9. Slower but impressive were Laos at 6.5 and Cambodia at 5.5. The very rapid rates of China and Vietnam resulted from high investment rates in China, and for both countries the dynamic gains result from initial introduction of market regulation in key sectors. As is well documented, the governments of both countries pursued a set of policies designed to closely manage the transition from central planning to market regulation: 1) regulated trading systems with managed exchange rates, 2) central role of public sector enterprises, 3) encouragement of foreign investment within tight regulation, and 4) expansionary macro policies.[12]

At the mid-1990s there seemed no reason to doubt that rapid growth in the East and Southeast Asian region would continue.[13] Even the weakest of the economic performers, Myanmar and the Philippines, displayed increasing growth rates. Yet, in the second half of the 1990s the market economies of the region would enter into collapse or severe recession. The IKMT group would be a miracle no more, with Indonesia and Thailand suffering almost unprecedented decline for countries not affected by armed conflict. The next section considers why this occurred and the economic consequences.

Table 1: Growth of GDP, 1960-1996

	1960-69	1970-79	1980-89	1990-96
Market-based				
Indonesia	3.7	8.2	6.4	8.0
Korea	8.3	8.1	7.6	7.6
Malaysia	6.5	7.6	5.9	9.5
Thailand	7.8	7.5	7.3	8.6
Average	6.6	7.9	6.8	8.4
Philippines	5.1	5.8	2.0	2.8
Transition				
Cambodia	nd	nd	7.7	5.5
Laos	nd	nd	4.1	6.5
Vietnam	nd	nd	4.5	7.9
Average	nd	nd	5.5	6.6
Other				
Myanmar	3.0	4.4	1.9	5.5
China	8.6	7.4	9.8	10.5

Source: World Bank, *World Development Indicators 2008,* online database. Notes: China from 1963; Laos and Vietnam from 1985; Cambodia from 1988.

Table 2: Gross Investment as share of GDP, 1960-1996

	1960-69	1970-79	1980-89	1990-96
Market based				
Indonesia	9.7	25.0	28.3	30.8
Korea	19.0	25.7	30.4	37.4
Malaysia	17.3	24.4	27.8	38.7
Thailand	20.5	25.8	29.4	41.2
Average	16.6	25.2	29.0	37.0
Philippines	19.5	27.0	22.5	22.9
Transition				
Cambodia	16.4	12.5	10.2	15.4
Laos	nd	nd	8.8	27.5
Vietnam	nd	nd	15.1	21.5
Average	nd	nd	11.4	21.5
Other				
Myanmar	12.1	13.3	16.1	13.5
China	20.8	30.6	35.4	38.7

Source: World Bank, *World Development Indicators 2008,* online database.
Notes: China from 1963; Laos and Vietnam from 1985.

Table 3: Gross Investment-Growth Ratios, 1960-1996

	1960-69	1970-79	1980-89	1990-96
Market based				
Indonesia	2.6	3.1	4.4	3.9
Korea	2.3	3.2	4.0	4.9
Malaysia	2.6	3.2	4.7	4.1
Thailand	2.6	3.4	4.0	4.8
Average	2.5	3.2	4.3	4.4
Philippines	3.9	4.7	11.2	8.1
Transition				
Cambodia	nd	nd	1.3	2.8
Laos	nd	nd	2.1	4.2
Vietnam	nd	nd	3.3	2.7
Average	nd	nd	2.3	3.2
Other				
Myanmar	4.0	3.0	8.3	2.4
China	2.4	4.1	3.6	3.7

Note: Calculated form previous two tables.

Figure 1: Absolute deviations of GDP growth rates from period average, four rapidly growing ESEA countries, 1960-1996 (3 year moving average)

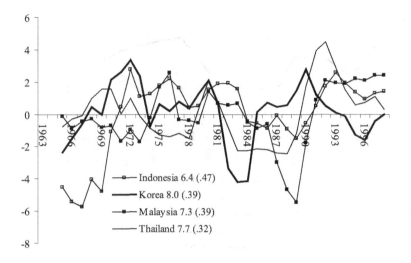

Note: The number after the country name is the average rate for the entire period, with the coefficient of variation in parenthesis.

Figure 2: GDP growth rates, Philippines and the high growth countries average, 1960-1996

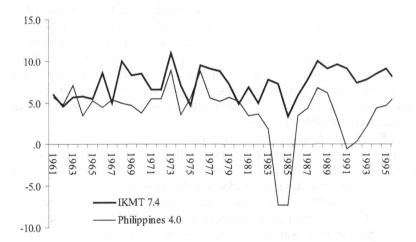

Note: The number after the country name is the average rate for the entire period

Figure 3: GDP growth rates, Asian transition countries and Myanmar

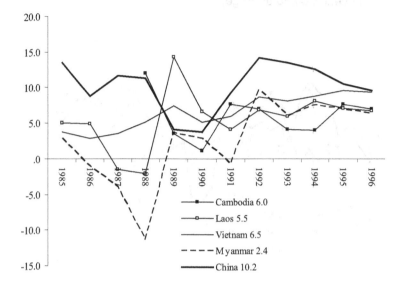

Note: The number after the country name is the average rate for the entire period.

Crisis and Collapse, 1997-2000

The form taken by the Asian financial crisis was sudden and massive capital flight. The explanation for the capital flight that swept the IKMT group of countries lies in three key aspects of what came to be called the "Asian financial crisis": 1) the suddenness with which it occurred in the four countries;[14] 2) the failure of this crisis to affect the other countries of East and Southeast Asia except for the Philippines to a much milder extent; and 3) the quickness of the subsequent recovery. Taken together, these three characteristics suggest that the crisis was not the result of fundamental weakness in the IKMT economies.

Figure 4 shows quarterly changes in GDP for Indonesia, Korea, Malaysia and Thailand for the first quarter of 1995 through the fourth quarter of 2000. As noted in the previous section, the Thai economy was in a downturn beginning in the last quarter of 1996, well before the crisis hit. In Korea a fall in growth occurred one quarter after Thailand's (first quarter of 1997) to 4.9 percent compared to over seven percent for the first quarter of 1996, but growth recovered to six percent in the second quarter. However, in the third quarter of 1997 the crisis hit Korea, and the year ended on a growth rate of less than three percent, to turn negative during every quarter of 1998. The downturns for Indonesia and Malaysia coincided with Korea's and proved more severe.

In 1998 growth was negative for all four countries in every quarter, but by the first quarter of 1999 Korea had begun its recovery, and in the second quarter growth was positive for all four countries. For Korea the recovery was spectacular, with growth averaging almost ten percent over seven quarters in 1999 and 2000. The recovery was quite strong for Thailand, but relatively weak for Indonesia and Malaysia. These recoveries, including Korea's, would prove uneven in subsequent years, as analyzed in the next section. However, by the end of 1999 the crisis was over for all four countries, having struck with virulent but brief force.

No other country in the region suffered as the IKMT group did. The next section, covering the economic recovery of the IKMT countries in the 2000s, looks at the performance of the transition countries and Myanmar. Here, quarterly data on the Philippines and China allow detailed inspection of those two countries during the Asian crisis, shown in Figure 5. While the Philippines suffered a contraction in 1998 and 1999, the downturn was considerably less than for the IKMT group, with only three quarters of slightly negative growth, a cumulative total for 1998 of less than one percent and positive growth rates subsequently. In the case of China, there appears to have been no effect, though the quarterly average for 1999 of 7.1 percent was almost one percentage point lower than the previous year.

Having established the brevity of the crisis, it is instructive to consider the orthodox interpretation of the causes of the crisis, as stated in an article in the IMF house journal, *Finance and Development*:

> To a large extent, these countries were the victims of their own success. Because of their strong economic performance throughout the early 1990s, the Asian countries were in denial when problems began to surface. Believing they were immune to the type of crisis that erupted in Latin America in the 1980s because they did not have the large fiscal deficits, heavy public debt burdens, rapid monetary expansion, and structural impediments that had made Latin America vulnerable....
>
> The underlying causes of the Asian crisis have been clearly identified. First, substantial foreign funds became available at relatively low interest rates, as investors in search of new opportunities shifted massive amounts of capital into Asia. As in all boom cycles, stock and real estate prices in Asia shot up initially, so the region attracted even more funds. However, domestic allocation of these borrowed foreign resources was inefficient because of weak banking systems, poor corporate governance, and a lack of transparency in the financial sector. These countries' limited absorptive capacity also contributed to the inefficient allocation of foreign funds. Second, the

countries' exchange rate regimes, exchange rates were
effectively fixed, gave borrowers a false sense of security,
encouraging them to take on dollar-denominated debt.
Third, in the countries affected by the crisis, exports were
weak in the mid-1990s for a number of reasons, including
the appreciation of the U.S. dollar against the yen, China's
devaluation of the yuan in 1994, and the loss of some
markets following the establishment of the North American
Free Trade Agreement.[15]

The quotation gives several "clearly identified" causes of the crisis: 1) complacency as a result of previous success; 2) excessive foreign borrowing by the private sector ("substantial foreign funds"); 3) weak banking systems, poor corporate governance and lack of financial transparency; 4) fixed exchange rates that encouraged foreign borrowing; and 5) weak export growth in the mid-1990s. The striking characteristic of all these explanations is their vagueness, which implies difficulty if not impossibility of verifying them.

The first "explanation", complacency, can be discarded as tautological (all expansions come to an end at some point) and beyond verification. The second, third and fourth explanations all refer to foreign capital inflows, which had been considered a virtue of the IKMT countries prior to the crisis. In 1996, in the section on managing capital flows in East Asia in the World Bank *Annual Report*, one finds the IKMT countries lauded for their capital inflows as well as complimented for "effectively" using the capital flows:

East Asian countries have been successful in integrating
with the world market for both capital and goods. Since
1990, the region has become the predominant destination
of private capital flows. In 1995 alone, developing countries
in the region received an estimated $108 billion in foreign
capital flows, of which $98 billion was from private sources,
including $54 billion in direct investment. The surge in
foreign capital flows was induced by rapid economic
growth, *sound economic fundamentals*, and a high level of
integration with the world market… [T]hese countries have
been able to use the foreign capital inflows more effectively
than other developing regions, thereby contributing to rapid
technological upgrading. [16]

Given the World Bank's favorable comments on capital flows and the domestic use of them, the argument in *Finance and Development* that institutional weakness was an explanation of the Asian crisis appears as a retrospective judgment, no doubt preferred to explanations linked to the capital account liberalization urged by the IMF.

The assertion that "export weakness" laid the basis for the crisis is more difficult to assess, because it requires one to define "weakness" in the specific context of each country in the mid-1990s, then explain why this would provoke a crisis of capital flight. Figure 6 shows annual export growth for the IKMT countries, and its interpretation is not obvious. Three of the four countries experienced falls in the rate of exports growth in 1996 (to a negative rate for Thailand). However, for two of the countries, Korea and Thailand, it was a one-year fall from several years of increasing or steady strong growth. Further, for two of the countries with declines, Korea and Malaysia, the rate of growth in 1996 was above ten percent.

If there were a link between export growth and capital flight it is reasonable to think this would be *via* foreign exchange reserves, which are shown in Figure 7 for 1981-1996, measured in months of import cover. For three of the countries the level of reserves in 1996 was close to the highest level of the sixteen year period, with the exception being Malaysia. Yet it was not Malaysia where the capital flight occurred first, but Thailand, whose reserves during 1994-1996 were at the highest level for the two decades.

While the reserve position of the four countries provides little indication of weakness, the same cannot be said for the current account balances, shown in Figure 8. For three of the countries, Korea, Malaysia and Thailand, a deterioration of the current account began in the second half of the 1980s, the first two countries moving from substantial surpluses into deficits. In the case of Thailand the deterioration began from a current account close to zero in 1986 to deficits well in excess of five percent of GDP, until a sharp improvement to about minus four percent in 1996, the year the crisis struck. Though the Indonesian current account was about the same from the late 1980s onwards, it remained negative for all years, due entirely to debt service payments, as a comparison of Figures 8 and 9 reveals.

The deterioration of the current accounts suggests an explanation for the crisis that swept the four countries. In 1994 persistent current account deficits resulted in a speculative run on the Mexican *peso*. Later in the decade Ecuador, Argentina and Russia would suffer speculative attacks, and the Asian crisis can be seen as one chapter in an unfolding drama of currency wars. The persistent deficit of Thailand made that country the obvious candidate for the initial speculative strike, which proved immediately successful from the speculators' point of view. The success of the speculative attack in Korea, Malaysia and Thailand is shown in Figure 10. Worse affected was Korea, whose exchange rate depreciated by over one hundred percent, with the greatest appreciation at the end of 1997. However, the appreciations of these three countries were minor compared to what occurred in Indonesia (Figure 11). In mid-July 1997 the Rupiah stood at 2452 to the US dollar, and by mid-December it had risen to over 5700. Massive increases in the central bank rate did nothing to check the collapse of the Rupiah, which reached over 11,000 in May 1998, to hit its peak two months later at over 14,000, a depreciation of over seven-fold.

The large depreciations undermined the stability of all four countries, perhaps most importantly by rendering private external debts unsustainable. Of the four countries only Indonesia, operating under strict IMF conditionalities, took no administrative measures to control capital movements. The consequence of the currency collapse proved devastating in Indonesia, compounded by the government decision to indiscriminately recapitalize private banks, which would prove to be the most expensive recapitalization in history. [17]

Figure 4: Quarterly GDP of the IKMT group of countries, 1997-2000

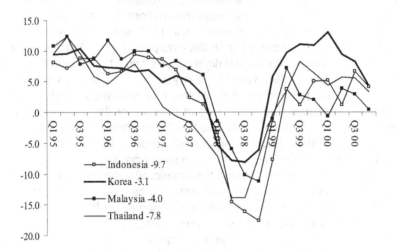

Note: Numbers next to the country names are average quarterly rates for the fourth quarter of 1997 through the first quarter of 1999. Sources: Abeysinghe & Rajaguru (2003, p. 24), http://www.econstats.com/r/rkor__q16.htm (Korea), http://www.econstats.com/r/indonesia__q12.htm (Indonesia), and for Malaysia, http://www.adb.org/documents/books/ado/2002/mal.asp. See also http://64.233.169.104/search?q=cache:1XgryMAOymsJ:siteresources.worldbank.org/INTEAPHALFYEARLYUPDATE/Resources/550192-1194982737018/AppendixTables-EAP-Update-Nov2007.pdf+indonesia+quarterly+gdp+2005&hl=en&ct=clnk&cd=15&gl=uk

Figure 5: Quarterly GDP, average IKMT countries, Philippines and China, 1995-2000

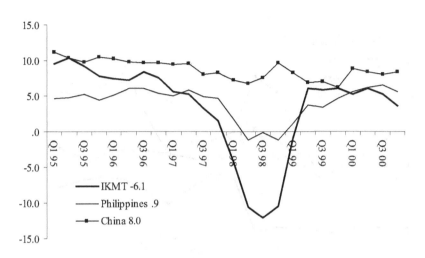

Note: Numbers next to the country names are average quarterly rates for the fourth quarter of 1997 through the first quarter of 1999.
Sources: see Figure 4.

Figure 6: Export Growth for the IKMT Countries, 1990-1996

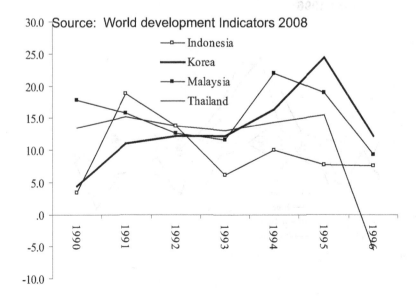

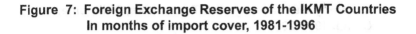

**Figure 7: Foreign Exchange Reserves of the IKMT Countries
In months of import cover, 1981-1996**

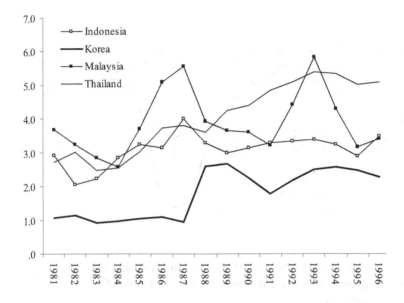

Source: World Bank, *World Development Indicators 2008,* online database.

**Figure 8: Current Account as percent of GDP of the IKMT Countries,
1981-1996**

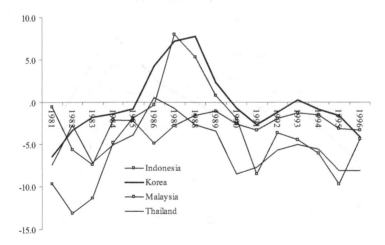

Figure 9: Current Account less Debt Service as percent of GDP of the IKMT Countries, 1981-1996

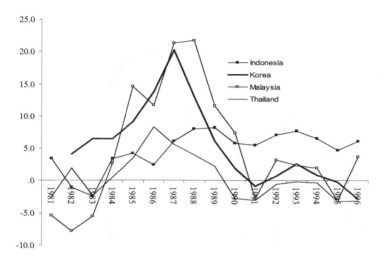

Figure 10: Nominal Exchange rates for Korea, Malaysia and Thailand, Quarterly 1997-1999 (4th quarter 1996 = 100)

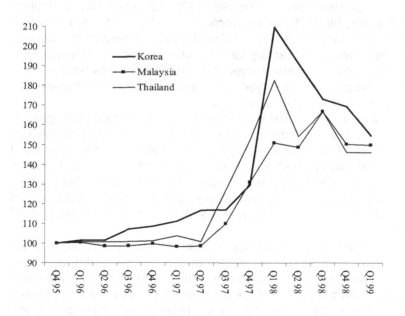

Source: http://www.ny.frb.org/xml/fx.html

Figure 11: Nominal Exchange rates for Indonesia, Monthly 1997-1998 (January 1997 = 100)

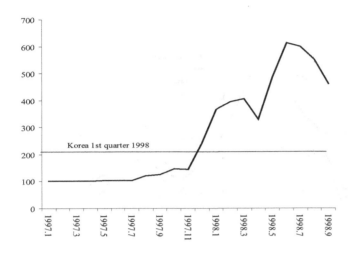

Source: http://www.ny.frb.org/xml/fx.html

Recovery, 2000-2007

Despite the severity of the 1997-1998 crisis, especially for Thailand and Indonesia, the IKMT countries recovered to what in other regions would be considered moderately strong rates of growth. However, the recovery did not come with equal rapidity for every country, with a sustained upturn in Malaysia and Indonesia delayed into the 2000s. Once recovery was achieved, the growth rates stayed at levels substantially below those during the long boom that preceded the crisis.

After the first quarter of 1999 the IKMT countries had positive growth rates, with the exception of Malaysia, a marginally negative rate in early 2000 and another in early 2001 (see Figure 12). The recovery of Korea was initially the most robust, with six consecutive quarters of extreme growth. Most delayed was the recovery of Malaysia, which after an initial growth burst of over seven percent apparently to start recovery in the second quarter of 1999, averaged 1.6 percent in 2000 and less than one percent in 2001.

The growth rate of all four countries fell in 2001, in part because of a sluggish world economy. What the IMF defines as the "advanced countries" grew at less than two percent during 2001-2003, and this had a clear impact on the exports of the IKMT countries, as Figure 13 shows. With investment still depressed, export demand now fuelled growth and strong export growth rates characterized 2000, averaging almost twenty percent across the four countries, driven by excess capacity left from the crisis and an almost unprecedented four percent growth of advanced country

GDP. In 2001 export demand collapsed, with Indonesia's export growth falling below one percent, and negative rates for the other three countries.

GDP growth rates after 2001 were moderately strong and sustained, but substantially below those of the boom years. This can be explained by the continued strong role of export growth in determining aggregate demand, with investment not yet recovered and a relatively passive fiscal policy. Weak growth of the advanced countries, less than three percent during 2007, partly explains the weak export growth of the IKMT countries. One consequence of the slower growth of the IKMT countries was their unexpected growth parity with the Philippines. For decades the Philippine economy had grown slowly or stagnated compared to its successful neighbors, but it suffered from the Asia crisis much less. By 2001 its growth rate matched that of the average for the IKMT countries, even exceeding it in 2007 (see Figure 14).

A potentially important factor in the slow-down of export growth for the IKMT countries was the rapid export expansion of other countries in the region, especially China and Vietnam. This rapid export expansion propelled the transition countries and Myanmar to growth that equal or exceeded those of the IKMT countries during their long booms (see Figure 15). For ten years, 1998-2007, Myanmar averaged an astounding twelve percent growth rate, China over nine percent, and Cambodia, Vietnam and Laos all over six percent. For this ten year period none of the IKMT countries grew as fast as Laos at 6.4 percent. The growth dynamics of China, and perhaps Vietnam,[18] differed from those of the other, smaller countries. These large countries had a greater potential to foster higher growth through stimulating domestic demand, which the Chinese government did towards the end of the 2000s.

Figure 12: Recovery, IKTM Countries, quarterly GDP growth 1997-2007

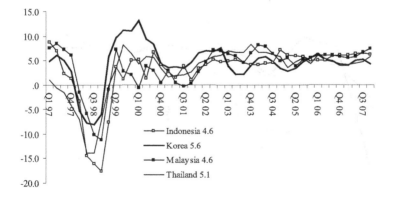

Notes: Numbers after the country name are rates of growth 1999 Q2 – 2007 Q4.

Figure 13: Annual Export Growth of the IKMT Countries, 2000-2007

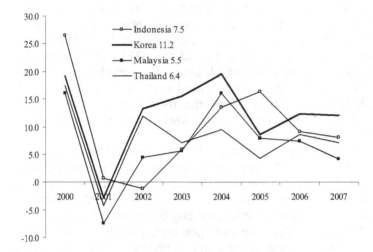

Note: Numbers next to the country names are export growth 2000-2007.
Source: ADB 2008.

Figure 14: Recovery, four high growth countries and Philippines, Annual data for GDP growth, 1998-2007

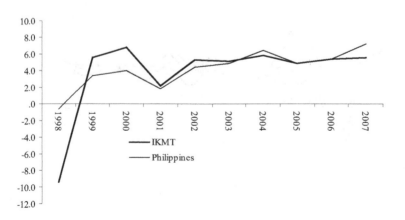

Figure 15: Annual growth rates of transition countries and Myanmar, 1998-2007

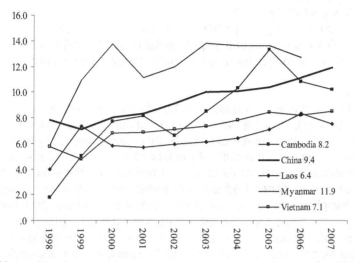

Note: Number next to country names are growth rates for 1998-2007.

Assessing the "Miracles", Old and New

For over three decades four countries of East and Southeast Asia experienced some of the highest growth rates in the world. These growth rates turned to depression and economic collapse during the Asia crisis at the end of the 1990s. Recovery came relatively quickly, strongly suggesting that the crisis did not arise from fundamental problems of the economies. However, the recovery was to lower average growth rates, growth rates which were substantially surpassed by a new group of "miracles", China, Cambodia, Myanmar and Vietnam.

The sustained, rapid growth of the IKMT countries, their slower post-crisis performance, and the emergence of new "miracles" in the region raises a fundamental question about the growth potential of underdeveloped countries: are growth rates in the range of six to ten percent relevant for most countries, and, if so, how long can they be sustained? The first step in answering these questions is to define what determines growth rates. The growth theory developed in the 1950s, both by Keynesians such as Harrod and Domar, and neoclassicals, for example Solow, agreed that the potential rate of growth was determined by three factors, 1) the rate of growth of productive capacity, 2) the productivity of that capacity, and 3) in a capitalist economy the rate of return on production. In algebraic models, the first was summarized in the investment rate, the second in technical change, and the third in the balance between the growth of the capital stock and the labor force.

A useful way of considering these three factors is by expanding the Harrod-Domar model. Let Y equal GDP, K = the net capital stock, and I equal net investment. The Δ symbol is an operator indicating change between two periods.

$\Delta Y/Y = y = [\Delta Y/\Delta K][\Delta K/Y]$

$\Delta K = I$, so $[\Delta K/Y] = [I/Y] = k$, the investment-GDP ratio.

$[\Delta Y/\Delta K] = v$, the 'marginal output-capital ratio. If v and k are fixed, either in the short or longer term, the identity changes into a behavioral relationship,

$y = vk$

Technical change primarily acts by affecting the productivity of the capital stock (k), and the rate of return influences the investment share. A frequently cited source of productivity change, especially for the IKMT countries, has been the skills of the labor force. We shall not deal with this influence because of its long term nature, and the difficulty of distinguishing among general educational levels, technical training, and work force discipline. However, we shall consider a broad interpretation of Leibenstein's "x-efficiency".[19] It follows from the growth equation that, were there no labor force constraint and no technical change, the growth rate would be determined by the net investment rate and the static capital output ratio.

On the assumption of aggregate depreciation rates of five and seven percent, an IMF study of the region in 2005 estimated capital-output ratios and net investment rates. It concluded the pre-crisis "potential growth rates" of Indonesia, Malaysia and Thailand to be five percent and Korea to be 4.7 percent. [20] In the event, these countries averaged growth rates of over seven percent for almost three decades (see Table 1). The "extra" two percentage points can be explained by three factors. First, each of the countries enjoyed growth gains through the reallocation of labor from relatively low productivity agriculture to industry, as Krugman argued. Second, the capitalists in these countries were able to gain the "advantages of backwardness" through the adaptation of the technologies of more advanced countries.[21] This advantage was realized in several ways, through foreign investment, early protection of domestic producers, and export competition. Third, "x-efficiency" gains were achieved through the transition to market social relations, including increased discipline of the work force.[22]

The characteristic of all three factors is their transitory nature; i.e., as their benefits are reaped, the potential to gain from them further declines. This characteristic is demonstrated in Figure 16, which shows as three-year moving averages the ratio of GDP to gross investment ratios for the IKTM countries, 1965-2006. In the diagram each country's time series is normalized to the average for the entire period. In the legend, the log-linear pre-crisis trend coefficients, 1965-1996, are reported with their level of statistical significance, with all significant at one percent probability or lower.

The time series for each country can be interpreted as an index of the growth rate achievable from a given unit of investment. For all the countries that statistic declines, by 3.4 percent annually in the case of Indonesia, and at about two percent for the other three countries. The declines should not be interpreted as falls in the "productivity of capital", but as the progressive exhaustion of the "advantages of backwardness", as each country gravitates to what the IMF study called "the potential growth rate", or, the long term sustainable growth rate.

It should be added that the extremely high investment shares in GDP in the 1990s before the crisis, over thirty percent for all four countries, were above sustainable levels. Table 3 compares the growth and investment shares in the seven years before the crisis with the seven years following it. It can first be noted that the recovery involved substantially lower investment shares, by forty percent in Malaysia and Thailand, thirty percent in Indonesia and twenty percent in Korea. In every country growth rates fell by even more, which supports the argument that the advantages of backwardness were being exhausted. It would appear that the crisis of 1997-1999 accelerated this process, in part by the elimination of less efficient enterprises. In any case, the post-crisis rates of growth were remarkably close to what the IMF study estimated to be each country's potential rate of growth.

If one accepts the advantages of backwards interpretation of the IKMT countries, it has important implications for the new miracles, China, Vietnam, Cambodia and, perhaps, Myanmar. The growth China and Vietnam from the late 1980s to the late 2000s proved even more phenomenal that for the IKMT countries. After twenty years of rapid growth, our analysis predicts that these two countries are exhausting the possible gains from technological up-grading and force discipline, though some scope would remain for transfer of labor out of low productivity activities. Equally important, it would be unlikely for China and Vietnam to maintain their investment shares. If the gross incremental capital output ratios reported for the 2000s in Table 3 were equal to the average, they imply that the capital stock in both China and Vietnam grew at eleven percent. This not a rate of investment that can be sustained, because the labor demand it creates will at some point overwhelm the process of internal labor force migration. Thus, it would be reasonable to expect growth in China and Vietnam to drop into the five-to-six percent range in the 2010s with Vietnam's post-crisis growth much closer to that level.

Whether Cambodia or Myanmar could emerge as "third generation miracles" would depend substantially on those two conflict-prone countries maintaining political stability: However, since neither country has generated investment shares even into the twenty percent range, miracle status is unlikely, though if, as some predict, large oil and gas reserves were found in Cambodia high investment rates would become a possibility. More likely would be a steady descent towards a potential growth rate of five percent as the gains from international migration, technological up-grading and x-efficiency are exhausted. The least likely candidate for miracle status would be the Philippines, which exhausted largely these growth sources without achieving rapid growth.

Figure 15: Growth Rates and Investment shares, IKMT countries, pre and post Asian financial crisis

Country	1990-96		2000-06		Ratio	
	growth	Inv/GDP	growth	Inv/GDP	growth	Inv/GDP
Indonesia	8.0	30.8	4.9	21.2	.61	.69
Korea	7.9	37.7	5.2	29.9	.66	.79
Malaysia	9.5	38.7	5.2	23.1	.55	.60
Thailand	8.6	40.4	5.0	25.1	.58	.62

Source: *World development Indicators 2008,* online database.

Figure 16: Index of growth-investment share ratios for the IKMT countries, 1965-2006 (3 year moving averages, GDP growth)

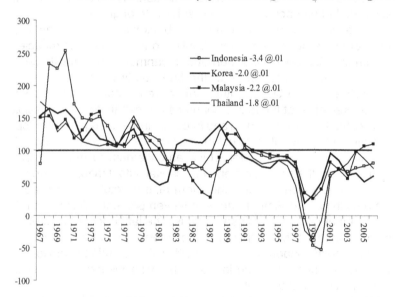

Note: The numbers following the country names are the log-linear regression trend for 1965-1996 (1966 for Indonesia), and the degree of significance of the trend term.

Closing Comments

The long period of steady, rapid growth of Indonesia, Korea, Malaysia and Thailand was possible because of high investment rates, plus the "advantages of backwardness". The severe crisis that brought this growth to a sudden stop did not result from basic flaws in the economies and governance of these four countries. It was the most virulent manifestation of the wave of speculative financial instability of the 1990s, which would be repeated in severe form on a global scale ten years later.

Partly by chance and partly as a result of the rapid development of the four countries that made them attractive to speculative attack, the crisis coincided with the approaching end of the "advantages of backwardness" that allowed unusually high growth rates. The decreasing contribution of the growth augmenting factors resulted in strong, but slower, growth rates following the recovery, with the fundamental cause of the decline obscured by the crisis. The "growth miracle" period had ended, and the countries approached maximum sustainable growth rates of about five percent.

The 2000s would bring the exhaustion of the same growth-enhancing factors for the next generation of "miracles", China and Vietnam, implying lower sustained growth rates in the following decade, again approaching five percent. The possibility of sustaining very high growth rates among the small countries of the region would be unlikely, since extended periods of rapid growth required investment shares considerably above actual ones.

Annex: Data sources

General Data Sources

Abeysinghe, Tilak, and Gulasekaran Rajaguru

2003 'Quarterly Real GDP Estimates for China and ASEAN4 with a Forecast Evaluation,' National University of Singapore, Department of Economics Working Paper 0404, http://nt2.fas.nus.edu.sg/ecs/pub/wp/wp0404.pdf

Asian Development Bank

2008 *Key Indicators for Asia and the Pacific 2008, 39th Edition* (Manila: ADB) http://www.adb.org/Statistics/Data/default.asp

International Monetary Fund, *World Economic Outlook 1996* (Washington: IMF, 1996) http://www.imf.org/external/pubs/weo/03devel.htm

2005 *Global Economic Outlook 2005* (Washington: IMF) http://www. deloitte.com/dtt/cda/doc/content/GlobalEconomicOutlook2005.pdf

World Bank: http://64.233.169.104/search?q=cache:1XgryMAOymsJ:siteresources. worldbank.org/INTEAPHALFYEARLYUPDATE/Resources/550192-1194982737018/ AppendixTables EAP-Update-Nov2007.pdf+indonesia+quarterly+gdp+2005&hl=en &ct=clnk&cd= 15&gl=uk

Sources by country:

Korea http://www.econstats.com/r/rkor__q16.htm

Indonesia http://www.econstats.com/r/indonesia__q12.htm

Malaysia http://www.adb.org/documents/books/ado/2002/mal.asp

http://www.statistics.gov.my/eng/images/stories/files/LatestReleases/PE/ petablesjune2008.pdf

Thailand http://www.tcf.or.jp/data/19990423_Chalongphob_Sussangkarn. pdf

Chapter 8

THE CHIMERA OF PROSPERITY IN POST-IMF SOUTH KOREA AND THE ALTER-GLOBALIZATION MOVEMENT

Seongin Jeong and Richard Westra [1]

South Korea (hereafter Korea) compressed into several decades the historical process of over a century of development from light to heavy/ chemical to consumer durable industry experienced by the developed countries. In the 1980s Korea's emergence as a prominent player in the world automobile industry embodied the dramatic shift that occurred in global automobile production during the last decades of the 20th century. While the export prowess of Korea is a well documented subject, the extent to which Korea constitutes an "automobile society" in the vein of North America, Europe and Japan is not generally appreciated. It ranked fifth in the world in 1998 in automobiles per 1000 population (163 in that year) and evidenced an exponential increase in automobile ownership of 2228.6 percent between 1980 and 1998—the largest of any country in the world during that period.[2]

There exists debate over the structural characteristics of Korean corporations, the *chaebol*. The way the argument goes is that Korean *chaebol* like the Japanese *keiretsu* are marked by business networks and multi-subsidiary structures, draw increasingly upon personal relations and "trust" among grouping affiliates to share investment responsibility and risk, spawn under the auspices of a single entrepreneur/family and flourish viz. political patronage. These features, it is claimed set East Asian capital apart from the impersonal modes of corporate governance of United States (US) capital with its more arms-length supply links and reliance upon a stock market dominated by individual investors for finance. However the sharp counter-posing to so-called "models" of post-World War II (WWII) corporate capital with the US capital set out as a so-called "market model" is deeply problematic. Studies of US capital reveal that in the late 1930s, ownership of almost 75 percent of the largest nonfinancial companies was marked by large controlling blocks of stock rather than some mythical democratic "people's" ownership. In 1959, 27 percent of corporate directors were either nonemployee large stockholders or representatives of financial institutions with significant controlling blocks of shares. While this differs *de jure* from the Japanese/German so-called "Nippo-Rhenish" model of capital (of which the *chaebol* is a species) with its direct bank ownership (*chaebol* were financed by the state controlled bank) it constitutes a *de facto* similitude in terms of the actual operation of corporate capital. Indeed, even by 1965, in about half of US corporate capital, control resided in the hands of founding families and their descendants through stock ownership. And, because in the post-WWII period to the early 1970s price to earnings ratios were quite low, stocks were held for long periods mimicking the penchant of so-called "patient" capital of the Nippo-Rhenish model of corporate capital.[3] We can add on the question of supplier links, indications are, particularly in the consumer durable/auto industry, that the tight coupling of tasks which optimally requires increased horizontal integration and fostering of long term relations with suppliers acts as a powerful force for industrial convergence across models of post-WWII capitalism.[4]

The conceptualizing of a "developmental state" in the context of so-called newly industrialized country (NIC) economic growth is not groundless. But the notion that its obverse in post war capitalism is a sort of "night-watchman" state *is*. As David Coates (2000, 223) puts it, no state can "free either itself or its class base from the generalized logics of accumulation which characterized world capitalism as a whole".[5] And, if world capitalism in the post-WWII era had a "logic" shaping state action, it was one that operated within the international institutional parameters of the Bretton Woods monetary system facilitating state governed projects of national development. This in effect rendered developmental policy a sort of mainstay of state policy *per se* for the period. Even the US state in the post-WWII period directed finance toward "picking winners", specifically in defense and agriculture. Also, the US state maintained a "de facto" industrial policy viz. its proclivity to bail out corporate capital when required and regulate industry with an eye to competitive international outcomes.[6]

Of course, it is not being argued that US policy and the Korean state policies of targeting industrial sectors and select businesses, allocating credit to same, favoring particular entrepreneurs, exerting authoritarian control, etc. are completely commensurate. But controlling for historical catch-up and the compressing of industrial epochs by Korea, we see that the strong view of the developmental state as constitutive of capital is drawn coincides with the growth of the *chaebol* around the steel/heavy chemical complex under the 1970s Yushin system of Park Chung Hee. In comparative perspective, it is precisely this period of the "great spurt" where West European development, for example, also experiences hypertrophied state participation in industry combined with authoritarian politics; a political profile which then changes as these economies shift to consumer durable production. The point here is that management of capitalist development in the consumer durable/automobile societies at the pinnacle of that development in the post-WWII period required extensive state support. And states of successful accumulators were equipped with an arsenal of interventions including: countercyclical demand management, investment in infrastructure, military expenditure, industrial targeting, social welfare and insurance programs, fiscal and monetary policy, and so forth.

If there is a signal distinguishing feature of international capital in the post-WWII period it is the internationalization of production including: foreign direct investment, international technology licensing, international subcontracting, leasing, management agreements and so on. The internationalization of finance and banking supported the internationalization of production, which in turn created the possibility for emergence of a genuine international division of labor for the first time in the history of capitalism. In prior eras of accumulation, international capital had been characterized by the concentration of global industrial production in the hands of a limited group of core states. Both so-called "early" and "late" industrializing states within this group followed much the same development sequence—exporting first light industrial commodities to foreign markets, then capital goods—and maintained a divide viz. the world at large which was relegated to a position of raw material supplier or outlet for foreign portfolio investment.

Korea's economic development synchronized with the transformations of international capital noted above. Korea gained a reputation firstly as an assembler and producer of low cost standardized products for mass consumption. In this process Korea benefited from the emergence in the 1960s of what has been proclaimed "[o]ne of the most significant developments" of the international economy—international subcontracting.[7] In particular, Korean development was marked by two facets of this, Original Equipment Manufacturing (OEM) and Own-design and manufacture (ODM). Through OEM Korean firms first gained valuable technical and organizational expertise under the auspices of foreign companies that market their products. With ODM Korean firms "reverse engineered" industrial processes, technology and components while producing under the design requirements of the foreign companies marketing the goods.[8] The growth in indigenous productive capacity which the foregoing engendered can be charted empirically in the upward spike of Korea's export-import ratio in trade of industrial goods with both Japan and the world, as well as in Korea's increasing rates of domestic investment as opposed to foreign investment.[9] In fact, a feature distinguishing Korea from other NICs has been the weight of domestic consumption; this propelled Korean *chaebol* up the technological ladder as global brands (so-called own brand manufacture OBM) and international competitors with global reach in their own right. [10] Korea is thus the *only* example approaching full scale industrialization from the third world as a whole as that world shed the yoke of direct colonialism in the post-WWII years.

What, it may be asked, have been the key ingredients of Korean development? One answer may be summarily dispensed with: Korean development in the post-WWII era had absolutely nothing to do with neoliberal mythology concerning the role of so-called "free markets" in development.[11] In fact, as has also been strongly argued, all economic development or "growth" among major economies in the post-WWII period was predicated upon extensive state/superstructure support; capitalism as a whole in the post-WWII period operated at a greater distance from so-called market or laissez fair principles than at any point in its history.[12]

Probably the most significant component of Korea's emergence from the pack of non-developed previously colonized states is its place on the front line of vehement US anti-communist global strategy. It is officially claimed that in the years 1945-65 Korea obtained $12 billion from the US, equal to 100 per cent of the Korean government budget during the 1950s. Calculating US taxpayer beneficence for the period 1945-76, one estimate has it that Korea was the recipient of $600 per capita each year for thirty years. And military aid was also considerable, amounting to $15 billion, equal to four times that directed towards all of Latin America during that time.[13] What is most significant however for the global economy and Korea's place within it was the global projection of anti-communism. US re-armament put a floor under its domestic economy while the Korean War contributed to the recovery of both Germany and Japan. Through the war in Vietnam, which removed the last vestiges of "old" colonialism from Asia, the world economy crystallized around three poles of capital accumulation. In the context of capital accumulation in Asia centered on Japan, capitalist development in Korea emerged as the "most significant…outside Japan because it was based on a deliberate linkage between the objective of creating a national capital in the country and the role of both Japan and the United States which accepted and sustained the above objective".[14]

Besides its direct position on a Cold War fault line Korea was bound further to US global anti-communism by sending 300,000 troops to Vietnam, more per capita than the US itself.[15] Korea's early export orientation noted above was thus part of US strategy seeking to reduce the dependence on aid of its anti-communist partner. By 1967, the share of Korea's total exports by sector going to South Vietnam was: steel (94.29 percent); transportation equipment (51.75 percent); non-electrical machinery (40.77 percent).[16] Finally, it is through Japan, also firmly under the US anti-communist security umbrella that, following a US-brokered rapport OEM and ODM transferred technology to Korea. The edifice as a whole was supported both by ever expanding domestic consumption of the US market and by the Japan/Korea rapprochement-based loan guarantees from Japan that undergirded Korea's success in heavy steel import substitution industrialization (ISI) by the early 1980s.[17]

A second, less widely acknowledged (though no less important) factor in the Korean development equation was the process of land reform.[18] The importance of land reform for development resides in the role it plays in transforming social class structures and the vistas that are thereby opened for varying sets of economic actors. The work of Robert Brenner on transitions from feudalism to capitalism in Britain and Western Europe is noteworthy for its explication of how the unraveling of landlord/ peasant social relations of production in agriculture and their replacement by modalities of owner-operated farms and hired labor, in turn synchronized with the emergence of capitalism and ascendency of a bourgeois class, producing the sort of income distributions and development of the social productive forces which led to the prominent early development of that region within the world economy as a whole.[19] Mainstream development economists working in the neoclassical tradition never gave this question much thought as their abstract models of economic "growth" largely took capitalism (what they refer to as "the market") as a *fait accompli*.

Thus, as we peer across the third world, among the post-WWII newly decolonized states which had followed US academic development studies exhortations, it is only Korea and Taiwan where land reform— the eviscerating of feudal landlord/peasant relations—was extensively implemented. However, land reform in Korea and Taiwan followed not from enlightened scholarship on the actual historical emergence of capitalism as a mode of production but from the hothouse of US and its client states anti-communist policy. Remember, it was precisely the promise of land redistribution to hundreds of millions of Chinese peasants that swept Mao Zedong and the Communists into power in China and which offered an alternative model of development for the masses of East Asia. Fearing the possibility of peasant armies sweeping across Asia, the US supported the former Chinese "Nationalist" government in Taiwan as it proceeded with land reform. And in Korea, the American Military Government (AMG), hastened by the land reform policies first instituted in North Korea, removed the final vestiges of landlordism and colonialism in the South and redistributed land, in effect creating a class of independent farmers in Korea. Successive Korean governments supported and extended the land reform and employed the so-called "reverse scissors" policy of Mao to transfer wealth to the countryside.

From the Asian Crises to the Wall Street Financial Meltdown

We need not trace out every causal component of the Asian economic crisis of 1997-98 here (given the plethora of writings on it) except to note, on the one hand, that its explosion at a time when international organizations were heaping praises upon the "miracle economies" of East Asia was sparked by precisely those neoliberal policies organizations like the International Monetary Fund (IMF) and World Bank (WB) touted as the solution to development problems in the third world as a whole. And on the other hand, it resulted from decades of US hegemonic force pushing to reorient the global financial architecture to suit circumstances where the US was no longer the world's major creditor but its largest debtor. Of general significance here is the US effort in restructuring economies of the third world to act as open hosts to torrents of speculative dollar denominated financial flows in ways that benefited Wall Street and the internationally predominant private financial intermediaries headquartered there, along with the social class cohort that battened on these global activities.[20] Of specific significance is the increasing dependence of the US during the 1990s on state directed financial flows from Japan which prompted the US to intervene more directly in Japanese domestic politics. The "blowback" from this was the fact that US pressure on Japan to correct the trade imbalance by compelling an appreciation of the yen contributed to the Japanese "Bubble". And then US pressure on the Bank of Japan (BOJ) to lower interest rates to spark a recovery contributed to the Asian crisis because of the favorable conditions this created in the region for newly "liberalized" economies' financial sectors to borrow yen at low interest rates to lend for all sorts of speculative excesses in their own economies.[21] We can also note that the international regulations for banking practices and lending, the so-called Basel Accord, contained capital adequacy provisions which predisposed banks to lend only short term outside the OECD[22] (and though Korea ascended to OECD status in 1996, the vulnerability to short term "hot money" flows had already crystallized).

Debate within the parameters of neoclassical economics (including its "institutionalist" offshoots) held that the Asian economic crisis sounded the death knell of "Korea Inc." with its structures of "crony capitalism" and suggested future Korean development demands that Korea fall in line with neoliberal market reforms as represented by the US model of accumulation. This strain of debate further sub-divides into arguments as to whether a) the continued policy efficacy of the Korean state belies claims of its neoliberal transformation; b) Korea is shifting to an increasingly market oriented economy as per neoliberal dictates, but this move is to be decried; or c) neo-liberalism conceived as simply about the exorcizing of the state is misunderstood, and Korea's post-crisis neoliberal policy orientation to build new market-enhancing institutions is a positive outcome. We have already touched on the fact however that the separating out of the US as a "market" model of capitalism where state activity recedes is a spurious characterization of US accumulation in the post-WWII period. We can add to this point the fact that under neoliberal compulsions there is also no tendency toward the diminution in state economic activity but in fact its acceleration, as figures on such activity as a proportion of GDP illustrate. At the time of the Asian economic meltdown, for example, government expenditure as a percent of GDP in Korea was 21.9 percent. By 2005, it had risen to close to 30 percent, and in 2007 as the current economic malaise was gestating it was almost 32 percent.[23] Korea represents no anomaly here as neoliberal policy the world over, including in its heartland, the US, has led to the state playing a greater role in economic life rather than the state sector "shrinking" as neoliberal ideology proclaims. In 2004 after decades of neoliberal policy the proportion of US GDP flowing from state economic activity was 37 percent.[24]

Critical/Marxist approaches to the Asian crisis and its aftermath take as their starting point the view that the crisis signals the "end" of NIC development *per se*, given how the specific constellation of politico-economic forces within which this development germinates no longer exist. In this perspective the internationalization of neoliberalism through the so-called "Washington Consensus" constitutes a war of attrition aimed at remaking the world economic hierarchy.[25] Given our understanding of neoliberalism as briefly touched on above, it is thus through the prism of critical/Marxist perspectives that we can better sort out questions of the crisis and current development of the Korean economy. The fact is, the neoliberal account of the crisis ends up as a case of trying to blow and suck at the same time. It is not clear how they are able to keep a straight face while explaining Korean development as following neoliberal market dictates while simultaneously characterizing the crisis in Korea as an example of not following these dictates. In fact, as short term speculative "hot money" began to flow out of the Korean economy, the impact was exacerbated by IMF policy itself.[26] We must critique simplistic renderings of the so-called state/market debate. The truth of the matter is that it is not a question of *either* states or markets but what precise polices hypertrophic state activity is following under the aegis of neoliberalism.

On the question of whether post-IMF intervention neoliberal policy thrusts have had a positive impact on the Korean economy, we have to remember that Korean development as the sole exemplar of full scale industrialization from the third world following the bout of post-WWII decolonization owed much of its overcoming of hurdles to industrialization to its strategic anti-communist alliance with the US and its existence on a major Cold War fault line. We also should keep in mind firstly that the *chaebol* form of corporate capital in Korea shared a strong family resemblance to other post-WWII forms of corporate capital and that the way its differences have been construed in neoliberal debates over "the market" in post-WWII capitalism are spurious. Secondly, as the world became ensnared in the US impelled neoliberal maelstrom, NICs, among which Korea was the most successful, were certainly less prepared to defend their gains than "late" industrializing forerunners such as Japan, and were in a much weaker position to defend their economies and government programs than Western European OECD states. So-called structural "weaknesses" in the Korean economy related to the *chaebol*, such as the latter's high debt to equity ratios (which by 1999, two years after the crisis, were halved—from 400 percent to 200 percent) and their holding of "peripheral" businesses in the *chaebol* group (which they shed or traded following the crisis)[27] were due less to some unique East Asian crony capitalism (Worldcom, Enron, Tyco and the list goes on were US companies on a crony scale defying belief) than to world political economic conditions and US/Japanese government bailouts. Most trumpeted as a success of "restructuring" was the reduction of non-performing loans in the banks and the consolidation in the Korean banking sector which followed. Here too, as has been pointed out, there is nothing necessarily unique to Korea in economic crisis fomenting institutional change. And in the case of both *chaebol* and bank restructuring it has been argued it was Korean government injections of funds and government initiatives rather than some opaque IMF directing of "market forces" that led to the post crisis economic upswing.[28]

What is in fact the dark underbelly of the post-IMF neoliberal change in Korea is the effect of broader changes not only in the modalities of Korean accumulation but of accumulation on a world scale on working people. Paralleling the process of democratization in Korea from the late 1980s, which in turn opened the door to labor to begin exacting wage increases in line with productivity gains, remuneration had begun to approach European/OECD standards, a factor important for the growth of the domestic market. In the aftermath of the Asian crisis as the Korean economy again began to grow, it did so under conditions where Korean workers were subjected to high rates of part-time, insecure contract work and limited wage gains. Within the OECD in the early years of the 21st century Korea had the longest working hours, lowest pay and highest rate of "irregular" work.[29] By mid 2005, as pointed out by a Korean Confederation of Trade Unions (KCTU) official, the number of workers subjected to insecurities, harassment and violation of labor laws in Korea was 8.5 million.[30] During this same period Korean capital began to increasingly locate production abroad, particularly to China. Beginning in the early 1990s with a relatively minor investment by Korean *cheabol* LG, by 2008 there were over 40,000 Korean companies investing in China to the tune of $100 billion. As a result China is the largest trading partner of Korea, importing $103.75 billion in 2007 while exporting $56.14 billion worth of goods to Korea in that year.[31] Such "hollowing" out of Korean industry and Korea's market flooding with cheap imports is a detrimental aspect of the current world economy to which Korean workers share exposure with workers around the world.

Another festering problem of the post-IMF neoliberal restructuring years has been the burgeoning of the Korean black market economy, including "legal", so-called "informal" economic activity where it is solely a problem of taxes being evaded, as well as the actual illegal economy where laws *and* taxes are being evaded. The total value of the Korean black market economy has been estimated to represent 27.6 percent of Korea's GDP in 2005; it is the largest black market among the 22 OECD states (Italy's black market economy, for example, comes in second at 23.2 percent of GDP). This also impacts negatively on the lives of working people as it forces the government to raise taxes on workers and the self employed, and devalues goods and services produced in the private and public sectors of the "formal" economy.[32] Higher taxes in the context of rising wages and benefits of course was at the root of "golden age" economic growth predicated upon mass consumption of consumer durables marking the post-WWII capitalist expansion in core OECD states. Within the 21st century Korean economic context of falling wages and diminishing benefits for workers, it further constricts domestic demand and adds but one more factor to the increasing export dependency of the Korean economy.

One immensely significant hangover from both the so-called deregulation of the Korean financial system in the lead up to the Asian crisis and its continued liberalization under the auspices of the IMF restructuring has been the vulnerability of the Korean economy to contagions beginning elsewhere. Unlike the Japanese economy or China's, Korea's financial system and investment environment has been quite open through the early years of the 21st century (the neoliberal jargon here is "transparent") and unlike Japan and China its economic restructuring as such was orchestrated by neoliberal wizards at the IMF. It is little wonder why after a bout of IMF tutelage it is South Korea which uniquely in the East Asian region is bearing such a severe brunt of the recent Wall Street meltdown. In fact, among so-called emerging market currencies the fall of the Korean won was second only to the South African rand.[33]

Part of the problem—as if nothing was learned from the Asian crisis (which follows from the fact that the IMF purportedly "misdiagnosed" its cause, disregarding international conditions to focus upon domestic so-called "crony capitalism")—has been Japanese yen borrowing at extremely low interest rates (2-3 percent compared to the Korean domestic rate revolving around 6 percent). To be sure, the reversing of the so-called "yen carry trade" from 2007 in which yen is borrowed to fund investments in high interest rate currencies impacted other states, particularly as interest rates were reduced in other major currencies to combat the turmoil spreading from Wall Street. However the combined exposure of Korea to that as well as Korean financial intermediaries' freewheeling and heavy reliance upon US dollar-denominated securities and related borrowing conduits under domestic conditions of so-called liberalization and "transparency" has created a kind of déjà vu situation. Once again, with deteriorating international economic circumstances, large hedge funds began liquidating Korean positions and retreating to the safe haven of the dollar. With the won in freefall against the dollar following major investors ditching won positions, Korean financial institutions' repayment of dollar denominated borrowings has become strained, even though Korea holds approximately $200 billion in foreign currency reserves and is projected to maintain a current account surplus of $13 to $15 billion in 2009 (thus is not *necessarily* facing a liquidity crunch).[34]

Remember too that there exist no straightforward circumstances in global credit markets as "loans" imbricate in complex webs of new-fangled financial instruments—derivatives and options. This has nothing to do with domestic Korean regulations. It is rather an integral aspect of the global financial architecture. But the strictures this places on domestic economic possibilities are debilitating as evident from medium-sized Korean business failures and bankruptcies springing simply from such businesses being on the wrong side of currency options contracts displays. (Without teams of business school graduates on their staff many Korean business owners could not even understand complex financial products like derivatives).[35]

The cumulative impact of already comparatively low wage conditions, job insecurity, spiraling layoffs from the current downturn and further attrition against labor is leading to family as well as business insolvency, This in turn is constricting domestic demand and further reverberating through the already taxed financial sector. As well, given the neoliberal-impelled high export dependency of the Korean economy, the diminution in demand from Korea's major trading partners—the US, Japan and China—due to their economies being embroiled in the Wall Street fiasco's spreading contagion, exacerbates problems of employment and financial institution viability.[36] And, once again, to add insult to injury, with the Korean Stock Exchange (KOSPI) valuation savaged, we are seeing foreign capital flooding in to purchase assets at the newly reduced fire sale prices.[37]

Looking into the economic conditions prevailing in the Korean economy in the last years of the 21st century's first decade the sight is hardly representative of any "miracle": From May 2008 to May 2009 219,000 "formal" market jobs disappeared. A brewing asset market bubble portends further potential household solvency pitfalls. From January 2007 to January 2008 267,000 temporary and daily workers were removed from the just over 7 million total of this shrinking cohort of vulnerable workers. Let us be clear, these workers are not transitioning to "good" labor jobs but to no job. And there are almost 1 million workers laboring under contracts of less than two years who have their contractual period ending summer 2009 and who, under current labor laws, may be dismissed without benefit.[38]

The Welling Up and Limitations of Anti-Neoliberal and Alterglobalization Protest

Lee Myung-bak, an avowed neoliberal, assumed the Presidency of Korea in February 2008. His ascendance to that position was based on the electoral promise to revive the Korean economy. This was embodied in his so-called "747 pledge" in which he promised to achieve an economic growth rate of 7 percent, average per capita income of $US40,000, and raise Korea to the world's seventh largest economy. This was nothing more than rhetoric spewing out in complete ignorance of the ongoing world economic crisis which was already festering in the US. In fact, the World Bank in July 2009 placed Korea in 15th place in global economic rankings based on GDP, behind Australia, Mexico and India (In 2003, Korea was the 11th largest economy in the world).[39]

However, it was not economic conditions but the signing by Lee Myung-bak of an agreement as part of the ratifying of the Korea-US Free Trade Agreement (FTA) to commence the importation of US beef at a time when the possible contamination of US beef products by so-called Mad Cow Disease (bovine spongiform encephalopathy) was a global issue, that sparked the "candlelight movement" of 2008, which became the biggest mass movement since the 1980s democratization struggles in Korea. [40] People were especially angry at the Lee Myung-bak government's neglect of the elemental right of health and its abandonment of quarantine sovereignty. From the beginning they demanded that Lee resign. The movement lasted more than 100 days from May 2 to August 15. On June 10th, to coincide with the anniversary of the "Great June Struggle" of 1987 which forced the military dictatorship in Korea to adopt a system of direct democratic elections of the President, an estimated 1 million people from all walks of life gathered at venues around the country with 500,000 massed in Seoul alone.[41] Indeed, the candlelight movement of 2008 erupted when the people felt that their democratic rights, which they had secured and taken for granted since "Great June Struggle" of 1987, were seriously compromised by the Lee Myung-bak government's bulldozing through legislation for the importation of US beef suspect of mad cow disease without democratic consultation procedure. Considering that the candlelight movement of 2008 sought to defend the representative democratic rights won through Great June Struggle of 1987, even as they demonstrated its neoliberal hollowness by having to resort to direct democracy in the street, it stands as a Great June Struggle II.

The candlelight movement of 2008 also can be seen as a Korean alterglobalization activism given that the FTA was a global issue. [42] Indeed, it shared the values of the international anti-neoliberal and alterglobalization movement, above all in calls for reclaiming the commons and "people before profit". This was evidenced by the fact that, from the first day of demonstration, the protests were directed not only against the importation of US beef but against all the attempts by Lee Myung-bak government to enclose the commons through privatization of public education, health insurance, public media, electricity, gas and water, and most importantly, construction of a vast transportation canal crosscutting the Korean peninsula (Grand Canal).

What is particularly interesting about the candlelight movement is the fashion in which it morphed from a protest against importation of US beef into a mass movement which included students, workers, activists, even Buddhist monks, all aligned to protest a wide range of issues mentioned above. Especially, it was the plan of "Grand Canal", given its potentially environmental destructive bent, which incensed the monks and brought them out on the streets. The movement was similar to other international alterglobalization movements since the "Battle of Seattle" of 1999 in that its major keyword was "spontaneism" or "direct democracy".[43] In fact, the candlelight movement of 2008 had not started with calls from the left political organizations. Many of these entered the scene late and in a timid way.

The potent aspects of the movement were the combination of online and off-line protests as well as the active participation of teenagers, reflecting their anger against the government's plan to privatize education. However, the inadequate participation of the organized workers movement was one of the weak points of the whole candlelight affair. It was also unfortunate that some sort of "autonomist" mindset dominated the movement, worshiping the "spontaneity" of a so-called multitude? The absence of the political leadership of the radical left was one of the reasons why the movement, which had erupted on such a splendid scale and continued tenaciously for several months, gradually flickered out during August 2008 without achieving any of the initial targets of the movement, particularly the renegotiation of US beef importation.

As the protests lingered, Lee Myung-bak's government also became increasingly heavy handed. The police arrested the activists of the movement. They also arrested a prominent "Left" professor (which was rescinded by the court) and several Socialist Workers League of Korea members under an antiquated National Security Law prohibiting "denouncing capitalism".[44] With the subsiding of the candlelight movement, the Lee Myung-bak government and the ruling class resumed their forward push of the neoliberal agenda. However, as at this writing, they have just refueled the protests, witness the recent explosion of demonstrations against the killing of 5 people by the police during the forcible demolition of downtown Yongsan in Seoul to forward neoliberal urban redevelopment. [45] Also, there is the ongoing factory occupation by about 1,000 Ssangyong car workers who were fired by the company as it tries to survive the economic crisis by sacrificing workers. [46] These events showed the limitations of the candlelight movement of 2008, where the issues of labor or poverty, crucial to the current conjunctures of deepening economic crisis, had been addressed only marginally. [47] Korean progressives need to formulate and promote the central roles of labor and radical politics in the anti- and post-capitalist struggles, while drawing upon or communicating with the new young generation of resistance, the so-called "Generation of Candlelight" which was the most important achievement of the movement of 2008.

Chapter 9

CONSEQUENCES OF NEOLIBERAL ECONOMIC GLOBALIZATION IN THAILAND

Ake Tangsupvattana

Introduction

It was following the British enforced signing of the Bowring Treaty in 1855 that the participation of Thailand in the world economy commenced and the process of transition to capitalism was sparked. The entrance of Thailand into the global trading system was accompanied by an influx of Chinese immigrants. Subsequently, many Thais of Chinese descent contributed to the evolution of an entrepreneurial class that marked the transformation of Thailand. Economic change soon led to political change with Thailand becoming a constitutional monarchy in 1932, though the constitution was not very democratic, supporting instead a form of bureaucratic-authoritarian-military rule.[1] Blazing a trail similar to that of Latin American states following their independence Thailand embarked upon a process of import-substitution industrialization (ISI). By the 1950s Thailand developed rudimentary domestic manufacturing and a modern banking system. The nascent capitalist development of Thailand was then given a major boost by United States (US) spending on the Korean War. A little over a decade later, US spending in Thailand for its Vietnam War adventure further contributed to the growth of the Thai economy.[2]

The demise of bureaucratic polity followed the 1973 students' upheaval. A democratic experiment ensued from 1973-1976. Then, in 1976, the conservative forces within the military regained their power by suppressing the nascent student movements. Nevertheless, the military also realized that they could not rule Thailand as they had in the old days. Therefore, a so-called semi-democracy, a regime of sharing political power between the military and other elites, was established in the 1978-88 period. One component of this semi-democratic regime was the invention of an (authoritarian) corporatist system where the military incorporated peak business associations and labor unions in the economic policy process. Thailand then changed its economic strategy from ISI as practiced through the 1960s and 1970s to export-oriented industrialization (EOI). With this economic policy Thailand deeply immersed itself into global trade and economic globalization. That is to say, the Thai economy relied on the global market trading area because of the limited size of its domestic market; a feature of its skewed income distribution.

From the end of the semi-democratic regime in the late 1980s through the early 1990s there was a second economic boom accompanied by the development of firm parliamentary politics,[3] albeit briefly interrupted by a coup attempt via the so-called National Peace Keeping Council (NPKC) instituted by the military. Following Black May 1992 protest against the NPKC attempt to seize political power, Thailand moved towards stabilized representative democracy which in turn contributed to a bout of stable economic development. The most important economic aspect pertaining to economic globalization was the initiation of the Bangkok International Banking Facilities (BIBF). In 1993 the Thai government introduced the BIBF—essentially at the behest of US impelled financial liberalization and deregulation—to facilitate the inflow and outflow of capital, and to position Thailand as a regional financial center.

The Uncontrollability of Global Finance
and the 1997 Economic Crisis in Thailand

Global "financialization" and foreign direct investment (FDI) in all its forms are at the center of what is dubbed globalization. FDI would reach three times as many countries in 2000 as it did in 1985. Multinational corporations (MNCs) came to account for about 25 percent of world production and 70 percent of world trade; with their sales equivalent to almost half of the world gross domestic product (GDP) at the turn of the 21st century.[4]

As the 21st century began, the turnover on the foreign exchange markets was over $1.2 trillion per day, and billions of dollars of financial assets were also being traded globally each day.[5] These transactions were then facilitated by utilization of digital technologies.[6] Anthony Giddens argued that there exists a fully globalized market at the level of finance which operates on a real-time basis. So-called "disconnected" capital—institutionally managed money—then increased by 1,100 percent from 1970 to the end of the century in proportion to other forms of capital.[7]

Within the contours of economic globalization, especially financial globalization, the state has become increasingly less efficient and effective in managing the "national" economy. In consequence, the state has "de-legitimized" its power in economic management. Therefore, the idea of "governance" is represented as an alternative to inefficient and ineffective forms of government. If government is connected to the state's formal authority, governance is related to the alleged "inter-subjectivity" of so-called stakeholders.[8] Therefore the notion of governance becomes subject to the stakeholders' participation in dealing with the consequences of globalization.

However, there are different stakeholders with differing interests, leading to different understandings of globalization, with this in turn leading to different interpretations and understandings of global governance. Due to so-called "globalists" strong belief in economic globalization weakening the state's power and transfiguring the state from decision maker to decision taker,[9] it is unavoidable that this weakening will impact the processes of economic globalization.[10] Globalists thus give prime importance to the role of the market as a governance mode of rule as opposed to a government mode of rule by the state. The globalist interprets globalization as merely economic globalization and thinks of global governance as economic global governance ruled and run by the market system.

This understanding of globalization and governance is criticized as an ideology put out by free-marketers who wish to dismantle welfare systems and cut back on state expenditures.[11] It is also considered to be a new mode of Western imperialism dominated by the world's major capitalist states, and an ideological construction of a neoliberal global project, bent upon creation of a global free market to consolidate Anglo-American capitalism within the world's major economic regions.[12] This neoliberal project is linked to Washington Consensus deregulation, privatization, structural adjustment programs (SAPs), and limited government, and is connected to key Western capitals and global institutions such as the IMF.[13]

Globalist/neoliberal ideology is severely criticized by George Soros as market fundamentalism. This "ism" believes that efficient markets assure the best allocation of resources and that any intervention, whether it comes from the state or from international institutions, is detrimental. The main problem with market fundamentalism according to Soros is that markets are not perfect. They only cater to narrow quantitative interests; taking care of qualitative social needs is beyond their scope. Financial markets are also inherently unstable and operate more like a "casino" than "rational" market. Soros thus argues that, as an extreme ideology, market fundamentalism is as mistaken as Soviet style communism.[14]

We can easily spot the linkages between market fundamentalism, neoliberalism, the Washington Consensus, the world's major economic powers, Western capitals and global institutions and their exhortations promoting global governance by markets. After the East Asian economic crisis of 1997, as has been pointed out,[15] there was an endeavor to replace the Washington Consensus by the post-Washington Consensus—to construct a more humanized governance project. Yet, by its roots, the post-Washington Consensus is still entangled with the Washington Consensus because of its panegyrizing of the market system. Neoliberal governance in the so-called post-Washington Consensus era continued to foster the juggernaut of global finance as the core of their "market system". It was precisely such narrow neoliberal policy concerns that caused the 1997 economic crisis in East Asia and Thailand.

Much of the literature on the Asian Crisis points to causes relating to negative cultural factors, such as patron and client relationships, Confucianism and the *guanxi*[16] system producing nepotism, favoritism and so-called "crony capitalism". Elsewhere I contend that there were two combined causes of the 1997 Asian Crisis in Thailand, specifically: the corrupt business culture *and* economic globalization.[17] The development of firm parliamentary politics after the period of semi-democracy brought about the increased power of provincial business-politicians, employing money politics through patron and client relationships to influence politics at the national level. Local money politics combining with "crony" operations of business-people and business-politicians at the national level added a negative cultural element to the 1997 crisis in Thailand.

Without the initiation of BIBF as mentioned above however, the 1997 economic crisis in Thailand would have not happened, or would hardly have been as severe. What the data shows is that following the speculative attacks between 1996 and early 1997 mounted by international hedge funds, the Bank of Thailand moved from the pegged to the floating currency system on 2 July 1997. The Thai baht immediately dropped from US$ 25/1 to US$ 30/1 and by January 1998, it dropped to US$ 55/1 then sprang back to US$ 45/1 by February.[18] Foreign exchange reserves dwindled from $40 billion in January 1997 to under $30 billion six months later.[19] Investment into Thailand was effectively reversed. Capital inflows of 7.7 percent of gross domestic product (GDP) in 1996 became a 12.6 percent capital outflow by 1997[20] and the stock exchange of Thailand (SET) fell by 51 percent from its 1993 high.

The BIBF was a necessary condition for such speedy inflows and outflows of global finance as it liberalized and facilitated the global financial movements. That was the wrecking ball which hit Thailand hard, reflecting the combined impacts of economic globalization and the neoliberals' mode of "market" global governance.

Natenapha Wailerdsak explains that when the value of the Thai currency bottomed out in January 1998 at about 47 percent of its former value the weight of foreign exchange liabilities on company balance sheets doubled, rendering many of them technically bankrupt. Their income and cash flow diminished as well: Consumers stopped spending and investors stayed away. The IMF imposed a severe deflationary package. Over the next year, consumer spending shrank by 20percent and overall GDP by 11 percent. Companies booked heavy losses and struggled to survive by cutting costs, exacerbating the downward spiral.[21]

In financial sectors directly hit by the crisis, only the five largest banks survived, in part through government assistance. In the three that were controlled by a dominant family, the family share was scythed down to below 5 percent, and foreign shareholders acquired major stakes, yet the families retained management control. Four medium-sized banks were sold to foreign owners—two Singaporean, one British, and one Dutch. Five small and medium-sized banks were seized by government. These were closed down and their assets merged with other institutions. The remaining two continued to operate under the control of the Ministry of Finance. Of ninety-one finance companies operating before the crisis, fifty-six were closed down by government order in December 1997. Others failed over following months.[22]

When the crisis began, the Thai economy quickly melted down. For foreign capital, turned the Thai economic crisis presented an opportunity. If financial liberalization and deregulation were part of the neoliberal playbook to dominate the global economy the victims were victimized again by neoliberals when the crisis began by further exacerbation of neoliberal policies. With its schemes of rescue packages and with it the neoliberal project of governance, the IMF opened an opportunity for foreign capital to shop for undervalued products in Thailand's grand fire sale. Instead of encouraging Thailand to resurrect its economy by meticulously addressing the details of its particular situation, the IMF foisted its one-size-fits-all solution on the Thai Government, forcing it to sell Thai properties cheaply to global investors.

Neoliberal Policy Impacts from the 1997 Economic Crisis to the Present

With reference to Higgott's contention concerning the post-Washington consensus above, after the 1997 economic crisis the dominant mode of global governance continued to be the neoliberal governance project of rule by market. Although this mode of governance tried to soften the dehumanized governance model as it had operated before the crisis, the core of neoliberal thinking, the market mechanism, was rigorously adhered to in the post-Washington Consensus.

Next, we will focus on two cases of local impacts of the neoliberal project. They are the FTA (free trade area) between Thailand and China, and the Tesco-Lotus "hypermarket" invasion cases.

FTA Between Thailand and China:
Pros and Cons of the Global Neoliberal World

The free trade area and free trade agreement are frequently quoted terms under globalization and the neoliberal global governance models. Multilateral agreements through the World Trade Organization (WTO), the regional trade agreement (RTA) and bilateral agreements are examples of how these models are forwarded. For Thailand, though bilateral agreements seem to be more popular, the cases studied here are the FTA with China, the RTA between the Association of Southeast Asian Nations (ASEAN),[23] and the ASEAN-China FTA (ACFTA). Like a double-edged sword, FTAs can bring prosperity to local people through the international division of labor or they can destroy the ways of life of local people as well as the local economy.

Thailand's first FTA was AFTA (ASEAN Free Trade Area) in 1993. Then, on 18 June 2003, when Thailand and China signed the "Agreement between the Government of the People's Republic of China and the Government of the Kingdom of Thailand on Accelerated Tariff Elimination under the Early Harvest Program of the Framework Agreement on Comprehensive Economic Cooperation between ASEAN and China", the agenda of FTAs became a major issue in Thailand. Under this framework, ASEAN and China agreed to pilot FTA on goods and products in chapters 01-08 of the Harmonized System (HS 01-08)[24]. In doing this, HS 01-08 tariff reduction was implemented on 1st January 2004 with the tariff to be reduced to 0 percent in 2006. However, the Government of Thailand, under Prime Minister Thaksin Shinawatra's Thai Rak Thai Party[25] (TRT), instead of reducing tariffs, voluntarily eliminated them under HS 07-08 on 1 October 2003, a few months earlier than the first step required by the ACFTA tariff reduction. It is thus interesting here to focus on the impacts of the FTA on Thailand in this context.

Comparing the trade balance of payments (BOP) between Thailand and China from 2000 to 2007 (before and after the FTA), Thailand's balance receded into negative territory with China. Between 2004 and 2007 Thailand's trade BOP dropped over successive years by $1,037 million, $2,001 million, $1,887 million and $1,396 million. However, the trade volume between Thailand and China dramatically increased from $6,532 million in 2000 to $31,055 million 2007. If we consider the trade BOP only in HS 01-08, Thailand's export value to China in 2000-2007 would be 118, 186, 187, 261, 343, 455, 592 and 597 million US$ and import value would be 46, 57, 88, 120, 151, 175, 226 and 281 million US$.[26]

Considering import and export values in HS 07-08 alone, the export value to China between 2006-2007 would be 524.2 and 477.4[27] and import value would be 161.4 and 202.3 million US$[28]. Therefore the BOP of HS 07-08 between Thailand and China in 2006-2007 would be 362.9 and 275.1 million US$.[29] However, the highest and also most concentrated volume of Thailand's export to China in HS 07-08 was potatoes. If we discount potatoes exported in 2006-2007 for 425 and 348 million US$,[30] the export volume between Thailand and China in HS 07-08 would be 99.2 and 129.4 US$ respectively. Then, if we reduce these numbers by import value, the trade balance would be (-62.2) and (-72.9) millions US$. One of the important reasons for China's import of potatoes, it may be noted, is that China wants to use potatoes to produce bio-energy as an alternative energy source due to the increasing price of oil.

However, if we turn to focus on the types of imported products in Thailand (such as fruits and vegetables grown in cooler climates), we can see that the majority of these are competing with products grown in the most northerly parts of Thailand, which has similar weather to Southern China. Therefore, when the Thai-China FTA was implemented, Thai farmers growing these products suffered the most negative impacts created by the FTA. Particularly affected were small household industries that provide enhanced livelihood and increased living standards within local communities (such industries supplementing major income garnered from rice production). Small agriculturalists comprise a major segment of the Thai population, and are important contributors to the country's food security.[31] These small farm enterprises were placed under harsh pressure by the FTA.

Low prices for the above mentioned agricultural products brought about by China's advantages of lower labor costs and economy of scale caused heavy problems for Thai agriculturalists. So when the Thailand-China FTA was signed and HS 07-08 reduced trade tariffs to 0 percent, domestic agricultural products suffered. According to reports studying the FTA impacts on the Thai agricultural sector, the local market for marginally competitive agricultural products will be seized by countries with a higher competitive advantage, leading to hardship for the small producer. This report delineates the FTA impacts into two levels. The first level directly results from free trade itself i.e. the inability of agriculturalists to sell their product at a higher price than the lower priced imports. The second level makes the fundamental problems in the agricultural sector more severe. This involves the increased use of agricultural chemicals, agriculturalists' increased debt, agricultural product imbalance between demand and supply, the feasible management role of agricultural cooperative organizations, etc. Due to these problems, the impact of the FTA is highly detrimental.[32]

Compared to other products marked after the FTA, growers of garlic, onions, shallots, cool climate vegetables and fruits have experienced the greatest negative impact and have had more difficulties in making adjustments. As a result, small, and already marginal farmers have had to turn to employment in the service sector. Better financially savvy farmers can still survive but only by reducing their cost of production, looking for additional income streams, or by turning to other crops. The wealthier farmers become middleman, while many farmers are at a loss as to future courses of action. However, all have suffered similar impacts, that is, the reduction of product prices and farm income.[33]

Other reports tell the same story.[34] In the case of garlic, onions, shallots and low temperature fruits and vegetables, a number of local products are being replaced by Chinese products, leading farmers to scale down, withdraw their previously grown crops from production, or encounter longer selling periods. As a result the volume of imports is dramatically increased. The decline of farm prices is also related to the FTA. This either results in an overall price plummet or lower price levels during the period when seasonal prices in the domestic market are supposed to increase. Although the export of fruits has increased, the values of other products conversely decreased. Thai farmers do not realize any benefits from the FTA as their farm prices and sales volumes remain more or less the same. In addition, farmers are encountering one-sided grading from the middlemen or exporters. This makes the benefits from the FTA on farmers highly questionable.

In the case of garlic, the Thailand-China FTA is used by middleman/

traders as a tool to control and curb the market price. After the FTA agreement, it seems that small traders have gradually disappeared from the market due to the expanding role of big traders, who are directly collecting agricultural products at their source. The change to growing fruits and vegetables by agribusinesses after the Thailand-China FTA provided positive results to the big enterprises through better management practices, enhanced purchasing power and increasing marginal profits. On the other hand small-scale entrepreneurs and farmers experienced negative impacts from losing their bargaining power in the new trading structure and in many cases finally ended their farming careers.[35] In reality, the FTA causes problems for the small producers in terms of resource access. This means the benefits from the agreement accrue to the big producers more than they do to the small agriculturalists. The FTA will make low competitive sectors suffer. There will be unemployment problems, changes in people's way of life, deterioration of traditional skills and lifestyles. These are issues which are hard to quantify.[36] Therefore, the question of whether Thai society gains from the FTA cannot be answered by only focusing on the reduction of tariffs between the countries but must be done through understanding the whole market structure, market power, and the impacts of the FTA on this market structure and market power.

The Tesco-Lotus Case:
When Transnational Corporations Rule, Business Becomes an Ethics-Free Zone
Another case of the impact of neoliberal economic globalization in Thailand is the case of Tesco-Lotus hypermarket.

In the retail sector MNCs rule the world. For instance, Carrefour (France) and Tesco (Britain) were ranked as number one and two, respectively, in the industry of food and drug stores in *Fortune's Global 500*. In 2007, Carrefour created revenues of $US115,585 million and made profits of $US3,147 million while Tesco created revenues of $94,703 million and made profits of $4,253 million.[37] With this economic power, they can negatively impact people's livelihood, unemployment and cause the fading away of jobs, etc., both in their home countries and in others. The big names, such as Wal-Mart, Tesco, Carrefour and Seven Eleven exist in almost every corner of the globe. Therefore, if neoliberal economic globalization and governance weakens the state's power of economic management, and, instead fosters that of MNCs, the impacts of economic management in their hands merits further study.

In *Captive State: The Corporate takeover of Britain*, George Monbiot argues that modern traders[38] make enormous negative impacts on the home territory. He claims that during 1990s the number of specialist shops fell by 22 percent in Britain. The smallest ones were hit hardest: between 1990 and 1996, shops with annual sales of less than 100,000 pounds sterling declined by 36 percent. By contrast, between 1986 and 1997, superstore numbers rose from 457 to 1,102. While most towns have suffered substantial losses, the impact has been even greater in the countryside: at the end of 1997 the

Rural Development Commission revealed that 42 percent of rural parishes no longer possessed a shop. Between 1992 and 1997 retail food sales in Britain increased by 18.6 billion pounds, or 30 percent. While small shops lost 8.5 percent of their trade between 1990 and 1996, larger retailers gained 18 percent. These two trends appear to be linked. From the Government's study on the impact of superstores, food shops in market towns lost between 13 and 50 percent of their trade when a supermarket opened at the edge of the town center or out of town. The result is the closure of some town center food retailers, an increase in vacancy levels, and a general decline in the quality of the environment of the center.[39]

The National Retail Planning Forum, a research organization financed by big chain superstores, contends that there is strong evidence that new out-of-center superstores have a negative impact on retail employment up to 15 kilometers away. Total employment in food selling within that radius, it found, decreased by 5.2 percent. As retail employment actually increased by 0.1 percent in Great Britain outside the 15 kilometer catchment areas, this decline could only be due to the new superstores in the sample. In other words, if the superstores had not opened, employment would have risen. All of the reduction in employment that occurred in the catchment areas is attributable to superstore openings. The 93 stores the researchers studied were responsible for a net loss of 25,685 employees. In other words, every time a large supermarket opened, 276 people lost their jobs. The New Economics Foundation has calculated that every 50,000 pounds spent in small local shops creates one job, whereas 250,000 pounds need be spent in superstores for the same result. It can be concluded that the supermarkets' expansion relies not only upon increasing the total volume of trade but also upon seizing trade from the purportedly economically less efficient—though indubitably more socially efficient—employers in the independent sector.[40]

If we shift from Tesco in the heartland to Thailand, we will see a similar or even worse situation because of the state's inability to tame the modern traders. The retail sector represents 15 percent of Thailand's GDP[41] and in 2006 it represented 1.4 trillion Thai baht (42 US$ billion)[42] and was estimated that total retail sales would be around US$78 billion in 2008.[43] With this much at stake, retail trade has created a clash between traditional and modern traders. The former are native and local businesses such as the small local retailers, the wet market and the wholesaler while the latter is the MNC form of hypermarket, super market, convenience store, cash and carry, category killer and specialty store.

The wave of modern trade in Thailand originated around the 1990s. In 1989, CP group joined the Dutch firm Makro to form the Makro to sell goods to retailers. However, the big impact on the Thai retail trade came in 1994 when the Central group established hypermarkets under the name of Big C, and the CP group formed the Lotus hypermarkets. When the 1997 Economic crisis began, it provided an opportunity for the MNCs such as Casino, (French), Carrefour (French) and Tesco (British) to take on crucial roles. By 2000, Casino had taken over 66 percent of Big C and Central also sold its shares of Carrefour to Carrefour, meaning that Carrefour had absolute control under the nominee structure. At the same time, CP group sold its 92 percent of Lotus to Tesco so Lotus was renamed as Tesco-Lotus.[44] Thus, one can observe that the first wave of the neoliberal impact, as mentioned above, not only brought about negative consequences to Thai financiers and bankers, but also to the businesses in the retail sector.

From 2000 to 2006, Tesco, Carrefour and Big C expanded their hypermarket outlets from 24, 23 and 11 to 75, 49 and 24 respectively.[45] Over the period 1998 to 2001, these MNCs expanded their branches around the Bangkok metropolitan area, leading to the market becoming saturated. Between 2002 and 2005, they opened 63 branches in 41 of Thailand's 76 provinces.[46] Then the conjunction of neoliberal economic globalization and Thai local people spread out from Bangkok and into the provinces. The hypermarket retail sector in Thailand represents 5 percent of store numbers but 45 percent of total retail sales. They have been increasing their sales levels by an average rate of 15 percent between 2000 and 2005 to reach a level of 405 billion baht (US$10 billion). [47]

The usual debates on the pros and cons of the impacts of hypermarkets are, on the pro side, that they create more efficient business and economic systems where the consumer will ultimately benefit from lower retail prices. In contrast, on the con side of the argument, local retailers and wholesalers will be eliminated from the retailing system, meaning that local livelihoods are put at risk. Monbiot's work mentioned above demonstrates how MNC superstores/hypermarkets jeopardize people in their originating countries. In Thailand, we have no in-depth statistical analysis of hypermarket impacts. However, by looking at this type of retailing systemically and their investment and profits in other markets, we can draw some conclusions as to the likely impacts. Moreover by looking at resistance from local people, we can draw further inferences.

Traditionally, the supply chain of retail business begins with suppliers, selling products to wholesalers, who may sell directly to consumers but more often to small retailers, who then sell goods to customers. Small retailers basically open their shop-houses/small grocery shops/small ma-and-pa corner shops which are places to live and to also do business with local households. At the same time, some retailers having lower capital may rent kiosks in the wet market for selling fresh vegetables, meats and day-to-day consumer goods. The wet market is normally surrounded by shop-houses, but shop-houses also exist everywhere along commercial roads outside the market. When the hypermarkets come, the players, such as wholesalers and small retailers in the retail business supply chain, are cut off because the hypermarkets sell their goods to consumers directly. Hypermarket outlets, with their more efficient modern management practices, and greater economic power, can sell varieties of goods and products at lower prices. Thus the greater expansion of MNC hypermarkets results in small local retailers suffering. From the survey and research on the impact of modern trade on small retail shops in Bangkok by the International Retail and Franchise Business R&D Center and Consumer Behavior Research Center, Faculty of Business Administration, Sripatum University, it was discovered, through a sampling of 400 shop-houses open more than one year, that every type of MNC retailing has a different impact. Hypermarkets make the most impact by 34 percent; 7-Eleven-type convenience stores impact by 26 percent; supermarkets by 14 percent. Proportionally, this perception is congruent with the data from Price Waterhouse Cooper indicating that, in 2005, hypermarket and warehouse clubs and convenience stores had a sale share of 22 percent and 11 percent out of the 45 percent sales share of modern trades in retail business.[48] Considering only the big three, Tesco-Lotus, Big C and Carrefour had turnover at 92.1, 58.0 and 23.1 billion baht respectively and gained a total retail market share of 173 billion baht.[49] By 2004 it was estimated that hypermarket outlets grabbed around a 20 percent share of local retail expenditure, resulting in local shops losing heavily.[50]

The survey above also found that around 40 percent of shop-houses in Bangkok closed down and that these small retailers were forced to change employment. The same survey also indicates that, at the time of survey, consumers bought goods and products at the ratio of 50:50 traditional vs. hypermarket. It is estimated that within 3-5 years the hypermarket cornering of consumer spending will increase to 80 percent of the total.[51] Some sources estimated that the number of small grocery stores have been steadily declining by 10-20 percent per year.[52] From the data of Ministry of Commerce between 2001 and 2006, the registration as juristic person to retail and wholesale business has declined to 60,529 from 90,681 or to around 60 percent of its previous total.[53]

From the above data, we can see very clearly how neoliberal economic global governance provides a super highway for MNC imperialistic economic gains from Thailand. In this context, with its strategy of rapid expansion and its increasing revenue, Tesco-Lotus is the big brother. Accordingly Tesco-Lotus is the prime target of so-called "anti-modern trade" movements in Thailand. The anti-modern trade movement, the movement for traditional trades to survive the onslaught of the MNC retail chains, can be categorized by two approaches: by pressuring the state to revise laws or enact new laws to protect traditional trades, and by directly fighting the MNC retail chains, especially the hypermarkets, through local direct action, or people power.

In the first case, when hypermarket style retailers tried to implement their rapid expansion plan from the Bangkok Metropolitan area to other provinces, local resistance was ignited. This initial movement was composed of local businesspeople who were capable of organizing and using legal methods to fight the expansion. They complained and protested to the TRT government. The government urged the local authorities to strictly enforce the Town Planning Act to control the hypermarket outlet expansion. However, MNC retail chains found a legal loophole in the Building Control Act of 1989 whereby if local government refused to process their applications for building permits they could petition the parliamentary ombudsman to investigate.[54] So MNC hypermarkets continued to expand their outlets to provincial areas despite the legal opposition.

Up to 2006 when the military coup ousted the TRT government and the new interim government was formed the Confederation of Thais Opposing Foreign Retailers, the representative of traditional trade, had fiercely protested against the MNCs invasion. The government initiated two legal plans: they were to enforce the Alien Business Law rigorously and to enact a new retail business law. In the case of the Alien Business law, this law had first been amended in 1999 and for the first time allowed foreign firms to have majority ventures in the retail trade on the condition that they invested more than 100 million baht. However, another clause of the law disallowed foreign-majority ventures from selling agricultural products, food and beverages.[55] In effect, people who can own more than 49 percent of retail businesses in Thailand must be Thai if they want to sell products mentioned above.

However, though MNCs could not own outright according to the law they could still arrange to have all management power vested in them. Thai authorities then turned a blind eye to such arrangements. They allowed MNCs to preserve an aura of Thai ownership over companies they controlled. Yet, via a loophole of complex, multilayered shareholding structures, foreign investors theoretically complied with the law, while in practice controlling their "Thai" businesses.[56]

In the case of new retail act legislation, there has been pressure brought to bear by the traditional trade groups. The core of this proposed legislation is imposition of expansion limits on MNC retailing. This was initiated by the military government, which had nationalist sentiments. However, the draft of this law is still being debated and has not been enacted at the time of writing. The criticism of the government is similar to that in the case of Alien Business Act, i.e. that this will be harmful for foreign investment.

In the second mode of resistance, traditional retailers and their alliances (other local businesspeople, local leaders, NGOs, local governments) have also taken up the battle against MNCs in their localities. In many provincial areas where Tesco-Lotus started to build its hypermarket outlets, local people even protested violently. Banners like "you build, I burn" and "disaster is coming" were carried in the demonstrations. A very interesting case was in Phrae Province, Northern Thailand, where the provincial chamber of commerce organized a coupon scheme whereby people buying in any of the participating local shops received coupons that qualified them for discounts and raffle prizes. Local radio stations also helped through free advertising. By the end of 2005 the number of participating shops rose from 90 (in 2004) to 150. Six million coupons were issued, and sales revenue grew by 600 million baht. Unlike in many other provinces, Tesco-Lotus failed to dominate in Phrea Province. It gained an estimated 30 percent share of the market, but the local retailers survived. At least, up to the end of 2006, no shop was forced out of the market by the MNCs.[57]

Conclusion

From the neoliberal first wave impact through the 1997 economic crisis to the second wave characterized by the FTA and invasion of MNC retailing we have seen the way so-called "market rationality" has replaced qualitative human interests. And, as has been pointed out the replacing of the Washington Consensus by the post-Washington Consensus after the 1997 economic crisis has done little to mitigate the poverty of the neoliberal global market system. Rather global business norms reign in an ethics-free zone. We can see this in the impact of global neoliberalism on small agriculturists and small retailers in Thailand. Our one hope is that that the era of the absolute control by neoliberal ideology is nearing its endpoint. And that the culture of greed at the core of the global capitalist system contains the seeds of its own destruction.

Chapter 10

COMPARATIVE STUDY OF NEOLIBERALISM IN SYRIA AND EGYPT

Angela Joya

Since their independence in 1952 and 1946, Egypt and Syria have pursued similar policies of economic development, albeit with different outcomes. Both countries implemented populist reforms that redistributed wealth and restructured the state and its role in society. However, postwar struggles over state building and economic development culminated in the failure of populist regimes, which gave way to the conservative military regimes of Anwar Sadat in Egypt and Hafiz al-Assad in Syria. The next phase of economic development occurred in the context of an oil boom that benefited Egypt and Syria either through direct aid or through workers' remittances. With the help of foreign sources of revenue, both regimes implemented development policies that resulted in the expansion of bureaucracy, military, infrastructure and services.

In the 1980s, the regimes faced economic crises as they over-stretched their budgets and relied on foreign aid and loans for fulfilling development goals. This decade represented a period of transition and struggle over the state and economy, and by its end the international context came to determine these struggles in favor of globally oriented interests that supported a free market economy model. That the new ruling classes in both countries did not face very strong resistance in the 1990s was due to the slow pace of austerity reforms. However, since 2004, both countries have intensified the pace of neoliberal reforms aimed at proliferation of the imperatives of the capitalist market throughout these societies through the subjection of small and independent producers, workers and peasants to the logic of the market. Despite the contradictions resulting from the shift towards neoliberalism, such as high levels of unemployment and poverty and an absence of meaningful and sustainable economic growth, the absence of any organized progressive forces has left resistance in the hands of Islamist groups such as the Muslim Brotherhood in Egypt. In Syria, Islamist groups have been suppressed by the state for a long time and at the moment it is difficult to determine the nature of popular opposition to state policies.

Comparing the paths of economic development in Egypt and Syria in the postwar period with a focus on the economic shift towards neoliberalism, this chapter will be divided into four sections. First, I will provide a history of Post-War developments in both countries and outline the development policies that were adopted by Egypt and Syria. Part two will examine the economic crisis that engulfed both regimes in the 1980s and the regimes' different responses to the crisis. Part three will outline the policy shift towards the neoliberal market models that were implemented in the early 1990s and examine the policies, the political nature of reform and the factors that determined the pace of these reforms. Section four will outline the contradictions of the neoliberal model and its failures in meeting the stated goals of both countries. Rather than responding to the needs of citizens, the neoliberal economic model has served the interests of a globally oriented class of powerful interests that has dominated the state in both countries in the course of the 1990s. As a result, neoliberalism has redistributed power within the ruling class away from the statist bureaucrats who had dominated the state in the 1970s and 1980s. However, political liberalization has not kept pace with economic liberalization, as the neoliberal model remains contested, with few beneficiaries and many losers. The last section will provide a balance sheet of attempts at political liberalization and identify the factors that shape the pace and nature of such struggles.

History

After independence, Egypt and Syria faced the dilemma of achieving social development with scarce resources and limited technology. Domestically, the populist regimes launched a struggle against the dominant landlord classes and internationally, they relied on aid from the Soviet Union as the US clearly objected to the independent development strategies of these regimes. Syria under the Ba'ath, and Egypt under Nasser and the Free Officers, accomplished a wide range of social reforms. Prior to independence, both countries had suffered from deep inequalities. To reverse the negative effects of such polarized wealth, the Ba'athist and Nasserist regimes implemented reforms aimed at enhancing the lives of peasants and workers. Thus, land reform and industrialization were implemented in the decades of the 1950s and 1960s. Egypt and Syria also struck an alliance between 1958-1961 with the goal of uniting the two countries and employing their resources towards a joint development program that would help both countries. The union broke off after three years due to opposition from conservative forces within Syria who did not agree with Nasser's vision of social change and reform.

In Egypt, Nasser's rule marked a radical shift away from a landlord class that had dominated the state and economy. Nasserist populism generated state revenue through land sequestration, nationalization of foreign owned banks, insurance companies, factories and the Suez Canal. Nasser implemented industrialization and expanded the state bureaucracy with the goals of achieving social justice and wealth redistribution. Thus, his economic policy of industrialization resulted in state control of the public sector, of investment decisions and of foreign currency flows in and out of Egypt.[1] Nasser's policies resulted in rising living standards for many Egyptian workers and peasants.[2] The agrarian reforms provided secure tenure to farmers and peasants, but also made 1.3 million peasants owners of the lands they had tilled. The total number of Egyptians that benefited from land reform reached 7.5 million, including peasants and their families.[3] Under Nasser (1952-1970) economic development was a national agenda that aimed at establishing social order by addressing the needs of all Egyptians.[4]

In Syria, a state building project proceeded with the nationalization of private firms. Close to 106 private firms, including oil companies, cotton companies and 70 per cent of export and import trade were nationalized. Tax laws and fiscal policy were modified in the interests of more egalitarian revenue generation and redistribution. Rent reductions also served the interests of workers and the poor.[5] Clearly, the regime aimed at using the state to guide economic development and redistribution. The most radical phase of Ba'athist rule was from 1966-1969. Forming a social base among the poor and the peasantry, the reforms of radical Ba'athists included a bigger role for the state in production, redistribution and consumption decisions.[6] At the same time, popular representation was facilitated through independent workers and peasants' unions whereby workers and peasants could participate in the decision making process related to production.[7]

However, defeat by Israel in 1967 marked the beginning of the end of populist regimes as their legitimacy was questioned by conservative forces in both Egypt and Syria. This resulted in a change in the balance of power within the military in favor of conservative forces that enjoyed the support of landlords and industrialists. Military defeat by Israel exposed the limits of the economic development policies of the regimes in both countries. Burdened with debt, the regimes were faced with increasing unemployment, slow growth and declining resources. The rise of conservative forces also revealed the degree of contestation over the state and the limited power of the populist regimes. It is noteworthy that the populist regimes' failure to nurture space for democratic political processes led to top-down, military-led regime change by Sadat and Hafiz al-Assad.[8]

In the 1970s a number of changes occurred which provided the context for the regimes of Sadat and Assad. Internationally, the oil boom provided an opportunity for both Egypt and Syria to attract revenue either through aid or through workers' remittances. A shift in economic policy towards infitah, or opening, in both countries occurred in the background of the 1973 war with Israel. Egypt and Syria had managed to win back parts of the lands that they had lost in the 1967 War and thus used the success in the war as a pretext to open their economies. While both countries pursued similar policies of liberalization, the outcomes were different and shaped by political and economic factors that reflected the balance of social forces in each society.

After Nasser's death in September of 1970, Anwar Sadat (1970-81) announced a shift in Egypt's domestic and foreign policy in response to both domestic economic crisis and opportunities presented by the regional oil boom.[9] A whole range of problems appeared on the horizon as the Egyptian economy faced a general crisis. Overall growth levels had dropped to 3 percent in 1973, while unemployment stood above 10 percent of the civilian labor force.[10] A solution to rising unemployment was the expansion of the public sector and the army, which absorbed a high portion of the educated unemployed population.[11] Despite these solutions, high levels of inflation intensified social conflicts in Egypt. In order to avoid an escalation of social conflict and disorder, Sadat continued to borrow and support price subsidies, leading to a dramatic rise in Egyptian external debt. Thus, a rising trade deficit combined with increasing external debt and high levels of inflation, formed the background for Sadat's 1974 infitah policy.

But the main goal behind the infitah was the attraction of Arab capital, which Egypt expected would happen as a reward for its war with Israel. Nonetheless, infitah remained contentious in policy circles and amongst cabinet ministers. Many were opposed to such a shift in policy and those who supported it only did so because they believed it would provide the liquidity needed to support the public sector.[12] Nevertheless, the infitah was criticized by many who saw it as a policy that gave a free hand to Sadat's friends and their clients to amass unprecedented levels of wealth. Sadat was seen to be using the state as his private realm of power and patronage. Infitah was criticized by ordinary Egyptians who viewed it as being responsible for unleashing greed and for giving rise to a consumerist class in society. Despite the creation of Tax Free Zones, development was stalled while the import of consumer goods supported by remittances and oil money flooded the shops and warehouses of Egypt.[13]

Sadat's policies have been interpreted as supporting a private market economy, but in retrospect his policies lacked a clear direction and intention. Indeed, economic planning was missing while the infitah provided the context for economic anarchy that not only created massive external debt, but also resulted in a decline in the living conditions of many Egyptians.[14] While an organized private sector did not emerge under Sadat, the public sector suffered. Although in terms of numbers the public sector expanded, the quality of production and services declined while wages stagnated. Declining wages in the public sector either resulted in a transfer of skilled workers and managers to the private sector and to other regional economies or to the expansion of corruption as a means of survival for public sector workers.[15] At the social level, Sadat's policies were met with protests, especially in 1977 when he announced an increase in basic food prices. A combination of the infitah and making a peace deal with Israel resulted in his death at the hands of Egypt's Muslim Brotherhood.[16]

In Syria, Hafiz al-Assad assumed power in the aftermath of defeat in the 1967 war. At this stage, Syria's economic crisis resembled that of Egypt's and thus the policies implemented by Assad also resembled those of Sadat's. The possibility of attracting oil revenues to Syria led to the announcement of infitah policies, which aimed to encourage foreign investment in Syria.[17] However, Syria differed from Egypt in that the Ba'ath Party had an economic program that was pursued by President Assad. Assad's strategy was one of maintaining a balance in society. Thus, on the one hand, he changed the social basis of the state by integrating peasants into the state. On the other hand, he developed local industry through active state support and planning.

Assad's economic development was a response to the disorganized planning of previous regimes, and the rising influence of the merchant classes. It was designed with the intent of expanding the political base of the new regime among the Sunni merchants.[18] With the stated goal of attracting Syrian capital back to Syria, a series of reforms followed. Economic pressures of state building forced Assad to encourage repatriation of capital and introduce incentives such as tax free zones which were part of the *infiraj* or *al-infitah ala ash-shab*—opening to the people.[19] State building also entailed centralization of authority through the co-optation of different forces in society. Labor and unions were absorbed within the newly created institution of the National Progressive Front (NPF). Other reforms included the establishment of economic courts to monitor economic activities within the state sector. Redistributive policies such as public housing, public health services, public education expansion, and state guaranteed employment,[20] were funded through the high rent received from oil sales, remittances and the geo-strategic rents of the Cold War era.[21]

As a gesture to the private sector, Assad radically increased the role of the private sector in the commercial and industrial sectors of the economy while reducing the role of the public sector by reorganizing it.[22] The private sector made a series of significant gains during different phases of economic liberalization. The autonomy and freedom that was awarded to the private sector went hand in hand with its newly established role in the overall economic development of Syria. Despite this, the liberalization policies of Assad only succeeded in evoking a "cautious response" from the private sector. Investment levels remained low although three major sectors of the economy—construction, tourism and transport—had been opened up to private investors.[23]

While the liberalization policies of the 1970s resulted in a boom in the service sector, agriculture's share of labor was reduced due to shifts to technology. At the same time, laws protecting labor were relaxed in order to encourage the repatriation of capital.[24] While the private sector failed to undertake viable economic development, heavy state intervention did produce a number of positive results that benefited the private sector and

Syrian society as a whole. Under Assad, Syria witnessed the development of major projects linked to infrastructure and road construction, railways, ports, and telecommunications facilities.[25]

The social crisis of the late 1970s and early 1980s reflected the displeasure of the traditional ruling classes with the state and its economic policies. Indeed, Syria represented a unique case whereby the state represented the broader interests of the peasants and workers, although not under the banner of socialism or communism. The merchants and their supporters expressed their anger against the rising influence of another class of traders and petty producers who had benefited from the *infitah*. The state's response was to maintain a balance by repressing the merchants, but also by imposing a measure of discipline on the fledgling private sector, petty traders and small producers. Taxes were increased on the private sector and raw materials were directed towards public sector enterprises. Tax evasion was punished by the state while state-run financial institutions became the central credit offering bodies.[26] Perthes argues that the measures taken by the state in no way represented a serious restriction on the private sector as the private sector was assured that no return to socialism and no expropriations would take place. The measures were aimed at facilitating the development of the economy in general. With the establishment of the Committee for the Guidance of Imports, Exports and Consumption in 1981, the state included the private sector in economic development and planning.[27] Intervention by the state was possible precisely because Assad had not abdicated his political powers in the course of economic liberalization.[28] At the same time, he did not want to alienate his newly established broad political base that included groups such as landlords, merchants, peasants and workers. The corporatist state had re-emerged once again as the private sector failed to carry out the task of economic development.

1980s Economic Crisis

While Egypt and Syria embarked on similar paths of development in the 1970s, the outcomes differed due to external and internal factors. At the end of the 1970s, Sadat's popularity was at its lowest point as Egyptian society was once again faced with economic crisis. The state had failed to launch a successful development strategy that would deal with the declining living standards and rising unemployment. Fear of social disorder forced Sadat to import food and other commodities through external borrowing. The state faced yet another crisis when Sadat signed the peace treaty with Israel, which resulted in Egypt's isolation from other Arab countries. Thus Egypt entered the 1980s with a discredited political leadership and a deep economic crisis that took the form of huge external debt. In the context of a deep credit crunch triggered by the unilateral interest rate hike by US Federal Reserve Chairman Paul Volker, Egypt's debt rose from $2 billion in the late 1960s to $21 billion by 1981.[29] Egypt's debt servicing obligations increased by an average of $1.7 billion a year, between 1984-87 and total debt exceeded $40 billion by June of 1987, equivalent to 112 percent of GDP.[30] At the same time, the dip in oil prices resulted in reduced workers' remittances.[31]

To deal with the crisis, Sadat's successor, Hosni Mubarak, adopted a paternalistic approach. Fearing an escalation of crisis in society, his economic reforms were implemented with an eye towards the general welfare of Egyptians. This policy pattern continued until the late 1980s at which point other influences came to dominate the state. During the 1980s, business interests organized themselves into chambers and committees thereby increasing its influence over public policy by the beginning of the 1990s.[32] The crisis provided economic justification for the transformation of the public sector despite the high productivity levels of public sector firms.[33] On the one hand, economic reform aimed at dispossessing the peasants and workers; on the other hand, interests linked to the official Egyptian economy launched an organized battle against those who operated in the informal economy. Thus, the economic crisis provided the context for intra-elite struggles, which ended with the defeat of *"sharikat tawzif al-amwal al-islamiyya"* or "Islamic Money Management Companies" (IMMCs) and the consolidation of the power of official state banks.[34] Thus, the official banks emerged as the winners with a monopoly over the Egyptian financial system at the expense of the IMMCs.

During the 1970s, unlike Egypt, Syria did not experience as deep a crisis due to a number of factors. First, Syria had maintained its strong stance against Israel and thus continued to receive aid from Arab countries. Secondly, the policies of economic liberalization adopted in the 1970s were more sectoral than structural and thus, the impact of liberalization was managed better in Syria than in Egypt. Volker Perthes has argued that, "[Syria was] one example of a variety of approaches adopted by Middle Eastern (and other) states to manage economic change without provoking disruptive political change."[35] Thirdly, the state was heavily involved in the economy and delivered social policies with the help of oil revenues and foreign aid. Unlike Sadat, Assad allowed restricted space for private sector activity and at the first sign of the private sector's failure, he asserted state control over the economy.[36] While Assad relied on the coercive powers of the state to crush opposition to his regime, he was well aware of Syria's delicate political situation and the vulnerability of his rule in a divided country; thus he maintained a balancing act in dealing with different groups' demands.

Arab aid and workers' remittances along with Soviet financial and military aid also helped Syria's industrialization under Assad. However, towards the latter half of the 1970s, Syria's industrialization became dependent on foreign sources, which led to the 1980s crisis.[37] While in the 1970s, industry received a major share of public investment by the 1980s it was marginalized and received a smaller share of public funding. The bulk of aid during the 1980s went to military spending, which had a negative effect on consumption.[38] State expenditure led to inflation and a growing external debt, which grew ten fold between 1970 and 1983. The $2.3 billion debt plagued the economy.[39] Hinnebusch writes that the Syrian state had overdeveloped with the help of rents and as soon as rents disappeared, it became impossible to support the large public sector. Austerity measures and cutbacks in public spending were pursued as a way of resolving the foreign exchange crisis. In response, the state actively encouraged the private sector to play a more central role in economic development. Faced with the option of going to the IMF and World Bank and subjecting the state to the conditionalities of these institutions or allowing a bigger role for the private sector, Assad opted for the latter.[40]

By mid 1980s, Syria began to shift towards an export-oriented economy not out of ideological commitment to the free market but rather as a pragmatic response to the crisis caused by international and regional factors.[41] This phase of liberalization did not simply encourage the private sector to participate in the economy; the private sector was encouraged to be the *main* agent of economic development.[42] Attempts to relieve the economic crisis led to export-oriented development and the privatization of the agricultural sector. However, the privatization of agriculture did not resolve a rising trade deficit in food, which stood at 3000 million (Syr.), a third of the total trade deficit of Syria.[43] An imbalance in the economy emerged as the contributions of agriculture and industry towards GDP decreased while those of services and trade increased. According to Hawwa, this sudden shift was the result of uncoordinated economic development. Thus, Syria was faced with four main problems as it entered the 1980s. First, there was a decline in aid due to a drastic drop in oil prices. Syria's economy was demonstrating signs of stagflation in this period. Second, Syria experienced a rising trade deficit. Third, the adoption of an export-oriented model was seen as a quick fix for the economic crisis and thus not much thought was put into the planning of the economy. In the absence of a viable private sector, Syrian officials opted for signing deals with multinationals which had its own problems given the concessions demanded by the MNCs.[44] However this policy resulted in the abdication of important powers of the state in favor of the private sector. Increasingly, the Central Bank of Syria gained power in determining not only monetary and fiscal policies, but also in making decisions about economic development. Thus, the economic crisis precipitated the loosening of state control over the economy.[45]

The reforms had an uneven affect on different social groups and classes. If we look at who gained and who lost, we will notice that at a general level the private sector clearly gained. However, scratching below the surface, we will notice that not everyone within the private sector gained. Those aspects of the private sector that relied on state protectionism for their survival lost to a newer private sector whose interests were more directly linked to external markets than to the domestic market. In a sense, Syrian reforms resembled structural adjustment policies that were often imposed by the International Monetary Fund (IMF) on many other economies in the same period or earlier.[46]

The period from 1985-1990 marked the beginning of increased competition between the public and the private sectors. The regime did not privatize state corporations; instead it imposed the logic of market competition on state firms. At the same time, the private sector was offered numerous incentives, including tax breaks and tax holidays, while the public sector was constantly scrambling to meet the social needs of the domestic population and keep up with profitability levels. The emerging weakness of the Soviet bloc further strengthened the shift to a market economy and the Syrian state pre-emptively sought a re-orientation in its economic policy through self-imposed austerity measures and reforms. The state has been increasing the influence of the private sector, while restructuring the political landscape to reflect the changed balance of social forces. This is a very sensitive task, which is reflected in the gradual and uneven nature of liberalization in Syria. Nonetheless, during the decade of the 1980s, the private sector made headway in the process of policy making by increasing their numbers in various organs of the state. In 1990, one-third of the seats in the People's Council were reserved for the private sector, highlighting the radical transformation of the Syrian state over the course of twenty years (1970-1990). This clearly marked the decline in the influence of traditional forces, namely the Ba'athists, in the state.[47] The socio-economic impact of the reforms fell unevenly on the shoulders of public sector workers and those who depended on state subsidies for survival such as small farmers, peasants, and the unemployed.

In short, the pace of economic liberalization in both Egypt and Syria was determined by the material interests of social forces. Depending on their gains and losses, powerful interests either supported a faster pace of liberalization or cautioned a slower pace, although the fear of social unrest and the absence of legitimacy remained important factors in determining the pace of economic reform in both countries.[48]

Economic Liberalization in the 1990s

When the Cold War ended Egypt and Syria faced a number of dilemmas. The loss of geopolitical rents and the success of the capitalist bloc had delivered serious blows to their economies. In this context of economic crisis, the first Iraq War presented Egypt and Syria with both economic problems as well as opportunities. The first took the form of declining remittances and returning migrant workers. The second took the form of inflows of Kuwaiti capital. In the meantime, both Egypt and Syria were still grappling with the economic crisis of the 1980s and had not fully overcome the challenges of unemployment and declining growth in the public sector. Internationally, both countries realized their structural weakness in an increasingly competitive global economy. With the rise of China and other East Asian economies, Egypt and Syria's unskilled labor force and low level of technological development meant that the countries would have to export primary commodities and develop their private sectors as part of launching a free market economy. Both Egypt and Syria began shifting towards a free market economy, but Egypt's record indicates deeper economic integration with the global economy whereas Syria has pursued a cautious form of economic liberalization without subjecting its population to severe dislocations. While pro-market voices have come to influence policy in both countries, economic liberalization has remained contentious as some see it as a threat and others view it as an opportunity.

The ideological support for free market economies comes from the powerful international financial institutions such as the World Bank and the International Monetary Fund. The underlying belief of the Post-Washington Consensus is that the market is a realm of objective price setting and so long as there are no distortions, such as state planning or state intervention in the economy, all commodities should get the right prices. Only competition and productivity gains should determine which firms will survive and what factors of production should be rewarded.[49] Based on this belief proponents of economic liberalization argued that Egypt and Syria's economic woes were due to irrational economic planning reflected in the large public sector and state intervention in setting wages and prices. Thus, they recommended that to solve the economic crisis in both countries, it was imperative that they liberalized their markets and removed the state from sectors that could be served by the private sector. There was no doubt in the minds of free market proponents that economic liberalization was the answer to the high levels of unemployment, poverty and inequality.

More specifically, it was argued that both Egypt and Syria would be able to pay off their external debts and regain credit worthiness if they implemented structural adjustment policies. First, they had to privatize their public sector firms so as to allow the market to determine the required number of workers for each sector. Second, it was argued that the state should encourage competition among privatized firms so as to increase productivity and economic growth. Third, they had to restructure their labor markets by removing subsidies to consumers, labor protection policies and legislation that increased the cost of hiring and firing workers. The outcome of these policies, it was argued, would resolve the problem of unemployment while at the same time reduce corruption and clientelism.

Following the advice of new institutionalists, Egypt signed its first important structural adjustment package known as the Economic Restructuring and Adjustment Program (ERSAP) in 1991. The ERSAP contained six components: a stabilization program, privatization, price liberalization, trade liberalization, investment-friendly policies, and a social fund for creating labor intensive employment and helping create micro-enterprise.[50] The signing of ERSAP was significant in that it resulted in over $20 billion of debt reduction, which radically brought down Egypt's interest payments, albeit future reductions in debt were directly tied to economic reforms.[51] Egypt was also the first country to negotiate a $6 billion Social Fund for Development (SFD) to cushion the cost of reforms, and to provide jobs for the 600,000 workers who had returned to Egypt in the wake of Iraq's invasion.[52] The Egyptian government introduced major cuts in general subsidies, introduced a new tax law, revived the stock exchange and liberalized land rents. Furthermore, a series of laws were issued that aimed at securing the confidence of foreign and domestic investors while at the same time limiting the role of the state in redistribution and social policy.[53]

In general, it can be argued that Egypt experienced two kinds of reforms: the first reforms which occurred in the late 1980s and early 1990s were mainly intended to boost investment by targeting the budget deficit and the external debt. The general direction of early reforms was a reduction of expenditure and thus fiscal restraint, which would affect prices of basic commodities as well as employment levels as a result of overhauling of the public sector.[54] The reforms of the 1990s and after aimed to introduce deep structural changes. In the case of Egypt, the IMF is purported to have wrongly assumed that a shift from the public to the private sector would mean an automatic emergence of a dynamic free market economy. Thus, while state investment in the public sector has shrunk, the private sector has not stepped up to fill this gap and thus Egypt suffers from deteriorating infrastructure and the erosion of public services.[55]

Similarly, the 1990s posed serious challenges to the Syrian regime. With the collapse of the East bloc, the dominance of the capitalist economy, and failing public sector performance, the Syrian regime reoriented its policy direction.[56] On the one hand, Syria managed to clear a big part of its external debt through the financial rewards that it received from Arab states in return for its opposition to Kuwait's invasion by Iraq in 1991. On the other hand, Syria introduced Investment Law No.10 with the hope of attracting Syrian, Kuwaiti and other Arab investors who fled Kuwait during the Iraqi invasion.[57] By introducing this law, the state offered favorable conditions to investors. The private sector could now engage in any sector of the economy while the public sector became more and more limited in its sphere of activity.

This freedom of the private sector is demonstrated in the opening of previously restricted economic fields for investment. Furthermore, the private sector is offered tax incentives and the freedom to repatriate profits while benefiting from exemptions in customs duties and import restrictions. The push for increasing exports is supported with tax incentives.[58] Taking advantage of the failing state of the public sector and a lack of vision for economic development, the private sector successfully strengthened its structural position within the Syrian economy. By the 1990s, the private sector had a bigger share of the Syrian economy in terms of investments in comparison to the public sector.[59] As Patrick Seale writes, Investment Law No. 10 served as a landmark on the path towards capitalist development in Syria.[60]

Maintaining the public sector as the producer of basic commodities speaks more to the socio-economic realities of Syrian society than to its lack of commitment to economic liberalization. Close to two out of nineteen million Syrians live below the poverty line according to a 2005 UN report. The official 14 percent unemployment rate does not include those who have precarious and insecure jobs. According to the Arab Human Development Report 2005, unemployment has increased from 9.5 percent in 2000 to 14 percent in 2004. Other reports calculate unemployment at 20 percent.[61] As long as the public sector remains in control of the production of basic commodities there will be a certain guarantee of political stability and social order, something that the fractured, but newly emerging elite seek.[62] Richards has also offered similar explanations for the slow pace of reform. Beside the fear of social disorder, the vested interests of the old bourgeoisie and state elite are other factors that have put a break on the pace of reforms in Syria, which Richards has called "dilatory" reforms.[63]

A number of challenges continue to exist for the Syrian regime, which forces it to remain involved in economic planning. The main reason for the public sector's involvement in the economy has been the inability of the private sector to take on the task of national economic development.[64] Social policies and state expenditure are often supported not by taxes but through the sale of oil, which according to the IMF will be depleted by 2020.[65] At the same time, the performance of the private sector has been marginal in terms of positive growth and redistributive measures. The rate of job creation has declined from 4.8 percent in 1990 to 2.9 percent in 2000. The Syrian regime was faced with a number of social problems and economic imbalances by 2000, which included a four percent growth in the labor force with a slow rate of one percent growth in the economy.[66] In order to deal with these problems, the Syrian regime has continued to both play a part in the economy and pursue economic integration through free trade deals, such as the Greater Arab Free Trade Area (GAFTA), and EU-Mediterranean, as well as through intergovernmental organizations such as the WTO. Bashar al-Assad's rule represents a crucial breaking point from his father's rule. This shift is reflective of a larger shift in the nature of ruling class interests and the economic dilemmas currently faced by Syria. The Syrian ruling elites have come to a crucial realization namely that the Ba'ath Party and its way of organizing the state and economy no longer represent the interests of the newly emerged factions of the ruling class.

In Egypt the stronger organization of business interests in the course of the 1980s concluded the intra-elite class struggles in favor of free market supporters. Other factors that consolidated the power of businessmen in Egypt included the close ties between the Egyptian ruling party, the National Democratic Party, and neoliberal-minded ministers and investors who dominated the inner circles of the Party. This alliance resulted in the signing of the Uruguay Round of GATT by Egypt in 1995, which laid the basis for the 2004 launch of even deeper reforms by Prime Minister Ahmad Nazif. By 2004, businessmen and neoliberal ideologues had taken over the key ministerial and cabinet posts and business oriented government services have expanded under the Nazif government. This marks the beginning of a new form of patronage that is masked in the language of the free market economy.

In the course of the 1990s reform-minded bureaucrats introduced tough reforms that radically altered the distribution of power within Egyptian society. After 2004, it was argued that the expansion of the global economy and the competitiveness that globalization had initiated forced Egypt to face many challenges. Domestically, it needed to provide jobs for its growing population, to reduce poverty levels and meet the social needs of its population. Those in power argued that foreign investment was the only way to meet all of the above goals. Thus modernization of Egypt in technology, infrastructure, resources and productive facilities was linked to foreign investment.[67]

In return for loans from the IFIs, the Egyptian regime committed itself to increase taxes on consumption and remove tariffs and subsidies, and abolish guaranteed employment for university graduates, which resulted in a youth unemployment rate of 25 percent. Privatization has been opposed by a fraction of the ruling class that had benefited from public sector firms. The Constitutional Court's ruling in support of privatization of public sector firms proved to be a major defeat for the Egyptian workers as it put an end to workers' rights employment in public sector firms and left no guarantees in place for similar employment once public enterprises were transferred to private hands. This ruling also meant that close to 180,000 workers were laid off in financial and administrative services. [68]

Neoliberalism in Egypt has led to the development of a market economy through reducing the role of the state in providing public services, fiscal and monetary regulations while encouraging and facilitating an increased role for the private sector in the economy and society. As such, the central bank has assumed "autonomy" from non-neoliberal interest groups in determining fiscal and monetary policies based on free market ideals and detached itself from the social concerns of the Egyptian producers. To that end, Egypt has signed bilateral deals with Israel and the US, introduced tax free zones, simplified its investment law, and provided businesses with 'free land"—communally held land, which has been under government attack since 1992—for projects in Upper Egypt. At the same time, the social safety net has been restructured with the goal of reducing the government budget through cutting subsidies and liberalizing prices. And to compensate for tax cuts for the private sector, the government aims to broaden the tax base by transferring the burden onto ordinary Egyptians.

Syria has been depicted as a closed economy by the IMF because of low levels of international trade and a lack of dependence on the global economy in terms of credit.[69] Its lack of integration into the capitalist world market is reflected in the low level of external debt. Syrian debt has remained at very manageable levels and its foreign exchange reserves can support its imports for up to 2.5 years. The IMF report of 2005 on Syria has identified declining oil prospects as a serious worry for the Syrian economy. The only way that the Syrian economy could sustain the burden of reduced oil revenues is to pursue a rapid process of liberalization. The report further argues that Syria has failed to solve its problems of unemployment and poverty as it has failed to provide an investment friendly environment for investors. The reforms suggested to help Syria would entail a radical shift away from state planning to a free market. This argument is premised on the lack of efficiency of public sector enterprise. State owned enterprises are irrationally organized, over staffed, under paid and cumbersome, argues the report. Although the argument for economic reform uses declining oil prospects as its main reason, oil constitutes only 15 percent of the GDP and the Syrian economy represents one of the most diversified economies in the whole Arab world.[70]

The current struggles over the path of development in Syria are being waged between elites who have conflicting interests.[71] Supporters of economic reform constitute different groups that gained their power during different phases of the infitah. The conflict between the military and the pro-infitah groups faced a showdown in the spring of 2000 when the military began to clamp down on civil society groups. While the regime put a break on the pace of reforms, it also resorted to extreme measures in order to eliminate the heavy influence of Ba'athist military and security forces in economic planning. These measures included the forced retirements of security and military forces as well as an increase in the number of private sector representatives in parliament. While the political economy of Ba'athism is facing a serious threat from rapid liberalization, the relevance of the military and security forces might not come to an end so easily,[72] although since 2000, the military and the Ba'ath Party have been faced with declining legitimacy because of some of the social and economic factors discussed earlier.

Developments that Syria has experienced during Bashar al-Assad's regime (2000-) are evidence of a qualitative transformation of the Syrian state. The growing influence of pro-reform factions and their participation in the political process since the 1990s has come to determine the course of economic development and state reform under Bashar. While the old guard, embodied in the Ba'ath Party, has resisted the fast pace of reform, a neoliberal logic has been dominant in shaping a wide range of political, legal and institutional reforms. Bringing together the emerging factions of the ruling class, along with the pro-reform Ba'athists, Bashar al-Assad has been engaged in the remaking of the Syrian state and economy. Unlike his father, Bashar did not hesitate to get help from the IMF and the World Bank.[73] In fact, his minister of finance is an ex-World Bank economist. From this point of view, the period of his rule is quite significant, especially in terms of the impacts this new path of economic development has on the process of class formation.

Although most of these reforms have been implemented by Syrian officials the IMF remains unsatisfied because of the slow pace of reform. Obstacles to reform come mainly from the military and security forces along with remnants of the old industrial bourgeoisie that demand a slower pace of reform and still require a certain measure of protectionism due to a lack of competitive edge vis-à-vis other global economic powers. Thus, while the Syrian elite agrees on the direction of reform, their concerns for political stability and their position of economic weakness caution them in favor of a gradual pace of reform.[74]

In light of IMF suggestions and the dilemmas of economic development, Bashar al-Assad has pursued further economic and political reforms that have expanded the realm of activity and freedom of the private sector. The economic reforms include further liberalization of trade, investment and other capital flows, all of which transfer political decision making to the hands of a minority in the Central Bank and the Ministry of Finance. An assessment of the liberalization period from 1990-2005 by the IMF tends to praise the series of reforms undertaken by the Syrian regime. According to the report, under Bashar's rule: "Prices have been largely liberalized, trade and foreign exchange regimes have been simplified and liberalized, the tax system has been streamlined, and the private sector's field of activity has been broadened to virtually all sectors of the economy, including banking and insurance."[75]

As it stands, Syria is gripped with massive unemployment and poverty, an expanding labor force and an incapable private sector that has failed to invest in sectors that could absorb this level of growth of the labor force. In the face of this reality, the report strongly advocates that the Syrian state take an interventionist role in the economy. In order to expand its revenues, the state must reform current taxation structures so that taxation becomes more equitable. The report also warns against liberalization due to the negative effect of the global economy on the smaller industries and the tariff protected industries such as consumer durables, pharmaceuticals, textiles and clothing industries. In spite of these warnings, the Syrian state under Bashar has been transferring economic decision-making powers to the private sector to a greater degree.

Contradictions of Economic Liberalization

Despite important differences between Egypt and Syria, a number of contradictory outcomes in both cases have resulted due to economic liberalization. First, the shift to a market economy has failed to meet the basic goals of achieving higher living standards through the provision of employment and public services while a shift towards democracy has not accompanied the process of economic liberalization.[76] Changes in state and society have resulted in a redistribution of power upward whereby privatization of state enterprises has resulted in monopolies and oligopolies. Thus, while a small group has amassed unprecedented levels of wealth because of privatization and liberalization, a majority of public sector workers and peasants have lost access to their means of survival. As scholars have pointed out, the shift from the public sector to the private sector and rising profits has not translated into more efficiency, transparency and higher standards of living for ordinary Egyptians; instead the shift has intensified corruption and increased the market power of a few at the expense of the many.[77]

While in Syria, the state has managed to maintain subsidies and a measure of wealth redistribution, in Egypt, there has been an increase in poverty and socio-economic crisis among a large section of the population.[78] Although the neoliberal project is contested by public sector workers, the main struggle exists between the old guard and the newly formed, dominant neoliberal fraction of the ruling class—or as referred to in the literature in positive terms— "civil society".[79] So far, reforms have assumed an uneven pace, and at times have been reversed due to political concerns of the ruling elite. The fear of social unrest and mobilization of the people by the Muslim Brotherhood, which has gained popularity among the majority of the poor, also cautions the ruling class about the fragility of their power.

In Syria, there are different obstacles in the path of developing a market economy, the most important of which include the structural constraints imposed by the global division of labor and the deeply integrated global economy. The Syrian economy lacks the institutions and skilled labor force needed to compete in the global economy. At the same time, fear of political instability and exposure to intense competition serve as two important factors as to why the Syrian elite does not support a fast pace of reform.[80] Furthermore, the experience of the last two decades of reforms suggests that the process of integration into the world market by attrition of the public sector is a messy process with undetermined outcomes. For a start, there is no guarantee that the private sector is capable of taking on the responsibilities for generating growth that will contribute to a better standard of living for the Syrian population. Many Syrian elites pursue speculative activities that only benefit the few at the expense of many. The productive sector of the economy would stagnate and the brunt of this economic crisis would easily fall on the workers and the poor. This would carry negative implications for the elite as the legitimacy of the regimes erodes with increasing social inequalities. This explains the caution that is displayed in implementing liberal reforms by the regime and the complicity of the Syrian ruling classes. And perhaps even the uncustomary solicitude of the IMF…

Nevertheless, Syria seems to have reached a critical impasse. There have been disparate attempts at finding a way out of the current impasse through opening up political space.[81] In the absence of any clear force to lead the economy, the regime is hesitant to give in to the demands of any particular group fearing a total collapse of the political order. Although most of the regime's faith is put in the private sector, its repeated failure to effectively organize the economy poses signs of worry among the resisters to reform. The situation has become grimmer in light of larger socio-economic problems that exist in Syria. Out of a population of 18 million, 1.5 million lives at poverty levels.[82] Despite these warnings, international financial institutions seem satisfied with the outcomes in Syria's economy. According to the most recent World Bank and IMF reports Syria's non-oil exports have risen, the trade deficit has been reduced and private investment has correspondingly increased.[83]

While little debate on political liberalization occurred in the 1980s, after the collapse of the Soviet Bloc, political liberalization has taken center stage, especially in the context of economic liberalization. Proponents of market liberalization claim that economic opening would be followed by democratization, a thesis that has been proved wrong in the cases of Egypt and Syria. Both countries have embarked on market reform since the 1980s and more decisively in the new millennium. However, there is little sign of political opening.

Conclusion

As we have seen, while Egypt and Syria have adopted a similar set of policies for economic development, the nature of political leadership, social organization alongside domestic and international socio-economic factors have determined the outcomes of economic policies. The shift to a market economy has been contested by various groups in Egypt and Syria, although proponents of free market seem to have declared their victory in Egypt for now. The Syrian state and society are still experiencing the beginnings of a more decisive shift towards a market economy; however, the level of organization of the peasantry and the role of the Ba'ath Party in policy making has prevented a rapid process of economic liberalization.

It is too early to determine the outcomes of economic liberalization in Syria in a definitive way; nonetheless the case of Egypt clearly demonstrates the class nature of market liberalization and its negative effects on ordinary Egyptians' social welfare. The shift towards a market economy has further intensified rather than reduced the arbitrary and unchecked power of the ruling class and the state, thereby reducing the space for democratic decision making. The state in Egypt has become more effective in facilitating surplus extraction and capital accumulation in the interest of landlords, developers and capitalists, while squeezing the peasantry, the small producers and the workers. Institutional reforms have aimed at limiting the power of the opposition to deliver any serious challenges to the existing ruling class. To say nothing of the widespread repression. In the absence of any other progressive alternatives and a space for democratic discussion and debate, the Egyptian public has thrown its support behind the Islamist groups.

While the logic of efficiency and cost-effectiveness has remained at the core of the shift towards a market economy, the experience of Egypt suggests that efficiency has come at an important social cost whereby peasants and workers have lost their sources of livelihood and have been subjected to market imperatives. Rather than achieve transparency and reduce corruption, the adoption of a free market economy has justified the power of a small elite that has come to dominate the state and the economy, and become more emboldened than before. Social policies have been dismantled and the state's role has been transformed to one of facilitating private sector activity while ignoring the needs of citizens and the general well being of society. The result has been great income gap and increased social tension as reflected in the recent protests in Egypt.[84] Given the disappointing performance of the free market economy and the continuing problems in both Egypt and Syria, the regimes have favored a slower pace of reform. Economic development will continue to remain contested, although alternative outcomes will depend on the balance of power of contending social forces and especially on the level of organization of peasants and workers in both countries. The cases of Egypt and Syria demonstrate that there is no one outcome as countries liberalize their economies and that each case has to be taken seriously on its own terms.

Chapter 11

THE EXHAUSTION OF NEOLIBERALISM IN MEXICO

Cliff DuRand

The world is now in the midst of a catastrophic crisis of capitalism that is global in its reach. The crisis of the 1970s had been temporarily resolved by a turn to global neoliberal economic policies. Now it is precisely those policies that have led to the present crisis and, as the countries of the global North are now discovering, there is no new "fix" in sight.[1] But the dead end of neoliberalism has been apparent in Latin America for some time and has opened the way for the Left there to experiment with new alternatives.

Mexico embraced neoliberal policies early and the political elite still holds to them in spite of their failure to deliver as promised. Under the North American Free Trade Agreement (NAFTA) Mexico became an ideal laboratory in which to observe the effects of corporate-led neoliberal globalization—both in its heyday, and now in its crisis.

First, a little historical context is needed. In the early 1980s an external debt crisis swept through Latin America when the US Treasury Department raised interest rates as a fix for the stagflation that had set in there. In the 1970s the banks had been awash in petrodollars and recycled them as loans to many developing countries—among them Mexico: But when interest rates shot up and the price of oil declined, Mexico found itself unable to even service its immense external debt. It was on the verge of default when Treasury engineered a bailout that was in actuality a bailout of the banks, not Mexico, since the money never even left the US. As part of the deal, the IMF imposed a Structural Adjustment Program (SAP) on Mexico that required it to:

- cut government spending, especially on social programs

- privatize public assets
- increase exports so as to earn foreign exchange to pay the North American banks
- open Mexico to foreign direct investment (FDI)

This was a drastic shift from the economic policies that had prevailed for decades. Since the 1930s the development of the Mexican economy had been protected by import substitution industrialization (ISI) policies. Following the example set by the industrialized countries of the North which had protected national capital against foreign competition, the Mexican state likewise favored the development of its own infant industry with protective tariffs and limits on foreign ownership. It also sought to ensure a minimal level of well being of its population through agricultural subsidies and low prices for basic food stuffs, public provision of social services, etc. All this was to change with Mexico's debt crisis.

There was a faction within the ruling political elite and its party, PRI, that was eager for such changes. Headed by Harvard MBA Carlos Salinas and other technocrats schooled in neoliberal economic thought, they pushed through the IMF reforms against the opposition of those in the PRI who upheld the principles of the Mexican Revolution as represented by Lazaro Cardenas. Salinas, who became President in the fraudulent 1988 election, consolidated this neoliberal turn with NAFTA. These neoliberal reformers constituted what the World Bank later called "an insulated technocratic elite" that the Bank said was an essential political condition needed to carry out such a transformation.

"Neoliberalism" refers to a renewed form of an ideology that goes back to the late 18th and 19th centuries, long before "liberal" meant "progressive". The classic expression of the liberal ideology of the time is Adam Smith's 1776 book *The Wealth of Nations*. The core idea there is an insistence on the separation of the political sphere from the economic sphere. An autonomous economic sphere is envisioned in which the market is supreme. The market is conceived of as made up of individual actors who freely engage in exchanges based on self-interest. Whether buyer or seller, each seeks to maximize their individual gain and enters into contractual agreements only if it is perceived to be to one's own advantage. The market is then the mechanism for summing up individual goods, producing the maximum good for the greatest number. This utilitarian calculus is performed through the invisible hand of the market a-la-Adam Smith.

But in order for the market to work its purported magic it must be free of social, i.e. collective, interference. A "free market" is one that is free of governmental action, which is seen as distorting the market and its outcomes. The only actors allowed are individuals who are guided not by altruism, conscience or compassion, or even enlightened self-interest, but only by their own individual self-seeking benefit-maximizing proclivities. In this view the best government is the one that governs least, a minimalist state. The only legitimate role for the state is to maintain or establish the conditions necessary for a market to operate. This includes establishing a common currency and standard weights and measures as well as enacting laws and accompanying institutions to protect private property and enforce contracts. Permissible state action might even extend to the public provision of necessary infrastructure like roads, ports, utilities and communications facilities that require large lumps of investment but where the benefits are long term and socially dispersed so that costs cannot be easily adduced. But in this case as well, the state should withdraw as much and as soon as possible so that these facilities could be privatized. Throughout, the underlying assumption is that the market is the sole effective means for integrating society and making the decisions that can determine its development.[2] Though, of course, we know that even if we supposed that markets worked "perfectly", they would still operate as a Stalinist-like dictator wielding individual self-seeking proclivities for the "social" purpose of profit-making.

In any case, broadly speaking, the above view of markets as the repository of individual freedom remained the predominant public ideology in the United States up until the collapse of capitalism in the Great Depression of the 1930s. Out of that crisis a new public ideology was born, often called "welfare liberalism" or sometimes "social liberalism". It recognized that the market is not always self-regulating and that there is a common good that can be promoted only through the collective action of the state. To save capitalism from its breakdown, decisive state intervention into the market was necessary.

Neoliberalism reflects the belief in the possibility of a return to the earlier form of 19th century liberalism. This belief was put into operation under Margaret Thatcher in Britain, in the US under Ronald Reagan and in Mexico under Carlos Salinas. Only this time it occurred in the context of the alleged new era of capitalism known as globalization. This marched onto the historical stage under the banner of "free trade." Free trade extended the neoliberal principles beyond individual national economies to a purportedly developing global economy. And it involved more than just trade in goods between countries. It also involved free movement of capital across borders as the way was opened for investment from abroad and for repatriation of profits. Capital became hypermobile as it was freed from national limits. And the primary actor in this drama of globalization was the transnational corporation (TNC).

For Mexico, globalization has meant opening up the country to penetration by these transnational corporations and abandonment of its earlier ISI, shifting to export oriented development (EOD) instead. At the same time there has been a withdrawal of the state from the market and its role in providing for the welfare of those less well off. Individuals and domestic businesses alike have been pushed into a market increasingly dominated by giant transnational corporations, while being given little social support from the state. This is the brave new world of neoliberal globalization.

The advocates of neoliberal globalization promised that it would raise the living standards of people worldwide and promote economic growth. A rising tide would lift all boats, those of rich and poor alike. As we will see, the results have not fulfilled the promise. The yachts of the rich have certainly risen to unprecedented heights, but the rowboats of the poor are sinking, and those in the middle are struggling to stay afloat.

Neoliberal globalization has not even led to significant growth of the world economy as a whole. Worldwide aggregate growth rates were around 3.5 percent in the 1960s. Even during the troubled 1970s they fell to only 2.4 percent. But as neoliberal globalization began to take hold in the 1980s and 1990s, global growth rates fell to 1.4 percent and 1.1 percent. Since 2000 they have been at a flat one percent. [4]

We see a similar lackluster pattern in the case of Mexico. Pre NAFTA the Mexican economy grew at a rate of 5 percent annually between 1960 and 1980.[5] Under neoliberal policies that growth rate dropped to 2.3 percent annually from 1980 to 2004. The picture is particularly stark in agriculture. Between 1945 and 1961 Mexican agriculture grew at an average annual rate of 5 percent. Since the 1980s it has been 1.5 percent and in the first trimester of 2008 it fell to a minus 1.3 percent.

Under EOD 40 percent of what Mexico now produces is exported. 80 percent of that goes to its nearest market, the US. On the other hand, 40 percent of Mexico's food is imported, whereas in 1960 Mexico was nearly food self-sufficient.[6]

Under NAFTA Mexico has pursued that trade in which it enjoys a comparative advantage. Under liberal trade theory each country should export that which it does best and import that which other countries can do better. In international trade Mexico enjoys two advantages: a low wage work force and proximity to US markets. Mexico has tried to build on this through NAFTA, but in order to preserve that advantage, Mexico has to keep wages low. At first it was a decisive advantage, until China, with wages only one quarter those in Mexico, joined the WTO. But Mexico still has an advantage in heavy items like automobiles where the shorter transportation routes are decisive: so too with fresh vegetables, especially in the off season.

One of the most significant market oriented reforms under NAFTA has been the privatization of *ejido* land. *Ejidos* are communally owned land that was guaranteed under the 1917 constitution. For the campesinos this was the crowning achievement of the Revolutionary cry for "land and liberty." However, as a condition for entry into NAFTA, Mexico had to amend Article 27 of the constitution, ending land reform and allowing for division of *ejido* land into private property which could then be sold.[7] To assure that it would be sold, the state withdrew much of its support for small-scale agriculture. State-regulated grain reserves and price-support programs were dissolved, farm credits and subsidies were drastically reduced, and tariff and quota protections on agricultural imports have been eliminated—even while US agriculture continued to receive lavish federal supports, amounting to 40 percent of net farm income. In Mexico agricultural subsidies dropped from $2 billion in 1994 to $500 million in 2000. From 1990 to 1994 farmers received 33.2 percent of their income from the government. From 1995 to 2001, that dropped to 13.2 percent. At the same time duty-free corn was imported from the US in ever greater amounts that was cheaper for consumers than Mexican grown corn. These conditions forced an estimated 2 million campesinos off the land in the first decade of NAFTA, swelling the supply of low wage labor.

The privatization of the commons and other neoliberal policies have been devastating for millions and millions of Mexico's campesinos, who made up 40 percent of the population 25 years ago but are now only 30 percent. They have been transformed into a low wage proletariat, migrating to urban areas and, as is well known, to the U.S. Much of the story is told in these two factoids: every hour Mexico receives $1.5 million in food imports; in that same hour, 30 farmers leave for the US![8]

As a result, 16 percent of Mexico's workforce in now in the US—a huge loss to the nation's economy, in spite of the $23.98 billion they sent home to their families in 2007. These remittances total more than the foreign direct investment (FDI) in the country ($23.23 billion in 2007).

This massive migration is in large part due to the lack of adequate employment in Mexico. Typically 71 percent of new workers entering the labor force each year cannot find work in the formal sector: If they don't emigrate, they eek out a living in the informal sector, which now accounts for 28 percent of employment. They may work as street peddlers or in mom and pop stores or find occasional off the books employment in construction or as gardeners or maids with little in the way of benefits. In spite of long hours the small-scale self-employed petty bourgeoisie on the average makes 2.5 times the minimum wage of 54 pesos per day. It takes four minimum wages to reach the poverty line.

As can be easily seen, underemployment and unemployment are endemic. Officially unemployment stands at 5 percent. But the official statistics do not tell the story since a person is counted as employed if they work just one hour per week. Even if this minimal definition of unemployment is accepted, the 16 percent of the labor force that is in the U.S. should be added to it, shedding light on the fact that the economy cannot employ at least 21 percent of its workers.

Poverty is widespread, although estimates vary widely. There is general agreement that between 47 percent and 67 percent of households are in poverty. Rural poverty is between 58 percent and 76 percent, according to Mexican economist Enrique Dussell Peters. The World Bank estimates it at 73 percent. At the same time there has been a concentration of wealth in the hands of a few. In July 2007 Carlos Slim became the richest man in the world, worth $67.8 billion, surpassing Bill Gates' measly $59 billion fortune. Slim's companies represent 40 percent of the total value of Mexico's Bolsa stock index. Mexico now has more billionaires per capita than almost anywhere else.

Industrial development has been sluggish at best. Under EOD it was expected that the maquiladoras would be the leading sector of economic growth. Industrialization has been heavily focused in the expanding maquiladora sector.[9] These "off-shore" production platforms for transnational corporations have spread from the border region to throughout Mexico. Tapping the country's abundant low wage labor force and using imported components, the maquiladoras assemble commodities for foreign (mainly US) markets free of duties. They account for 80 percent of Mexico's exports, although by rights these exports should be counted as intra-firm transfers.[10]   The only thing Mexican in their production is the labor. As offshore production platforms for US TNCs, maquiladoras lack the backward and forward linkages that could stimulate peripheral development of other firms. They do not rely on domestic inputs, nor do they produce for domestic markets. In a very real sense, they are not part of a national economy. They belong to a global economy—the economy being constructed under the aegis of transnational capital.

Their main contribution to the Mexican economy is the wages they pay to their workers. Of the four million firms in Mexico, only 3500 account for 97 percent of the exports. But they employ only five percent of the workforce! Foreign direct investment (FDI) has undermined endogenous development rather than contributing to it.[11]

Another important sector of the industrial economy is the auto industry. Since the 1990s foreign direct investment in this area has averaged $2 billion a year and grew rapidly as Ford and General Motors struggled to cut costs. Auto exports rose by 68 percent from 2004 to 2007. Seventy-five percent of Mexican auto production is for export. Mexico has been able to attract this investment because of the two main competitive advantages it enjoys: proximity to the US market and abundant cheap labor: But apparently not cheap enough. While Ford announced last summer that it was moving production of the popular Fiesta to Mexico, creating 4,500 new jobs here, the deal requires the union to accept a two-tier wage structure under which new workers will be paid at half the current wage of 45 pesos per hour. The union leader said, "We agreed to it. We need to be more competitive. That's the truth. That's a reality."[12] This is after the United Auto Workers had accepted a two-tier wage structure in hopes of saving US jobs. Ford is pitting Mexican workers and U.S. workers against each other in a race to the bottom—with even cheaper Chinese workers being kept in reserve. Such is the dynamics of globalizing capitalism. In the long run only the transnational corporations win.

In sum, what we find in Mexico under NAFTA is a classic case of dependent development. It continues the pattern of combined and unequal development that has afflicted the global South for centuries. It is what economist Andre Gunder Frank called "the development of underdevelopment".[13] *Under*development (as distinct from *un*development) is a process whereby a country is developed (economically, culturally and otherwise) as a dependent appendage to the benefit of a core country. In the era of colonialism, this defined the relationship between colony and mother country. In the post-independence era of neocolonialism, it defined the relationship between the agricultural Third World and industrial First World. Now in the era of globalization, not even the core nations of the North benefit from the exploitation of the nations of the South. Transnational corporations are freeing themselves from the nation-states that gave them birth.[13] They now move freely around the globe extracting wealth from all they encounter. It is a game that enriches the few at the expense of the many.

This is documented in Wage-Productivity charts (below) that show the widening gap between what workers have received over the first decade or so of NAFTA compared with their productivity. The pattern is remarkably similar in Mexico, the US and Canada.

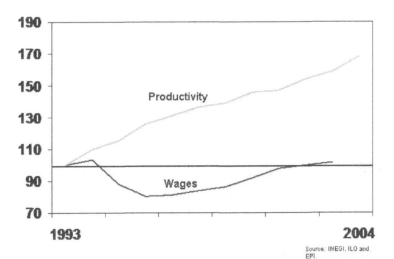

Source: INEGI, ILO and EPI.

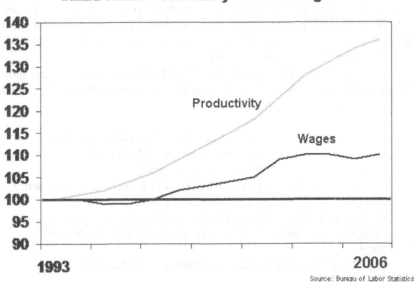

Source: Bureau of Labor Statistics

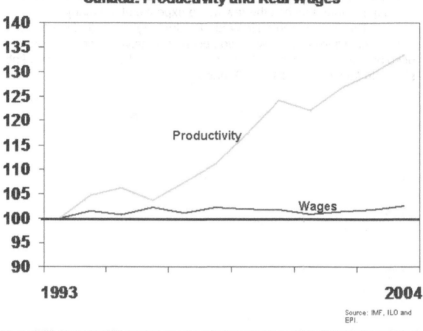

Canada: Productivity and Real Wages

Source: IMF, ILO and EPI.

Crisis: Whither Mexico?

I have focused on neoliberalism's impact on Mexico when it was working as designed—that is, working for transnational capital. But now neoliberalism is in crisis, and much of that story is told in those wage-productivity charts. Capital accumulation has soared while worker income has stagnated resulting in a crisis of over-accumulation. The fix of neoliberalism is no longer sufficient.[14]

What will this exhaustion of neoliberalism mean for the global South, particularly Mexico? It's too early to tell in any detail. But so far the indicators are all negative:

- the peso is falling faster than any other major currency
- inflation, mild at 6 percent so far, is likely to increase
- exports are declining as markets abroad contract
- oil prices are declining. Oil is the #1 foreign exchange earner and provides 40 percent of the government's budget.
- Tourism (the #3 foreign exchange earner) is declining as foreigners tighten their belts and are scared away by fear of crime
- FDI is declining as investors look for safe harbors

- remittances (the #2 foreign exchange earner) are declining as immigrants have less money to send home
- emigrants are returning (so far in modest numbers) to an economy with few jobs to offer
- the drug war has added to growing crime and a sense of insecurity
- a legitimacy crisis. Can a political elite that has low legitimacy even in good times govern effectively in the face of multiple unresolved problems?

Mexico is not a failed state. But there is potential for revolutionary upsurges in the years ahead. In 1810 Mexico started its war for independence from Spain. In 1910 it had a major revolution. Many think of 2010 as the next turn of the cycle. And then there is 2012, the year when the Mayan calendar runs out, heralding the end of an era and an opening to a new world. Coming as that does on the heels of the next presidential election, the mass psychology of that time may lead the popular classes to expect major changes.

Another possible scenario is for Mexico to recover from the ravages of neoliberalism by joining other countries of Latin America in a strategy for endogenous development within a regional trading alliance based on solidarity and mutual benefit. The crisis of global capitalism and the resulting contraction of trade could force Mexico in this direction and to a return to an import substitution industrialization strategy. Mexico will have to look for ways to free itself from transnational capital if it is to move ahead.

ENDNOTES

INTRODUCTION

1   See M.P. Cowen and R.W. Shenton, *Doctrines of Development* (London: Routledge, 1996) on this question.

2   See Jorge Larrain, *Theories of Development* (London: Polity Press, 1989) pp. 18-27.

3   David P. Levine, "Political Economy and the Idea of Development", *Review of Political Economy*, 13, 4 (2001) p. 524.

4   The use of terminology to describe capital such as "extra-human force" is *not* intended as an expression of the problematic "Kantian" antimony between the social and natural worlds. Rather it exists as an expression of the phenomena of commodity economic reification in the sense that capital, though a socially and historically constituted object, at a certain point *takes on a life of its own* as it wields human material reproduction and the self-seeking proclivities of "free" economic agents for the satisfaction of its abstract purposes. As put by Robert Albritton, "The Unique Ontology of Capital", *Poznan Studies in the Philosophy of the Sciences and the Humanities*, 60 (1998) p. 70: "One of the peculiarities of capital is that it is a subjectified object that objectifies subjects. It is an object in which self-expanding value takes on the properties of *SUBJECT* writ large, and in the process converts human subjects into commodities or mere objects used by value to expand itself".

5   Larrain, *Theories of Development*, pp. 45ff.

6   See, for example, A. K. Dasgupta, *Epochs of Economic Theory* (New York: Basil Blackwell, 1987).

7   The notion of "three worlds" spawned during the Cold War to capture the division of the globe in terms of a developed West, developed along alternate lines Communist Bloc, and the rest of the recently decolonized world. It has been fashionable over the years to describe that mass of previously colonized states as "developing countries", "emerging markets", "global south" and so forth. However I retain the notion of a third world in this chapter because despite the disappearance of the so-called second Communist "world" the conditions of existence of the vast swathe of humanity in the third world has grown more dire rather than improved in the years following WWII; though it may have improved among a few select cases and for certain elite groups within third world states.

8   What follows draws heavily upon Larrain, *Theories of Development*, pp. 102-10.

9   See the discussion in Ron Ayers and David Clarke, "Capitalism, Industrialisation and Development in Latin America: The Dependency Paradigm Revisited", *Capital & Class*, 64 (1998).

10   See Larrain, *Theories of Development*, pp. 115ff.

11   See Fernando Henrique Cardoso and Enzo Faletto, *Dependency and Development in Latin America* (Berkeley: University of California Press).

12   See, for example, the discussion in Anthony Brewer, *Marxist Theories of Imperialism: A Critical Survey* (London: Routledge & Kegan Paul, 1980) chapter 11.

13   An extended elaboration upon the foregoing is found in Ray Kiely, *Sociology and Development: The Impasse and Beyond* (London: UCL Press, 1995).

14   See the excellent discussion in Keith Griffin and John Gurley, "Radical Analyses of Imperialism, the Third World, and the Transition to Socialism: A Survey Article", *Journal of Economic Literature*, 23 (1985).

15   See the discussion in Richard Westra, *Political Economy and Globalization* (London: Routledge, 2009) chapter 4.

16   See Peter Gowan, *The Global Gamble: Washington's Faustian Bid for World Dominance* (London: Verso, 1999) pp. 20-3.

17 Gérard Duménil and Dominique Lévy, *Capital Resurgent: The Roots of the Neoliberal Revolution* (Cambridge, Mass: Harvard University Press, 2004) pp. 86-8.

18 Quite simply, monetarism refers to the neoliberal fixation upon inflation targeting and the view that it is the money supply which is the cause of inflation. Keynesianism, the economic doctrine animating policy making in the post-WWII golden age of growth, countenanced inflation because it supported long-term business investment/profit strategies, expanding effective demand or mass consumption of consumer durables and state social wage and countercyclical spending. Neoliberals love deflation because, as will be discussed further below, the economy that they have come to superintend is one in which growth no longer devolves from material goods production and long term industrial investment/profit strategies but from short term arbitrage and money games. Hence preserving the value of money for the institutions gaining from these games is what is really at the root of monetarism. So-called supply-side economics refers to the reversal of Keynesian support for bolstering effective demand and social wage redistribution designed to spur continued mass consumption. Supply-side policies in practice meant tax cuts for big businesses and wealthy individuals in the seemingly common sense but hugely misguided belief that this would provide an incentive for savings and investment. The fact, as we shall see, that the US as an economy has NO savings, is mired in gargantuan debt, and is relinquishing the last vestiges of its post-WWII material production economy is empirical testimony to the folly of neoliberal doctrines. Indeed, we should all be clamoring for those who won Nobel Prizes for neoliberal gibberish to return them.

19 See, in particular, the publication: World Bank, *The East Asian Miracle* (Oxford: Oxford University Press, 1993).

20 Westra, *Political Economy and Globalization*, chapter 4 treats what follows in greater length.

21 Richard Stubbs, *Rethinking Asia's Economic Miracle* (Basingstoke: Palgrave, 2005) is the key reading here.

22 Richard Westra, "The Capitalist Stage of Consumerism and South Korean Development", *Journal of Contemporary Asia*, 36, 1 (2006).

23 See Richard Westra, "Globalization: The Retreat of Capital to the 'Interstices' of the World?" in Richard Westra and Alan Zuege, *Value and the World Economy Today: Production, Finance and Globalization* (Basingstoke: Palgrave, 2003) for a succinct summary and critique of the formative literature.

24 See, for example, Jeffery Frieden, *Global Capitalism: Its Fall and Rise in the Twentieth Century* (New York: W.W. Norton & Co, 2007) pp. 288-95.

25 Westra, *Political Economy and Globalization*, chapter 4.

26 We would digress too far here to get into debate over all the components of the economic crisis befalling the US economy from the late 1960s. For competing views of the cause(s) see Dumenil and Levy, *Capital Resurgent*; and Robert Brenner, "The Economics of Global Turbulence", Special Issue, *New Left Review*, 229 (1998).

27 See on this, and related issues, Raphael Kaplinsky, *Globalization, Poverty and Inequality: Between a Rock and a Hard Place* (London: Polity Press, 2007).

28 See Jane D'Arista, "The Role of the International Monetary System in Financialization", in Gerald Epstein (ed.) *Financialization and the World Economy* (Cheltenham: Edward Elgar, 2005) pp. 222-3.

29 Eric Toussaint, *Your Money [or] Your Life: The Tyranny of Global Finance* (Chicago, Illinois: Haymarket Books, 2005) pp. 125-6.

30 See, on this question, Ronen Palan, *The Offshore World: Sovereign Markets, Virtual Places, and Nomad Millionaires* (Ithaca, NY: Cornell University Press, 2003).

31 On what is summarized below, see the discussion in Adrian Leftwich, "Politics in Command and the Rediscovery of Social science", *New Political Economy*, 10, 4 (2005).

32 See Arturo Escobar, *Encountering Development: The Making and Unmaking of the Third World* (Princeton: Princeton University Press, 1994.

33 Maria Mies and Veronika Bennholdt-Thomsen, *The Subsistence Perspective: Beyond The Globalized Economy* (London: Zed Books, 1999) constitutes an exemplar of this literature.

34   Arif Dirlik, *The Postcolonial Aura: Third World Criticism in the Age of Global Capitalism* (Boulder: Westview Press, 1998) develops this point.

35   Neil Thomas, "Global capitalism, the anti-globalisation movement and the Third World", *Capital and Class*, 92 (2007).

36   See for example Roy Bhaskar, *Reclaiming Reality* (London: Verso, 1989)

37   See Richard Westra, "Kautsky, Lukacs, Althusser and the Retreat from the Economic in Marxism – with the Return in Uno", *Political Economy Quarterly*, 44, 2 (2007); idem, "The Capitalist Stage of Consumerism and South Korean Development".

38   *Levels of analysis* in Marxian political economy entails the view that the political economic study of capitalism as a whole requires that the movement in thought from the basic theory of capitalism (Marx's project in *Capital*) to the study of capitalist history be mediated by a *stage theory* of capitalist development; the latter focusing on periodizing capitalism in terms of discrete historically contingent production structures and non-economic support systems capital accumulation proceeds through to manage the use value space of society in a world-historic phase or stage of capitalist development.

39   One of the most widely read Marxist accounts of the global economy is David Harvey, *Spaces of Global Capitalism: Towards a Theory of Uneven Geographical Development* (London: Verso, 2006). While this, and other current writings by Harvey certainly have much to offer Marxian debate, that Harvey's work never adequately treats the unit of analysis question in the study of capital accumulation as it cropped up initially in early development debate over characterizing capitalism as a "world system" constitutes an impoverishing weakness. As argued elsewhere (and those interested in pursuing this are encouraged to refer to that), Westra, *Political Economy and Globalization*, chapter 4, adequate treatment of the unit of analysis question in the Marxian research agenda demands both the specification of Marx's project in *Capital* as well as close argument on how that project relates to the study of capitalist history. My position, quite simply, is that resolution of the unit of analysis question in the study of capitalism can only be resolved through *levels of analysis* in Marxian political economy.

40   See the discussion in Cliff Durand, "The Exhaustion of Developmental Socialism: Lessons from China", *Monthly Review*, 42, 7 (1990).

41   On questions of socialist construction see Richard Westra, "Marxian economic theory and an ontology of socialism: a Japanese intervention", *Capital & Class* 78 (2002); idem, "*Green* Marxism and the Institutional Structure of a Global Socialist Future" in Robert Albritton, Robert Jessop, and Richard Westra (eds.) *Political Economy and Global Capitalism: The 21st Century, Present and Future* (London: Anthem, 2007); idem *Political Economy and Globalization*, chapter 5.

42   As noted by Sally Matthews, "Attaining a Better Society: Critical Reflections on what it means to be 'developed'", *Theoria* (April 2005), there has been a paucity of discussion surrounding this question and a rather blithe assumption that there need not be any as a tacit consensus exists over it.

43   C. Feinstein, "Structural Change in the Developed Countries During the Twentieth Century", *Oxford Review of Economic Policy*, 15, 4 (1999).

44   ILO, *Global Employment Trends* (Geneva: International Labor Office, 2008) p. 11 and table 4.

45   United Nations, "World Urbanization Prospects: The 2007 Revision Database", http://esa.un.org/unup/

46   See Mike Davis, *Planet of Slums* (London: Verso, 2006) pp. 14-16, 24-8.

47   *New York Times*, "Where Sweatshops are a Dream", http://www.nytimes.com/2009/01/15/opinion/15kristof.html?_r=1&ref=opinion

48   See for example Ray Kiely, *The New Political Economy of Development: Globalization, Imperialism, Hegemony* (Basingstoke: Palgrave, 2007) pp. 131-43.

49   See also Peter Edward, "Examining Inequality: Who Really Benefits from Global Growth?" *World Development*, 34, 10 (2006).

50   Kiely, *The New Political Economy of Development*, p. 137.

51   *United Nations,* "World Economic Situation and Prospects 2009: Update as of mid-2009", http://www.un.org/esa/policy/wess/wesp2009files/wesp09update.pdf
52   International Food Policy Research Institute (IFPRI), "Food and Financial Crisis: Implications for Agriculture and the Poor", *Food Policy Report* 20 (December 2008) http://www.ifpri.org/pubs/fpr/pr20.asp
53   "World Economic Situation and Prospects 2009", pp. 3-4.
54   Economic and Social Council, http://daccessdds.un.org/doc/UNDOC/GEN/N09/311/42/PDF/N0931142.pdf?OpenElement
55   *New York Times,* "Job Losses Pose a Threat to Stability World-Wide", http://www.nytimes.com/2009/02/15/business/15global.html?_r=1&th&emc=th
56   "Food and Financial Crisis"; IFPRI Policy Brief 13 (April 2009) http://www.ifpri.org/pubs/bp/bp013.asp

Chapter 1

1   I would like to thank Elena Arengo, Danilo Fernandes, Marcelo Diniz, and Joe Smith for helpful comments and feedback on this chapter, though any errors or oversights are fully the responsibility of the author.
2   The most ardent defenders of laissez-faire, known as the Mount Pèlerin Group, began meeting in 1947 in   Switzerland. This group included well-known intellectuals, such as Milton Friedman, Hayek, von Mises, Popper, etc.
3   See Paul Cooney, "Evaluando el Neoliberalismo en América Latina: Los casos de Argentina, Brasil y México", presented at the XII Encontro de SEP, June, 2007 and "Uma avaliação empírica da lei geral da acumulação capitalista no período atual de globalização neoliberal", *Revista de Economia* UFPR, v. 35, n.1, (2009).
4   Much of the material for this section on ISI is based upon the excellent historical analysis done by Wilson Cano, *Soberania e Política Econômica na América Latina,* (São Paulo: UNESP, 1999), Chapter 3.
5   Saad Filho, A. and Morais, L., "Neo-Monetarismo Tropical: A Experiência Brasileira nos Anos Noventa", *Revista de Economia Política,* vol. 22, n° 1 (85), janeiro-março, (2002), p.4.
6   For example, in the case of Mexico, the trade balance was positive if one excluded foreign TNCs. Given the high level of imports by transnational corporations, the resulting overall trade balance for Mexico was negative, which led to the balance of payments problems during the 1970s.
7   An example of the growing role of finance in the global economy is the increase in the percentage of US investment in finance compared to overall investment: after having a roughly stable level of 15 percent from the 1950s through to the 1970s, it grew steadily from the end of the 1970s and peaked at around 27 percent in 1989. See Brenner, Robert, *O Boom e a Bolha,* (São Paulo: Editora Record, 2002), p.133.
8   Given the fact that the second world no longer exists for all practical purposes, the term 'third world' seems outdated, and many advocate using the term 'global south' or 'developing' countries. Unfortunately, all suffer from the problem of over generalization. Despite its limitations, the term 'third world' is linked with the concept of center and periphery and is still associated with an alternative political project. Given the lack of an ideal term, the several terms mentioned are often used interchangeably throughout this chapter.
9   Inter-American Development Bank
10   Examples from a liberal or neoliberal view abound over the years; consider W.W. Rostow back in the 1950s or authors such as North or Krueger in the present-day.
11   With regard to exchange rate policy, there is a difference between the interests of neoliberals in the first world, which are at times defenders of devaluations and at other times defenders of convertibility or the pegging of a currency with the dollar.
12   See Paulo Gala, "Dois padrões de política cambial: américa latina e sudeste asiático" or Bastos, P.P., "Controle de capitais: uma comparação internacional" both presented at the third Latin American Political Science Congress, Unicamp, Campinas, Brazil, September, 2006.
13   See Paul Cooney, "Dos Décadas de Neoliberalismo en México- Resultados y Desafíos", presented at the V Coloquio de Economía Política de América Latina,

Mexico City, October, 2005, and Paul Cooney, "Argentina's Quarter Century Experiment with Neoliberalism: From Dictatorship to Depression." *Revista de Economia Contemporânea*, Rio de Janeiro, Vol. 11, Nro.1, jan./abr., (2007).

14   See Basualdo, E.M. "Historia económica: Las reformas estructurales y el plan de convertibilidad durante la década de los noventa, El auge y la crisis de la valorización financiera". *Revista Realidad Económica*, Número 200, 16 de noviembre -31 de diciembre (2003), Buenos Aires. or Guillén Romo, Héctor , 'México: del desarrollo "hacia adentro" al desarrollo "hacia afuera"', *Realidad Económica* 191, octubre/ noviembre, (2002): 56-77 on the issue of capital flight for the cases of Argentina and Mexico, respectively.

15   Chang, Há-Joon, "Kicking Away the ladder: the real history of free trade" in *Globalization and the Myths of Free Trade: History, Theory and Empirical Evidence*, ed. Anwar Shaikh (New York: Routledge, 2007).

16   Ibid., p.23. For a more extensive reading on this issue, see Chang, Há-Joon, *Kicking Away the Ladder-Development Strategy in Historical Perspective*, (London: Anthem Press, 2002).

17   The *Plano Cruzado* (Cruzado Plan) was a monetarist economic plan aimed at reducing inflation, which was out of control in 1986, and which also introduced the new currency—the cruzado. For a brief and concise summary, see Filgueiras, L., *História do Plano Real*, (São Paulo: Editorial Boitemp, 2000)

18   In 1992, Collor was impeached due to a corruption scandal, forcing him to leave office two years early.

19   Rocha, G.M. "Neo-Dependency in Brazil", *New Left Review*, v.16, July-August, (2002), p.6.

20   Ibid., p.7.

21   De Oliveira, F.A & Nakatani, P, "The Brazilian Economy under Lula: A Balance of Contradictions", *Monthly Review*, vol. 58, nr.8, February, (2007).

22   From 2005 through the third quarter of 2008, there was a clear increase in GNP growth: roughly between 4 and 5 percent, but as of the fourth quarter of 2008, there was a drop of 3.6 percent due to the world economic crisis.

23   The trade liberalization and deregulation which Collor implemented were in fact conditions for restructuring Brazil's foreign debt under the Brady Plan. See Rocha, (2002), p.6.

24   Ibid., p.9.

25   Ibid., p.6.

26   IBGE - Instituto Brasileiro de Geografia e Estadística-Brazilian Institute of Geography and Statistics (www.ibge.gov.br/home/).

27   Ibid., p.14.

28   Ibid., p.3.

29   See Saad Filho, A. and Morais, L., (2002), for a good discussion about Brazil's external vulnerability as a result of neo-monetarist policies.

30   Much of the analysis related to internal debt is based on two articles by Carlos Eduardo Carvalho: Carvalho, C.E., "Dívida pública: um debate necessário". In: Sicsú, João; Paula, L.F.R.; Michel, R. (orgs.). Novo-Desenvolvimentismo: Um projeto nacional de crescimento com eqüidade social. (Rio de Janeiro: Fundação Konrad Adenauer, 2004) pp. 379-399 e Carvalho, C.E., "A Dívida Interna: Custos, Restrições ao Crescimento, Alternativas", IEEI versão revista 24.04.(2007).

31   **Carcanholo, R., "La Experiencia Brasileña: Deuda Externa, FMI y Política Económica",** *Revista de SEPLA*, nro. 1, set/, (2007).

32   Carvalho, (2007), p.82.

33   See *Folha de São Paulo*, May 5th, 2009, "Commodities puxam alta no saldo comercial", where it is clear that Brazil is barely obtaining a trade surplus because of its exports of raw materials and agricultural products in contrast to manufacturing exports.

34   See BNDES, André Nassif et. al. (2006). Ha Evidencias de Desindustrialização no Brasil? or Folha de São Paulo (09.09.2006**) "BNDES aponta risco de desindustrialização".**

35   See Folha de São Paulo 10.11.2007.

36   Pochmann, Mario. (1996). "Efeitos da internacionalização do capital no mundo do trabalho no Brasil". in: NAFTA y MERCOSUR: Processos de Apertura Econômica y Trabajo, Enrique de La Garza Toledo y Carlos Salas (eds), (Ciudad de México: CLACSO, 2003).

37   For an excellent analysis of globalization, denationalization and the growing influence of foreign firms in Brazil, see Reinaldo Gonçalves, *Globalização e Desnacionalização*, (São Paulo: Paz e Terra, 1999).

38   See De Oliveira, F.A & Nakatani, P, (2007).

39   See Marquetti, A., "A Economia Brasileira no Capitalismo Neoliberal: Progresso Técnico, Distribuição, Crescimento e Mudança Institucional", Seminário USP/IPE, (2004).

40   According to DIEESE (Inter-Union Department for Statisitics and Socio-economic Studies), although the minimum wage is now R$ 415/month, they estimate that the necessary minimum wage corresponds to R$ 2,026 as of August 2008 (see www. dieese.org.br).

41   The measure of unemployment used here is including underemployment, which is actually a more accurate measure of the lack of available jobs in an economy.

42   For an analysis of the deterioration of the labor market in Brazil and the growth of the informal economy see Pochmann, M. *O Trabalho sob Fogo Cruzado* (São Paulo: Editora Contexto, 1999).

43   SEADE (Fundação Sistema Estadual de Análise de Dados) translated as the State Foundation for Data Analysis, which is based in São Paulo.

44   See Cano, (1999), p.277.

45   The two data series are open urban unemployment, which is inclusive of underemployment, however, prior to 2001; the values for Brazil are clearly lower compared to subsequent years and also for São Paulo. This is because a new methodology was adopted by the IBGE in 2001, using a broader definition for the open unemployment series.

46   The difference between the general index for inflation and the index of food items only was roughly 70 percent during the period 2007-2008.

47   See Pogge, Thomas and Reddy, Sanjay, "Unknown: The Extent, Distribution, and Trend of Global Income Poverty" (http://www.socialanalysis.org/), (2003).

48   ECLAC (Economic Commission for Latin America and the Caribbean), *Statistical Yearbook for Latin America and the Caribbean*, (www.eclac.cl), (2004).

Chapter 2

1   Poverty rates refer to 2004-5; foreign exchange reserves and investments are as of 2006-7. Government of India, *Economic Survey 2008*, accessed at http://indiabudget.nic.in

2   National Common Minimum Programme, Government of India, May 2004. http://pmindia.nic.in/cmp.pdf

3   The National Association of Software and Services Companies (NASSCOM) factsheet http://www.nasscom.in/upload/5216/IT%20Industry%20Factsheet-Aug%20 2008.doc, August 2008.

4   "RIL tops, Tata steel debuts on Fortune 500", *Express India*, July 9, 2008. Accessed online at http://www.expressindia.com/latest-news/RIL-tops-Tata-steel-debuts-on-Fortune-500/333467/

5   See "Jaguar Land Rover (JLR) is in secret talks with the British government for a £1 billion loan, just nine months after Tata bought the luxury-car marquee", See "Tata's Jaguar seeks £1bn loan from UK govt□, *Times of India*, November 23, 2008. http://timesofindia.indiatimes.com/Tatas_Jaguar_seeks_1bn_loan_from_UK_govt/ articleshow/3748925.cms. Tata Motors also floated the *nano car project*, a cheap car intended for 'the masses', which has become the center of intense political conflict and resistance against neoliberalism, ironically, in the Indian state of West Bengal, where a Left front government has been in power since 1977.

6   See "India Inc finalises $26 bn overseas mergers, acquisitions:, *The Economic Times*, October 9, 2008. Nayyar, D. (2008) "The Internationalization of Firms From India: Investment, Mergers and Acquisitions", *Oxford Development Studies*, Volume

36, Issue 1, pp. 111 – 131; Nagaraj, R (2006): 'Indian Investments Abroad: What Explains the Boom?, *Economic & Political Weekly,* Vol XLI, No 46, pp 4716-18

7   http://www.tatamail.com

8   See "India Inc. finalizes $26 billion overseas investment", *The Economic Times* http://economictimes.indiatimes.com/News/Economy/Foreign_Trade/India_Inc_finalises_26_bn_overseas_mergers_acquisitions/articleshow/3577139.cms

9   "GDP share: Indian billionaires beat Americans", *Financial Express,* March 9, 2008. http://www.financialexpress.com/news/GDP-share-Indian-billionaires-beat-Americans/282207/: According to latest data available with International Monetary Fund (IMF), the GDP size of India, China and the US for 2007 are estimated at 1,089.9 billion dollars, 3,248 billion dollars and 13,794 billion dollars respectively.

10   See the Bank's first major update to its 2005 *International Comparison Program,* August 26, 2008, accessed online http://siteresources.worldbank.org/NEWS/Resources/Poverty-Brief-in-English.pdf

11   *Household Consumer Expenditure Survey,* Poverty line as of 2004-5 was Rs.356.30 and 538.60 (rural and urban consumption expenditure per capita per month http://pib.nic.in/archieve/others/2007/mar07/2007032102.xls

12   Patnaik, U. "The Republic of Hunger", Public Lecture on the occasion of the 50th Birthday of Safdar Hashmi, organized by SAHMAT (Safdar Hashmi Memorial Trust) on April 10, 2004, New Delhi. http://www.networkideas.org/featart/apr2004/Republic_Hunger.pdf

13   Government of India, Planning Commission, "Towards Faster and More Inclusive Growth: An Approach to the 11th Five Year Plan", New Delhi, December 2006 http://planningcommission.nic.in/plans/planrel/app11_16jan.pdf

14   Report on the Conditions of Work and Promotion of Livelihoods in the Unorganised Sector, National Commission for Enterprises in the Unorganized Sector, New Delhi, September 2007. http://nceus.gov.in/Condition_of_workers_sep_2007.pdf

15   Sen, A.and Himanshu "Recent Evidence on Poverty and Inequality in India", IDEAS, New Delhi (2006). Accessed online at http://www.networkideas.org/themes/political/oct2006/po29_Abhijit_Sen.htm

16   Ananya Mukherjee Reed, *Human Development and Social Power* (London: Routledge, 2008)

17   See Table 4.1 (p. 54); Table 10.2 (p.203); Table 10.5 (p.206); Table 10.10 (p.210); Appendix Table 10.4 (p.381). Estimated from NSSO (2004-05) 61st Round, Schedule 10. Notes a. percentage of population of 6+ years; b. percentage of population of 20+ years.

18   Deshpande S. and Y.Yadav, "Redesigning Affirmative Action Castes and Benefits in Higher Education", *Economic and Political Weekly,* June 17, 2006, pp.2419-24.

19   Nagraj, K. "Farmer suicides in India: Magnitudes, Trends and Spatial Patterns", *Macroscan,* March (2008). http://macroscan.org/anl/mar08/pdf/Farmers_Suicides.pdf

20   See Focus on the Global South, http://focusweb.org/india/index.php?option+com_content&task=view&id=739%Itemid=30.

21   Nagraj, "Farmer Suicides".

22   Jha, P. "Some Aspects of the Well-Being of India's Agricultural Labour in the Context of Contemporary Agrarian Crisis", *Macroscan,* February 2007, http://macroscan.org/anl/feb07/Agrarian_Crisis.pdf

23   Chandrasekhar, C.P. and Jayati Ghosh, "Agriculture's Role in Contemporary Development", *Macroscan,* May 23rd 2006, http://macroscan.org/the/food/may06/fod230506Agriculture.htm

24   Chandrasekhar, C.P., "The Progress of Reform and the Retrogression of Agriculture", *Macroscan,* April 2007, http://www.macroscan.org/anl/apr07/pdf/Agriculture.pdf

25   Bagchi, A.K *The Political Economy of Underdevelopment,* (Cambridge: Cambridge University Press, 1982).

26   Bagchi, A.K "Public sector industry and the political economy of India's development", in T.Byres (ed.) *The State, Development Planning and Liberalisation in India,* (New Delhi: Oxford University Press, 1988); Mukherjee Reed, A. *Perspectives on the Indian Corporate Economy: Exploring the Paradox of Profits,* (Basingstoke:

Palgrave, 2001).

27   See note 19.

28   Tagnas, Rey AL and V.Kaul, "Innovation Systems in India's IT Industry: An Empirical Investigation", *Economic and Political Weekly*, September 30, 2006, pp.4178-86.

29   Kumar, N. (2001) 'Indian Software Industry Development in International and National Development Perspective', *Economic and Political Weekly,* Vol 36, No 45, November 10.

30   Mohanty, M., "Political Economy of Agrarian Transformation: Another View of Singur", *Economic and Political Weekly,* March 3 2007, 733-45.

31   West Bengal Industrial Development Corporation (WBIDC), "Agreement between Tata Motors Ltd., Government of West Bengal and WBIDC" available at http://www.wbidc.com; Basu, D. "Singur: The costs and benefits of neoliberal industrialization", Radical Notes, October 5, 2008. http://radicalnotes.com/journal/2008/10/05/singur-the-costs-and-benefits-of-neoliberal-industrialization

32   "Statement from Concerned Citizens: On the Shameful Events in Nandigram in the last few days", http://www.counterviews.org/Web_Doc/Nandigram/statement_on_nandigram.pdf

33   "People's Tribunal of Nandigram, A report presented to the Governor of West Bengal", August 2007. http://sez.icrindia.org/files/nandigram_final_report.pdf, p.26

34   *Ibid*, p.20.

35   Santos de Sousa, B. (ed.) *Another Production is Possible*, London: Verso (2006).

36   See Jessop, B "The Crises of Neo-Liberalism, Neo-Neo-Liberalism, and Post-Neo-Liberalism", public lecture organized by the Historical Materialism collective in Toronto, September 18, 2008. McMichael, P. "Reframing development: global peasant movements and the new agrarian question", *Canadian Journal of Development Studies*, XXVII, 4 (2006), pp. 471–483. See also McMichael, P., "Can we interpret the anti-globalisation movement in Polanyian terms?", Keynote address prepared for Twenty-five Year Anniversary Celebration & Symposium: "Globalization and its Discontents: Re-embedding the Economy in the 21st Century", Comparative Development Studies Programme, Trent University, October 12-14, 2001)

37   See Friedmann, J. *Empowerment: the politics of alternative development*, (Cambridge, Mass: Blackwell, 1992); Young, I. M. *Justice and the Politics of Difference* (Princeton, N.J: Princeton University Press, 1990); idem *Inclusion and Democracy* (Oxford: Oxford University Press, 2000); idem "Taking the Basic Structure Seriously", *Perspectives on Politics* 4, 1 (2006) pp. 91-7.

38   Young, *Justice and the Politics of Difference*, p. 19.

Chapter 3

1   Data are from World Bank, *World Development Indicators Online*. Website: <http://devdata.worldbank.org/dataonline> (retrieved October 1, 2008).

2   Data are from China's National Bureau of Statistics. Website: <http://www.stats.gov.cn/tjsj/ndsj> (retrieved October 1, 2008).

3   Joe Quinlan, "Why We Should Not Bank on the Chinese Consumer," *Financial Times*, October 3, 2007, p.24.

4   Total labor income is defined as the sum of urban wage incomes and the rural residents' net incomes.

5   Martin Wolf, "China changes the whole world," *Financial Times*, January 23, 2008, Special Report: The World in 2008, p. 2.

6   Data are from International Labour Office, *Yearbook of Labour Statistics 2006* (Geneva: International Labour Office, 2006), pp. 763-838, 933-1031. Wage rates are converted into US dollars using prevailing exchange rates.

7   Zhang Yi, "*13 Yi Zhihou Zhongguo Renkou de Xin Tezheng* (New Characteristics of the Chinese Population after 1.3 Billion)," in Ru Xin, Lu Xueyi, and Li Peilin (eds.), *2006 Nian: Zhongguo Shehui Xingshi Fenxi yu Yuce* (2006: Analyses and Predictions of China's Social Situation) (Beijing: *Shehui Kexue Wenxian Chubanshe* or Social Science Academic Press, 2006), pp. 97-107.

8   Data for China's coal, oil, natural gas, nuclear, and hydro production are from BP, *BP Statistical Review of World Energy*. Website: <http://www.bp.com/statisticalreview>

(retrieved October 20, 2008). Imports and stock change are derived by subtracting the total production of coal, oil, and natural gas from their total consumption. Renewable contribution is estimated by this author. Following the practice of the International Atomic Energy Agency, nuclear contribution is measured by its thermal equivalent, but hydro and renewable contributions are measured by the electrical energy they represent. Traditional biomass (such as wood burning in the rural areas) is excluded from the total primary energy supply.

9   Cui, Minxuan, *Zhongguo Nengyuan Fazhan Baogao* (Annual Report of China's Energy Development) (Beijing: *Shehui Kexue Wenxian Chubanshe* or Social Sciences Academic Press, 2008), p. 33.

10   Ibid. p. 33.

11   Ibid. p. 33.

12   Energy Watch Group, *Uranium Resources and Nuclear Energy*, EWG-Series No. 1/2007, Website: <http://www.energywatchgroup.org/fileadmin/global/pdf/ EWG_Uraniumreport_12-2006.pdf> (retrieved January 1, 2007).

13   Ibid. p. 34.

14   Colin J. Campbell, *Oil Crisis* (Brentwood, Essex, UK: Multi-Science Publishing Company Ltd, 2005).

15   The Association for the Study of Peak Oil and Gas Ireland, *Newsletter No. 94 – October 2008*, Website: <http://www.aspo-ireland.org/contentFiles/newsletterPDFs/ newsletter94_200810.pdf> (retrieved October 20, 2008).

16   Dave Rutledge, "Hubbert's Peak, the Coal Question, and Climate Change," Presentation at the Annual Conference of Association for the Study of Peak Oil and Gas USA, Houston, Texas, October 19, 2007.

Chapter 4

1   José Luis Rodríguez, "The Road to Economic Recovery" in Max Azicri and Elsie Deal (eds.), *Cuban Socialism in a New Century. Adversity, Survival and Renewal* (Gainesville: University of Florida Press, 2004), p. 151.

2   Technically, one other former COMECON member, the Socialist Republic of Vietnam, still claims to be building socialism. It is not the topic of this essay, but this author maintains that like China's much more written about "socialism with Chinese characteristics," Vietnam has restored capitalism, notwithstanding its still large state sector. On China, see the short paper by Al Campbell, "Is China's Market Path a Road to Socialism?" 2008, accessible at www.nodo50.org/cubasigloXXI, or the more developed argument in the book by Martin Hart-Landsberg and Paul Burkett, *China and Socialism. Market Reforms and Class Struggle* (New York: Monthly Review Press, 2005).

3   Fidel Castro, *Granma Weekly Review*, August 23, 1995, p. 6.

4   *ibid.*, p. 11.

5   *ibid.*, p. 9.

6   Fidel Castro, *Cubainfo*, September 14, 1995, p. 5.

7   Fidel Castro, *Granma Weekly Review*, November 23, 1997, p. 10. For one of a number of collections of his speeches from this economically difficult period that all contained this continued rejection of capitalism and commitment to socialism, see Fidel Castro, *Cuba at the Crossroads* (Melbourne: Ocean Press, 1996).

8   There is broad participation in these congresses. There is a lead up period to the congress with meetings in nearly all workplaces. There were 70,000 concrete suggestions in response to the 1996 preliminary draft that were presented and recorded in these meetings, and many of them were incorporated into the final draft.

9   The sample came from across the island except, due to bureaucratic hurdles, from the eastern part, where support for the revolution has always been strongest.

10   In the context of Cuba, being a "revolutionary" almost always means identifying with the process led by the revolutionary government, and hence being anti-capitalist. Along the same lines, in the poll 58 percent said they considered the revolution on balance to have more achievements than failures, while 31 percent responded the opposite way. The poll was conducted by the Costa Rican associate of Gallup, CID-Gallup, and a review of a number of the results can be found in *Cuba Update*,

February, 1995, p 9.

11   Francisco Soborón Valdés, "El Socialismo no es para los cubanos una opción coyuntural," *Diario de la Juventud Cubana*, December 23, 2005, accessed on 7/26/2008 at www.juventudrebelde.cu/2005/octubre-diciembre/dic-23/cuba_intervencion_index. html. The translation is by this author.

12   *ibid.*

13   In the case of the second argument here, many supporters.

14   Economist Intelligence Unit. *Cuba, Dominican Republic, Haiti, Puerto Rico Country Report.* 1997(3), p 7.

15   *ibid.*, p. 12.

16   Carmelo Mesa-Lago, *Are Economic Reforms Propelling Cuba to the Market?* (Miami: University of Miami, 1994), p. 68.

17   It is important to note a sleight-of-hand used continually by the advocates of a restoration of capitalism. When they become convinced that new economic reforms are no longer potentially beneficial to a capitalist restoration, they talk of "an end of reforms" instead of "a change in the type of reforms to ones less agreeable to capitalism." The process of economic reform in Cuba has never stopped (and rarely even paused) since 1959.

18   Here I will present only enough for the points I will be concerned with. As an example of more complicated issues, consider the issue of "free trade" which is associated with neoliberal theory. Since capitalism is still organized (primarily) through nation states, the different nation states and the capitals connected to them often try to pursue (if they are strong enough) a policy of 'open your markets to my goods but I will protect my markets from your goods,' as opposed to free trade. And they pursue this, as obviously inconsistent as it is, in the name of the universal benefits from free trade and neoliberalism. Three good books that give a rich picture of neoliberalism consistent with the brief presentation here are Gérard Duménil and Dominique Lévy, *Capital Resurgent* (Cambridge: Harvard University Press, 2004); David Harvey, *A Brief History of Neoliberalism* (Oxford: Oxford University Press, 2005); and Andrew Glynn, *Capitalism Unleashed* (Oxford: Oxford University Press, 2006). For a shorter introduction to neoliberalism, see Al Campbell, "The Birth of Neoliberalism in the United States: A Reorganization of Capitalism" in Alfredo Saad-Filho and Deborah Johnston (eds.), *Neoliberalism. A Critical Reader* (London: Pluto Press, 2005).

19   Duménil and Lévy, *op. cit.,* p 1.

20   I have already discussed in endnote 18 the limitations of neoliberal "free trade" in practice.

21   By the nature of capitalism "reduced government" or "free markets" need to be something very different in practice from their form as an ideological battering ram. Markets are not "natural," they cannot exist "by themselves" or "free." They require both a specific set of definitions of what is legal and what is not, and a force capable of enforcing those norms. Both of these capitalist needs require a state and government. In practice "reduced government" and "free markets" mean campaigns to eliminate all services that the state provides to labor that could be profitably commodified, and in particular those that strengthen the position of workers in the labor market.

22   Although the large majority of people consider Cuba to be non capitalist, a small group of people do consider Cuba to be "state capitalist." While this author strongly rejects that characterization, even that would leave it non neoliberal, considering the role the government plays in their concept of so-called state capitalism.

23   "Other planned economies" include Eastern European countries, China, North Korea, Vietnam and Mongolia. Comité Estatal de Estadísticas, *Anuario Estadístico de Cuba, 1987* (no publishing data given), Table XI.2, pp. 416 and 418. Calculations by the author.

24   North Korea of course still has a planned economy, but it constitutes only 0.004 percent of Cuba's merchandise trade. While as I have indicated above I consider Vietnam capitalist, it in any case constitutes only 1.6 percent of Cuba's trade. More important is that Cuba's trade with its two largest trading partners, Venezuela (20.6 percent) and China (14.9 percent) is very extensively planned by trade agreements,

notwithstanding their capitalist nature. While trade per se is not a concern of this essay, it is worth noting that the next largest trade partners operate according to more standard capitalist trading practices: Spain (8.2 percent), Canada (7.3 percent), Netherlands (6.9 percent), Germany (5.3 percent), USA (4.0 percent), Brazil (3.7 percent), and Italy (3.5 percent). Comité Estatal de Estadísticas, *Anuario Estadístico de Cuba, 2006*. Table VII.2, accessed on 7/26/2008 at www.one.cu/aec_web/paginas_de_tablas/p_vii/vii_2_3_4.htm. Calculations by the author.

25   Article 18, cited in Elena Álvarez and Jorge Mátter (coordinators), *Política social y reformas estructurales: Cuba a principios del siglo XXI* (México, D.F.: CEPAL, INIE and PNUD, 2004), p. 22.

26   Which then had to generate sufficient sales in hard currency to pay for their needed imports.

27   Which not only is inappropriate for social processes, but it is also neither appropriate for biological evolutionary processes nor was it Darwin's theory of evolution.

28   Omar Everleny Pérez Villanueva, "The Role of Foreign Direct Investment in Economic Development: The Cuban Case," in Jorge I. Domínguez, Omar Everleny Pérez Villanueva and Lorena Barberia (eds.), *The Cuban Economy at the Start of the Twenty-First Century* (Cambridge: Harvard University Press, 2004), p. 172.

29   Marc Franc, "Foreign investment projects in Cuba down: official," Reuters, July 9, 2008, www.reuters.com/article/idUSN0942151920080709.

30   While they indeed have been important, and in particular for earning foreign exchange in the 1990s, their image of dominating joint ventures is overblown. In 2002 they constituted only 76 of the 403 joint ventures, while there were 85 in basic industry, 48 in construction, 140 in 12 other fields and 53 more. Elena Álvarez and Jorge Mátter, *op. cit.*, p. 20. For the 2003 distribution see Omar Everleny Pérez Villanueva, *op. cit.*, p. 177.

31   As argued above, and as continually argued by advocates of a return to capitalism, Cuba made extensive 'market favorable reforms' from about 1993 to 1996, and then that process stopped. As already noted, reforms have continued in Cuba since then, but they have not been considered appropriately 'market friendly' by these advocates of capitalist restoration. It is because of this "stalling" that most figures concerning the share of these 'market friendly' reforms in the total Cuba economy, while they have changed some, remain today of the same order of magnitude as they were then. Because of this, using those figures (released very infrequently both then and today, and mostly in speeches) as qualitative indicators is generally appropriate.

32   Figure presented by Carlos Lage, the Vice President generally considered to be in charge of the economy, cited in the London-based newsletter *Cuba Business*, special edition on the seminar "Tightening the US Trade Embargo on Cuba: Implications for Trade and Investment," July 8-10, 1996, p. 4. Since roughly half of each joint venture belongs to Cuba, even that 3 percent is much more than what comes from 'foreign capital in joint ventures.'

33   *Cuba Business, op. cit.*, July/August 1996, p. 3.

34   Omar Everleny Pérez Villanueva, *op. cit.*, p. 173.

35   *ibid.*, p. 175.

36   It also ended the state monopoly on foreign trade, which most foreign capital considered necessary. For a listing of all the articles in the new constitution related to economic issues, see Comisión Económica para América Latina y el Caribe and Fondo de Cultura Económica, *La Economía Cubana. Reformas estructurales y desempeño en los noventa* (México: Comisión Económica para América Latina y el Caribe and Fondo de Cultura Económica, 1997) pp. 413-6.

37   The whole law is given in *ibid.*, pp. 417-40.

38   *ibid.*, p. 418.

39   *ibid.*, p. 418.

40   They have the final word. Each project has been studied and discussed by several layers in the approval process before it reaches the Executive Committee, and they then review those studies to see that everything is in order, and sometimes to consider the project from a broader social-political perspective.

41   See the two references in endnote 2 for this data.

42   Artisanal production is one part of the allowed self-employment (most concern services), which will be discussed below as part of the changes in the domestic economy. Below I will also discuss private property in the agricultural sector, which has been there throughout the Revolution.

43   The latter two are central to the discussion today. The former was important to this same discussion in the mid 1990s, but for the reasons indicated here it is not much discussed today in Cuba, although the changes made then are still in force.

44   See Comisión Económica para América Latina y el Caribe and Fondo de Cultura Económica, *op. cit.*, pp. 499-519 for the 1993 law, an original list of allowed professions, and extensions in 1995.

45   While called "taxes" they were really more of a licensing fee, in that they were fixed independent of revenue.

46   Statistics from the Ministry of Labor and Social Security, cited in *Cuba Business, op. cit.*, July/August 1996, p. 3. The Ministry of Economy and Planning gave similar but slightly different figures for the end of 1995, cited in Economist Intelligence Unit, *Cuba, Dominican Republic, Haiti, Puerto Rico Country Report*, 1997(3), 1996(3), p. 12. It is important to note that there were already 41,200 registered self-employed in 1989 (under a 1978 law) before the beginning of the special period reforms.

47   The intention to keep these as markets of self employed workers is exactly an attempt to keep these from becoming real capitalist markets, where owners of capital hire wage labor and extract surplus value from their work.

48   No evaluation is made here of whether, on net, such self employment brings more benefits to the revolutionary process than dangers, for example if the state indeed cannot adequately provide those services at this time. The point here is that independent of it, if they are on net desirable, they involve a threat to the socialist project.

49   *Granma Weekly Review, op. cit.*, October 12, 1994, p. 5.

50   The state will still have significant contracts as it also distributes food through schools, hospitals and workplaces.

51   Philip Peters, "Raul the Reformer?" Lexington Institute, September 25, 2007. Accessed 8/30/2008 at http://lexingtoninstitute.org/1177.shtml.

52   *Granma International*, 43(15), April 13, 2008, p. 6.

53   Al Campbell, "The Cuban Economy: Where It Stands Today," *Review of Radical Political Economy*, 40(3), Summer 2008, p. 279.

54   See Philip Peters, "State Enterprise Reform in Cuba: An Early Snapshot," Lexington Institute, July 2001. Accessed on 8/30/2008 at http://lexington.server278.com/docs/cuba6.pdf. Note that as Peters indicates this was written before any results could be evaluated, but it nevertheless gives a detailed look at what is involved in the program. Note also that while Peters consciously tries to discuss what he considers to be both the strengths and weaknesses of the program, he also operates with a very strong mainstream 'markets-are-optimally-efficient' bias.

55   Marc Frank, "Cuban official nixes Russian and Chinese reforms," Reuters, August 30, 2007. Accessed 8/30/2008 at www.reuters.com/article/idUSN3025851720070830. Frank correctly notes that some of the companies are joint ventures, and without giving some indication of what contribution to the numbers given come from that and what part comes just from the enterprise improvement effect, the numbers given have an unknown bias.

56   Notwithstanding the obvious possible different interpretation from the words themselves, the Cuban discussions of this issue use the expression "payment according to results" interchangeably with "payment according to work."

57   This also made a secondary contribution in the Chinese case, where as opposed to being key to the transformation the privatization of state owned enterprises (SOEs) is an issue being fought over today in the situation that capitalism has been reestablished. Again see the two references on China in endnote 2.

58   This was one of the first capitalist practices Deng reestablished in China, already in the early 1980s, understanding it as necessary for his intended restoration of capitalism. Again, see the two references on China in footnote 2.

59   Economist Intelligence Unit, *op. cit.*, p 8. In line with their wishful thinking in the mid 1990s discussed above that the leadership was engaged in the restoration of

capitalism, they explained why this barrier would be overcome. "This limitation is likely to subside, however, as the need to integrate the domestic economy with the external sector increases the use of international pricing." Ten years later many domestic prices in Cuba, still controlled by the state, in fact have not been forced to conform to international prices.

60   *ibid.*, p 3. It should be noted these were two of the first "reforms" promoted by Deng in China. See Al Campbell, *op. cit.* in endnote 2.

61   Given the importance and the resources the Cuban government has attached to this program, it is surprising how few articles on it have been written outside of Cuba. For an introduction to the specifics of the program, see Áquilas Mendes and Rosa Maria Marques, "Cuba and the 'Battle of Ideas': A Jump Ahead," *Review of Radical Political Economics,* forthcoming.

62   For a short introduction to the strong recent economic performance, see Al Campbell, "The Cuban Economy: Where It Stands Today," *op. cit..*

63   Keep in mind that Cuba neither is nor claims to be socialist, they only claim to be in the transition from capitalism to socialism.

64   Raúl Castro, *Granma International,* 43(9), March 2, 2008, p. 6

65   For a deeper discussion of this issue, see Al Campbell and Ufuk Tutan, "Human Development and Socialist Institutional Transformation: Continual Incremental Changes and Radical Breaks," *Studies in Political Economy,* forthcoming.

Chapter 5

1   Amartya Sen, *Development As Freedom* (New York: Anchor Books, 1999)

2   Martha Nussbaum, another founder of the "capabilities approach" to development lists ten capabilities. See: Martha C. Nussbaum, *Women and Human Development: The Capabilities Approach* (Cambridge: Cambridge University Press, 2000)

3   Franklin Tugwell, *The Politics of Oil in Venezuela* (Stanford: Stanford University Press, 1975), p.182

4   Banco Central de Venezuela: www.bcv.org.ve/indicadores

5   Terry Lynn Karl, *The Paradox of Plenty* (Berkeley: University of California Press, 1997)

6   Fernando Coronil, *The Magical State* (Chicago: University of Chicago Press, 1997), p.76 ff.

7   Ibid., p.100

8   Ibid., p.167

9   Ibid., p.180

10   Ibid., p.182

11   2003 OPEC Statistical Bulletin

12   Venezuela's urbanization rate was 88 percent in 2001 (World Bank Development Report), which is second only to Uruguay, which is practically considered a city-state, because most of its population lives in Montevideo.

13   Julia Buxton, *The Failure of Political Reform in Venezuela* (Aldershot, England: Ashgate, 2003), p.114

14   OPEC Annual Statistical Bulletin, 2003

15   Buxton, p.115

16   Banco Central de Venezuela

17   Karl (1997), p.125

18   This economic disease is caught whenever a commodity brings a sudden increase of income in one sector of the economy, which is not matched by increased revenues in other sectors of the economy. What happens is that this sudden sectoral increase causes severe problems in other sectors. The increased income from the oil sector causes a distorted growth in services and other non-tradables, while discouraging the production of tradables, such as industrial and agricultural products. The reason for this disparity is that the greater income rapidly raises the demand for imports, since domestic production cannot meet demand quickly enough, and also raises the demand for services, which the domestic market has to supply since services cannot be imported as easily as tradables can. The increased demand for imported goods and domestic services, in turn, causes an increase in prices, which ought

to cause domestic production to increase, but doesn't because the flow of foreign exchange into the economy has caused a general inflation of wages and prices.

19   Real per capita income (Real GDP Chain per equivalent adult, in 2000 constant dollars) declined from $11,869 in 1979 to $8,675, in 1999, (Penn World Table Version 6.1, Center for International Comparisons at the University of Pennsylvania (CICUP), accessed September 2008). Only Peru suffered a decline, of 17 percent, while Argentina, Bolivia, Brazil, Colombia, and Ecuador increased their per capita GDP in that time period. Venezuela's real GDP per worker declined far more dramatically, by 36 percent (compared to 27 percent for Peru), indicating that inequality also increased during this time period.

20   Universidad Católica Andrés Bello, "Proyecto Pobreza" http://www.ucab.edu.ve/investigacion/iies/pobreza.htm

21   Buxton, p.115

22   For imports the devaluation was 39 percent, for other types of activities, such as tourism it was much greater. Real incomes declined by 20 percent in the six-year period that the exchange rate control was in place.

23   Lopez-Maya, Margarita, *La protesta popular en Venezuela entre 1989 y 1993 Lucha popular, democracia, neoliberalismo* (Caracas: Nueva Sociedad Lopez-Maya, 1999) says that the most credible figure, provided by the human rights group COFAVIC, stands at 396 deaths.

24   According to Coronil, this crisis was ten times as severe, relative to the sizes of the economies, than the U.S. savings and loan crisis of the early 1990's (Coronil, p.381)

25   Edgardo Lander and Pablo Navarette, "The Economic Policy Of The Latin American Left In Government: Venezuela," Transnational Institute Briefing Paper 2007/02. Steve Ellner (in *Rethinking Venezuelan Politics: Class, Conflict, and the Chávez Phenomenon*, Boulder: Lynne Rienner, 2008) has a slightly different periodization, where he divides the last period into two phases,

26   See Gregory Wilpert, *Changing Venezuela by Taking Power* (New York: Verso Books, 2007), pp. 87-93

27   OPEC Annual Statistical Bulletin, 2004 (www.opec.org)

28   "Sancionan Ley de Contribuciones sobre Precios Extraordinarios de Hidrocarburos," Noticias Asamblea Nacional, April 15, 2008 (www.asambleanacional.gob.ve)

29   Juan Carlos Boué, *La internacionalización de PDVSA: una costosa illusion* (Caracas: Fondo Editorial Ramírez, 2004)

30   "PDVSA está completamente recuperada," by Prensa PDVSA, posted on aporrea. org, November 230, 2006 (http://www.aporrea.org/energia/n87232.html)

31   "Líneas Generales del Plan de Desarrollo Económico y Social de la Nación 2001-2007," Ministry for Planning and Development (www.mpd.gov.ve), p.56

32   "Venezuela Creates New State-Owned Petrochemical Company," Venezuelanalysis. com, June 27, 2005 (http://www.venezuelanalysis.com/news.php?newsno=1674)

33   "Venezuela and Brazil to Build Shipyard in Venezuela," by Steven Mather, Venezuelanalysis.com, August 3, 2006 (http://www.venezuelanalysis.com/news/1867)

34   This figure is according to an interview with Chavez's brother, Adán Chavez, who was the president of the National Land Institute in 2002.

35   Banco Central de Venezuela (www.bcv.org.ve/c2/indicadores.asp). The exact percentage is difficult to determine because offical figures lump agriculture together with various other sectors, such as hotels and restaurants, which have boomed in recent years.

36   Ibid., own calculations, based on the table, "Producto interno bruto, Por clase de actividad económica, 'A precios constantes de 1997'"

37   Data based on Finance Ministry and *El Universal*, March 27, 2005, "Gobierno que se niega a ahorrar" and Ministry of Finance data (www.mf.gov.ve).

38   Venezuela's total public debt (foreign and domestic) of 32 percent compares favorably to those of Colombia (44.2 percent), Brazil (50.2 percent), U.S. (64.7 percent), Germany (68.1 percent), and Argentina (69.7 percent). Only Guatemala (26.9 percent), Mexico (21.2 percent), and Chile (8.1 percent) have lower rates of public indebtedness in Latin America. (Source: CIA World Fact Book)

39   In 1998 foreign debt was 25.2 percent of GDP and domestic was 4.4 percent. By 2004 foreign was at 25.1 percent and domestic debt at 13.9 percent of GDP. (source: Finance Ministry)

40   In 1983 Venezuela's debt to GDP ratio was 22 percent, according to Karl (1997), p.268

41   Source: Central Bank of Venezuela (www.bcv.org.ve)

42   Banks also have to maintain at least 16 percent of their credit portfolio for agricultural loans, 10 percent for home loans, and 2.5 percent for tourism.

43   According to the magazine *America Economia*, Sept. 23, 2005.

44   Sunacoop data (http://www.sunacoop.gov.ve/estadisticas/cuadro1.htm)

45   Mission *Vuelvan Caras* was renamed to Mission Che Guevara in 2007.

46   This ministry has since been renamed as the Ministry of Popular Power for the Communal Economy.

47   For a review of these efforts, see: Jonah Gindin (2005), "Made in Venezuela: The Struggle to Reinvent Venezuelan Labor," in: *Monthly Review*, Vol. 57, No. 2.

48   The Revolutionary Front of Workers of Co-Managed and Occupied Businesses (Frente Revolucionario de Trabajadores de Empresas en Cogenstión y Ocupadas – FRETECO) says it represents 2,000 workers at 18 factories (http://www.controlo-brero.org/content/view/261/1/).

49   For a discussion of the problems with co-management, see: "Constructing Co-Management in Venezuela: Contradictions along the Path," by Michael Lebowitz, Venezuelanalysis.com, Oct. 27, 2005 (http://www.venezuelanalysis.com/articles.php?artno=1587) See also: "Invepal: desorden administrativo o algo más," by Luisana Ramirez, Aporrea.org, Aug. 8, 2006 (http://www.aporrea.org/endogeno/a24269.html)

50   Based on a presentation given by the Ministry for the Popular Economy at the Regional Andean Conference on Employment in Lima, Peru, November 22 and 23, 2004

51   According to an interview with Popular Economy Minister Elias Jaua, www.redvoltaire.net, "El pueblo es el principal actor del camino hacia el progreso," March 11, 2005

52   Ministry of the Popular Economy, Misión Vuelvan Caras (http://www.minep.gov.ve/)

53   Elias Jaua interview, "El pueblo es el principal actor del camino hacia el progreso," Voltairenet.org, March 11, 2005 (http://www.voltairenet.org/article124173.html)

54   Michael Lebowitz, *Build it Now: Socialism for the 21st Century* (New York: Monthly Review Press, 2006) quotes Chavez's June 2005 speech in Paraguay, where Chavez said, "Workers often demand a fair salary and other benefits, and they have the right to demand this. But the working class is obliged not just to demand its rights, but to constitute itself into a factor for the transformation of society." Chavez went on to add the analogy, "If you are traveling with your three children and your wife in your air conditioned car and pass by an eight year old child, that is on the street, at midnight, isn't this a problem of yours too?"

55   István Mészáros, *Beyond Capital* (London: Merlin Press, 1995), p.758, also cited in Lebowitz (2006). Chavez referred to Mészáros in his Alo Presidente program of July 17, 2005.

56   Article 3 of Decree No. 3,895, of September 13, 2005, published in Gaceta Oficial No. 38,271

57   "Empresas de Producción Social," article in PDVSA's corporate magazine, *Siembra Petrolera*, Issue, No. 1, Jan.-Mar. 2006, p.55

58   Source: personal communication with PDVSA's public affairs department.

59   For a recent study of Mondragon see: George Cheney, *Values at Work: Employee Participation Meets Market Pressure at Mondragon* (Ithaca: Cornell University Press, 1999)

60   Source: Instituto Nacional de Estadistica (www.ine.gov.ve)

61   Source: Ministry of Planning and Development (www.sisov.mpd.gob.ve)

62   Source: World Bank, Millennium Development Goals website (www.development-goals.org)

63   Source: Ministry of Planning and Development (www.sisov.mpd.gob.ve)

64   This is an area fraught with controversy inside and outside of Venezuela. For an evaluation of the political human rights situation in Chávez's Venezuela, see "A Decade Under Chávez: Political Intolerance and Lost Opportunities for Advancing Human Rights in Venezuela," Human Rights Watch, September 18, 2008 (http://www.hrw.org/en/reports/2008/09/18/decade-under-ch-vez) and my in-depth rebuttal to the report, "Smoke and Mirrors: An Analysis of Human Rights Watch's Report on Venezuela," by Gregory Wilpert, Venezuelanalysis.com, October 17, 2008 (http://www.venezuelanalysis.com/analysis/3882)

Chapter 6

1   Walden Bello, "A Primer on Wall Street's Crisis", *MRzine*, 3 October, 2008; Robert Brenner, "Devastating Crisis Unfolds", *Against the Current*, January-February 2008; John Bellamy Foster, "Can the Financial Crisis be Reversed?", *MRzine*, 10 October 2008; Lauren Goldner, "Fictitious Capital and the Transition Out of Capitalism", Self-published, 14 October 2008.

2   Yash Tandon, "Global Financial Meltdown and Lessons for the South", *South Bulletin*, 24, 1 October 2008.

3   Dani Nabudere, *The Rise and Fall of Money Capital* (London: Africa in Transition Trust, 1990); Patrick Bond, *Uneven Zimbabwe: A Study of Finance, Development and Underdevelopment* (Trenton: Africa World Press, 1998).

4   Walter Rodney, *How Europe Underdeveloped Africa* (Dar es Salaam: Tanzania Publishing House and London: Bogle L'Ouverture Publications, 1972).

5   http://www.reservebank.co.za/internet/Publication.nsf/LADV/0256A81189F3E772 4225742D0041E31F/$File/C.pdf

6   *Economist*, "Economics focus: Domino theory", 26 February 2009, http://www.economist.com/research/articlesBySubject/displayStory.cfm?story_id=13184631 &subjectID=348918&fsrc=nwl

7   Freedom of Expression Institute and University of Johannesburg Centre for Sociological Research, "National Trends around Protest Action", Johannesburg, 2009.

8   Christelle Terreblanche, "No changes, Zuma vows," *Independent-on-line*, 9 December 2007.

9   Jeremy Cronin, "The current financial crisis and possibilities for the left", paper presented to the Chris Hani Institute's Joe Slovo Memorial Lecture, 28 January 2009.

10   *Business Times*, 21 September 2008.

11   Brian Khan, "A Perspective from South Africa", Correspondence, 15 October 2008, p1.

12   International Monetary Fund, *Global Financial Stability Report*, Washington, 2006, pp. 1,2,26,36.

13   John Wakeman-Linn, "Private Capital Flows to Sub-Saharan Africa: Financial Globalization's Final Frontier?", Presented as part of the Spring 2008 *Regional Economic Outlook for Sub-Saharan Africa*, African Department, International Monetary Fund, Washington, DC, 2008.

14   Leonce Ndikumana and James Boyce, "Capital Flight from Sub-Saharan Africa", *Tax Justice Focus*, 4, 1 (2008), p.5.

15   International Monetary Fund, *Africa Economic Outlook*, Washington, DC, April 2008, p.36.

16   Jubilee Research, "Debt relief as if justice mattered: A framework for a comprehensive approach to debt relief that works", London, 2008, http://www.jubileeresearch.org/news/debt%20relief%20as%20if%20justice%20mattered.pdf (accessed 15 October 2008), p.1.

17   Yash Tandon, *Ending Aid Dependence* (Oxford: Fahamu, 2008).

18   Nastasya Tay, "Reaching the Summit? Aid Ineffectiveness", Civicus, Johannesburg, 7 September 2008.

19   Patrick Bond, *Looting Africa: The Economics of Exploitation* (London: Zed Books, 2008).

20   Andre Gorz, *A Strategy for Labor* (Boston: Beacon Press, 1964).

21   World Economic Forum, *Global Risks 2009*, Davos, World Economic Forum, January 2009.

22   The Commission of Experts of the President of the United Nations General Assembly on Reforms of the International Monetary and Financial System, "Recommendations for Immediate Action", New York, 2009.

23   Bond, P. (2004), *Talk Left Walk Right: South Africa's Frustrated Global Reforms*, Pietermaritzburg, University of KwaZulu-Natal Press.

24   Peter Mandelson, "European Commission Presents Roadmap for Negotiating Trade Agreements with ACP Countries", Strasbourg, 23 October 2007, http://trade.ec.europa.eu/doclib/docs/2007/october/tradoc_136541.pdf

25   Patrick Bond and Richard Kamidza, "How Europe Underdevelops Africa (But how Some Fight Back)", *Znet Commentaries*, 8 June 2008.

26   Rajendra Pachauri, "Testimony to the US House of Representatives Select Committee on Energy Independence and Global Warming,' Washington, DC, August 2007.

27   Ray Bush, "Scrambling to the Bottom? Mining, Resources and Underdevelopment", *Review of African Political Economy*, 117 (2007).

28   Bond and Kamidza, "How Europe Underdevelops Africa".

29   Patrick Bond and Jackie Dugard, "The Case of Johannesburg Water: What Really Happened at the Pre-paid 'Parish pump'", *Law, Democracy and Development*, 12, 1 (2008).

30   Bond, *Talk Left Walk Right*.

31   Larry Neumeister, "Lawsuits Seeking Billions from U.S. Companies in South Africa Dismissed", Associated Press, 29 November, 2004.

32   Peter Fabricius, "Apartheid Victims' US Legal Battle Rages On", *Sunday Independent*, 18 November 2007.

33   Robert Meers, "Dismiss Apartheid Suits, White House urges Supreme Court", CNN, 2 February 2008.

34   Francois Rank, "US firms to pay for apartheid", *The Times*, 14 May 2008.

35   Miles Larmer, "The Zimbabwe Arms Shipment Campaign", *Review of African Political Economy*, 117 (2008).

36   World Bank, *Where is the Wealth of Nations?*, Washington, DC, 2006.

37   Samir Amin, *Delinking* (London: Zed Books, 1989); Walden Bello, *Deglobalization* (London: Zed Books, 2002).

38   Jeremy Scahill, "This is change? 20 hawks, Clintonites and neocons to watch for in Obama's White House", AlterNet, 20 November 2008.

Chapter 7

1   The word comes from the title of the book, World Bank, *The East Asian Miracle: Economic Growth and Public Policy* (Oxford: Oxford University Press, 1003)

2   For brevity and to avoid repeated use of the dubious term 'miracles', these four countries are called the IKMT group.

3   See the discussion in Wan-wen Chu, 'The "East Asian Miracle" and the Theoretical Analysis of Industrial Policy,' (http://www.sinica.educ.tw/~wwchu/SURVEY.pdf, no date).

4   It is inaccurate, because a majority of the countries in the study were not in East Asia, but Southeast Asia.

5   Bulmer-Thomas argues that it is a exaggeration to characteristic the region by this term, see Victor Bulmer-Thomas, *Life After Debt? The New Economic Trajectory in Latin America* (London: Institute of Latin American Studies, 1992.

6   The phrase 'Asian financial crisis' is inaccurate because most of the Asian countries were hardly affected by it. Because of the terms general currency, it will be used here.

7   For more detail, see John Weeks, "Latin America and the "High Performing Asian Economies": Growth and Debt,' *Journal of International Development* 12, 5 (2000), pp. 625-654.

8   A brief but useful summary of the debt crisis of the Philippines is found at http://www.country-data.com/cgi-bin/query/r-10471.html

9   This statistic is not the "marginal capital-output ratio", since the denominator is gross not net investment.

10   The high investment argument might be judged too simple, even simplistic, expla-
      nation for the rapid growth of the IKMT countries, but it is one of two stressed by
      Krugman, the other being rapid labour force growth due to rural to urban migration.
      The latter cause challenges the World Bank emphasis on the growth of 'total labour
      productivity'. See Paul Krugman, "The Myth of Asia's Miracle", *Foreign Affairs* (Nov./
      Dec. 1994).

11   During 1970-1996 the GDP of Indonesia grew at 7.3 percent per year, and exports
      at seven percent. Over the same years, Malaysia and Thailand grew at almost the
      same rate, 7.5 and 76.7 percent, and exports at 10.5 and 11.8 percent. Only Korea
      was a clear case of export growth well above GDP growth, 7.9 and 16.2 percent,
      respectively.

12   For a detailed discussion of the policies of the Vietnamese government, see John
      Weeks, Nguyen Thang, Rathin Roy & Joseph Lim, *Macroeconomics of Poverty
      Reduction: Case Study of Viet Nam, Seeking Equity within Growth* (Hanoi: UNDP,
      2004).

13   In its World Economic Outlook 1996, the IMF considered the major problem of the
      IKMY countries to be inflation ('overheating') and called for demand restraint:
      ...[T] he combination of widening deficits on current account and rapid growth
      testifies to excess demand pressures, as opposed to problems of external com-
      petitiveness, in countries such as *Indonesia, Malaysia,* and *Thailand.* Moreover,
      preliminary staff work to assess the level and growth rate of output that appear to
      be consistent with stable inflation suggests that the current levels of activity in these
      countries may be above their sustainable long-term trends. These countries have
      already taken measures to restrain demand, but further action may be needed to
      avoid the emergence of excessive pressures on capacity and to contain external
      imbalances. *Korea* has also been facing a risk of overheating, although growth has
      been moderating toward a more sustainable pace and pressures on resources ap-
      pear to be easing. (International Monetary Fund, *World Economic Outlook 1996*,
      Washington: IMF, 1996)

14   If any prominent observer predicted the crisis there is no record of it. The IMF
      admitted failure to anticipate it:
      The IMF could, of course, be faulted for not having accurately predicted the depth
      of the recession, but there was no systematic bias in the IMF's growth forecasts,
      which were broadly in line with the consensus forecast. It is perhaps too early to
      know definitively why no one foresaw the severity of the recession... (International
      Monetary Fund, *World Economic Outlook 1996* (Washington: IMF, 1996)

15   B. B. Aghevli, "The Asian Crisis: Causes and Remedies", *Finance and Develop-
      ment* 36, 7 (1999)

16   The passage is from World Bank, annual Report 1996 (Washington: World Bank,
      1996), with emphasis added. No page numbers on the web version. Note the
      implicitly positive emphasis on private capital flows. As in almost all its reports,
      here the World Bank uses 'East Asia' incorrectly to refer to Indonesia, Malaysia and
      Thailand as well as the Republic of Korea.

17   See Terry McKinley, John Weeks, B. Khattry, R. Oktaviani, H. Saparini, J. Lim,and
      B. Santoso, *Pro-Poor Macro Policies in Indonesia,* UNDP Regional Project on the
      Macroeconomics of Poverty Reduction (Kathmandu: UNDP, 2003).

18   While China's population of 1.3 billion in 2005 was fifteen times greater and Indo-
      nesia's almost three times greater than Vietnam's, the latter country had a larger
      population than Thailand (65 million) and the Republic of Korea (48 million).

19   See Harvey Leibenstein, "Allocative Efficiency and X-Efficiency", *The American
      Economic Review,* 56 (1966), pp. 392-415

20   Taken from IMF 2005, Table 2.6, p. 121.

21   Gerschenkron set forth a list of alleged advantages of "backwardness" or being a
      "later-comer" to development in essays published in the early 1960s (see Alexander
      Gerschenkron, *Economic Backwardness in Historical Perspective: A Book of Essays.*
      Cambridge, USA: Belknap Press of Harvard University Press, 1962).

22   An important factor in increased labour discipline was the coercive power of govern-
      ments in the IKMT countries. See F. C. Deyo and Kaan Agartan, "Markets, Workers

and Economic Reforms: Reconstructing East Asian Labor Systems Political Opposition Can Be Contained by Some Combination of Economic Coercion, Market Disorganization, Tactical Retreat, and Police Suppression, but the Institutional Tensions That Underlie That Opposition Persist", *Journal of International Affairs* 57, 2003.

Chapter 8

1   The research for this chapter was supported by a Korea Research Foundation Grant (KRF-2007-411-J04601).

2   John A. C. Conybeare, *Merging Traffic: The Consolidation of the International auto Industry* (Lanham: Rowman & Littlefield, 2003) p. 66.

3   Lawrence E. Mitchell, *The Speculation Economy: How Finance Triumphed over Industry* (San Francisco: Berrett-Koehler, 2007) pp. 271-5.

4   Richard Westra, "The Capitalist Stage of Consumerism and South Korean Development", *Journal of Contemporary Asia*, 36, 1 (2006).

5   David Coates, *Models of Capitalism: Growth and Stagnation in the Modern Era* (Malden, MA: Polity, 2000) p. 223.

6   Ibid p. 222-3.

7   Peter Dicken, *Global Shift: Transforming the World Economy*, Third Edition (London: The Guilford Press, 1998) p. 223.

8   Biplab Dasgupta, *Structural Adjustment, Global Trade and the New Political Economy of Development* (London: Zed Books, 1998) pp. 268-72.

9   Toshio Watanabe, *Asia: Its Growth and Agony* (Hawaii: University of Hawaii Press, 1992) pp. 95-103.

10   James C. Abegglen, *Sea Change: Pacific Asia as the New World Industrial Center* (New York: The Free Press, 1994).

11   This point is belabored in Martin Hart-Landsberg, Seongjin Jeong and Richard Westra, "Introduction: Marxist Perspectives on South Korea in the Global Economy" in Martin Hart-Landsberg, Seongjin Jeong and Richard Westra (eds.) *Marxist Perspectives on South Korea in the Global Economy* (Aldershot: Ashgate, 2007).

12   Westra, "The Capitalist Stage of Consumerism and South Korean Development"

13   Meredith Woo Cumings, *Race to the Swift: State and Finance in Korean Industrialization* (New York: Columbia University Press, 1991) pp. 44-6.

14   See Joseph Halevi, "The accumulation process in Japan and East Asia as compared with the role of Germany in European post-war growth", in Bellofiore, R. (ed.) *Global Money, Capital Restructuring and the Changing Patterns of Labour* (Cheltenham: Edward Elger, 1999) and Joseph Halevi and Peter Kriesler, "History, politics and effective demand in Asia" in Joseph Halevi and J-M Fontaine (eds.) *Restoring Demand in the World Economy: Trade, Finance and Technology* (Cheltenham: Edward Elgar, 1998) p. 88.

15   Meredith Woo-Cumings, "The Political Economy of Growth in East Asia: A Perspective on the State, Market, and Ideology" in M. Aoki, H-K Kim and M. Okuno-Fujiwara, *The Role of Government in East Asian Economic Development* (Oxford: Clarendon, 1998) p. 335.

16   Halevi and Kriesler, "History, politics and effective demand in Asia".

17   ee Richard Stubbs, *Rethinking Asia's Economic Miracle* (Basingstoke: Palgrave, 2005) p. 156ff.

18   See the discussion in Sang-Hwan Jang, "Land Reform and Capitalist Development in Korea", in Hart-Landsberg, Jeong and Westra (eds.) *Marxist Perspectives on South Korea in the Global Economy*.

19   See for example Robert Brenner, "The Agrarian Roots of European Capitalism", in T.H. Aston and C.H.E. Philpin (ed.) *The Brenner Debate: Agrarian Class Structure and Economic Development in Pre-Industrial Europe* (Cambridge: Cambridge University Press, 1987).

20   See Peter Gowan, *The Global Gamble: Washington's Faustian Bid for World Dominance* (London: Verso, 1999).

21   See Richard Westra, "Phases of Capitalism, Globalizations and the Japanese Economic Crisis" in James Busumtwi-Sam and Laurent Dobuzinskis (eds.) *Turbulence*

and New Directions in Global Political Economy (Basingstoke: Palgrave, 2003).

22   This often overlooked point in debates over the Asian economic meltdown is made in John Eatwell and Lance Taylor, *Global Finance at Risk: The Case for International Regulation* (New York: The New Press, 2000) p. 167-8.

23   See OECD Economic Surveys: Korea (Paris: OECD, 1999; 2007; 2009)

24   See Peter Dicken, *Global Shift: Mapping the Contours of the World Economy*, Fifth Edition (London: Guilford Press, 2007) p. 208.

25   On the aforementioned views of the Asian crisis see Westra, "The Capitalist Stage of Consumerism and South Korean Development".

26   See James Crotty and Kang-Kook Lee, "Was the IMF-Imposed Economic Regime Change in Korea Justified? The Political Economy of IMF Intervention", *Review of Radical Political Economics*, 41, 2 (2009).

27   See Jang-Sup Shin and Ha-Joon Chang, "Economic reform after the financial crisis: a critical assessment of institutional transition and transaction costs in South Korea", *Review of International Political Economy*, 12, 3 (2005) p. 411.

28   Ibid. p. 415.

29   OECD Economic Survey: Korea (Paris: OECD, 2004).

30   Ignacio Ramonet, "Korean Blues", *Le Monde Diplomatique*, http://mondediplo.com/2005/07/01leader

31   *China Daily*, "South Korea Investment Grows with China", http://www2.chinadaily.com.cn/bizchina/2008-06/23/content_6787090.htm

32   *Korea Times*, "Black Market Accounts for 28 percent of GDP", http://www.koreatimes.co.kr/www/news/biz/2008/10/123_32276.html

33   *Financial Times*, "Volatile 2008 for foreign exchange", http://www.ft.com/cms/s/0/aa2a6c74-d72a-11dd-8c5c-000077b07658.html

34   *Korea Times*, "South Korea's Financial Jitters Deepening", http://www.koreatimes.co.kr/www/news/biz/2009/02/123_39771.html

35   Bloomberg, "Korean Corporations Court Bankruptcy With Suicidal KIKO Options", http://www.bloomberg.com/apps/news?pid=20601109&sid=aDQ1pZabcylo&refer=exclusive

36   See Jung-Woo Kim, "Export Performance and Outlook Amid the Global Recession", *Samsung Economic Research Institute*, Monthly Focus 2 (2009).

37   *Korea Times*, "Foreigners Underpin Korean Market", http://www.koreatimes.co.kr/www/news/biz/2009/06/123_46740.html

38   *Korea Times*, "Temps, Daily Workers Fall Below 7 Million", http://www.koreatimes.co.kr/www/news/nation/2009/02/123_39612.html

39   *JoongAng Daily*, "Korea drops four places in world ranks", http://joongangdaily.joins.com/article/view.asp?aid=2907077

40   For the detailed narration of the candlelight movement of 2008, refer to Kwang-Il Kim, □nterview: Korea's Summer of Discontent? *International Socialism*, 120 (2008), http://www.isj.org.uk/index.php?id=480&issue=120

41   *Korea Times*, "Candlelight Vigil Draws Record Numbers", http://www.koreatimes.co.kr/www/news/nation/2008/06/117_25630.html

42   ndeed, the candlelight movement of 2008 has evolved from the protests of 2006 against the Korea-US Free Trade Agreement, the first frontal confrontation by the disillusioned progressive forces with the previous Roh Mu-hyun government which openly pursued the Korea-US Free Trade Agreement, the completion of neoliberalization of the Korean society.

43   For more discussion of the ideas of alterglobalization movements, refer to Seongjin Jeong, The Ideas of the Alterglobalization Movement: A Marxist Perspective? 2008, Conference Proceedings, Institute for Social Sciences, Gyeongsang National University.

44   *Korea Times*, "Arrest Warrant Rejected for Progressive Economist", http://www.koreatimes.co.kr/www/news/nation/2008/08/117_30227.html

45   *Hankyoreh*, "6 Killed in Clash Between Police and Protesters in Yongsang", http://english.hani.co.kr/arti/english_edition/e_national/334510.html

46   Terry Cook, South Korea: Clashes Erupt at Ssangyong Factory Occupation? World Socialist Web Site, http://www.wsws.org/articles/2009/jul2009/kore-j01.shtml

47   In this respect, we disagree with Loren Goldner who regards organized labor in Korea, represented by the Korea Confederation of Trade Unions, as reactionary and believes they should be excluded from the roster of progressive forces. Refer to his paper, The Korean Working Class: From Mass Strike to Casualization and Retreat, 1987-2008? http://home.earthlink.net/~lrgoldner/korea.html

Chapter 9

1   Fred Riggs, *Thailand: The Modernization of Bureaucratic Polity* (Honolulu: East West Center, 1966).

2   See the discussion in Richard Stubbs, *Rethinking Asia's Economic Miracle* (Basingstoke: Palgrave, 2005).

3   Pasuk Phongpaichit and Chris Baker, "Power in Transition: Thailand in the 1990's", in Kevin Hewison (ed.) *Political Change in Thailand: Democracy and Participation* (London: Routledge, 1997).

4   Cited in "Introduction". David Held and Anthony McGrew (ed.) *Governing Globalization: Power, Authority and Global Governance* (Cambridge: Polity, 2002) p. 3.

5   Ibid.

6   Anthony Giddens, *Runaway World: How Globalization Is Reshaping Our Lives.* (London, Profile Books, 1999) p. 10.

7   Cited in Giddens, A. *The Third Way: The Renewal of Social Democracy.* (Cambridge: Polity, 1998) p. 30.

8   J. N. Rosenau, "Governance, Order, and Change in World Order" in James N. Rosenau and Ernst-Otto Czempeil (eds.) *Governance without Government: Order and Change in World Politics* (Cambridge: Cambridge University Press, 1992) p. 4.

9   D. Held, "Introduction" in D. Held (ed.) *A Globalizing World? Culture, Economics, Politics* (London Routledge, 2000) p. 3.

10   Cochrane, A. and Pain, K. "A Globalizing Society?" Ibid, 22.

11   Giddens, *Runaway World*, p. 9.

12   David Held and Anthony McGrew, "The Great Globalization Debate", in David Held and Anthony McGrew (eds.) *The Global Transformations Reader: An Introduction to the Globalization Debate*, 2nd edition. (Cambridge: Polity, 2003) p. 5.

13   Ibid.

14   G. Soros, *Open Society [Reforming Global Capitalism].* (New York: Public Affairs, 2000) p. xxiv.

15   R. Higgott, "Contested Globalization: The Changing Context and Normative Challenges", *Review of International Studies* 26 (2000).

16   A Chinese term which translates as connection.

17   Ake Tangsupvattana, "Driving the Juggernaut: From Economic Crisis to Global Governance in Pacific Asia" in Simon S.C. Tay (ed.) *Pacific Asia 2022: Sketching Futeres of a Region.* (Tokyo: Japan Center for International Exchange, 2005).

18   In time of writing, as the world is enmeshed in the 2008 Global Financial Crisis, the Thai baht is around $US33-35. However, the crisis is still going on and currencies around the globe are still volatile.

19   Warr, P.G. "Thailand" in Ross H. McLeod and Ross Garnaut (eds) *East Asia in Crisis: From Being a Miracle to Needing One?* (London: Routledge, 1998). 58.

20   Fukushima Kiyohiko, "Regional Co-operation: Security Implications of the Instability in International Finance". in Mely C. Anthony and Mohamed Jawhar Hassan (eds.) *Beyond the Crisis: Challenges and Opportunities* (Kuala Lumpur: Institute of Security and International Studies, 2000) 131.

21   Natenapha Wailerdsak, "Companies in Crisis" in Pasuk Phongpaichit and Chris Baker (eds.) *Thai Capital after the 1997 Crisis* (Chiang Mai: Silkworm Books, 2009) 18.

22   Ibid. pp. 27-28.

23   ASEAN 10 member countries are Brunei Darussalam, Cambodia, Indonesia, Lao PDR, Malaysia, Myanmar, Philippines, Singapore, Thailand and Vietnam.

24   HS chapters 01-08 refers to: 01 live animals, 02 meat and edible meat offal, 03 fish, 04 dairy produce, 05 other animals products, 06 live trees, 07 edible vegetables and 08 edible fruits and nuts.

25   Literally translated as Thai love Thai Party.

26   Ministry of Commerce, cited in Chaiyanut Jatiyanuwat, *Good Governance in Thailand's FTA under Globalization*, Ph.D. paper, Chandrakasem Rajabhat University. 2007.

27   Http://www2.ops3.moc.go.th/hs/export_yearly/report.asp, accessed 25th October 2008.

28   Http://www2.ops3.moc.go.th/hs/import_yearly/report.asp, accessed 25th October 2008.

29   Http://www.2.ops3moc.go.th/hs/tradebalance_yearly/report.asp, accessed 25th October 2008.

30   Ministry of Commerce, cited in Chaiyanut Jatiyanuwat.

31   "Executive Summary" in *Report on the Impacts of FTA on Agricultural Sector*, The Office of Agricultural Economics, Ministry of Agriculture and Cooperation.

32   Ibid.

33   Ibid.

34   "Executive Summary" in *Report on the Impact of Thailand-China FTA (under ASEAN-China FTA) on the Adaptation in Fruits and Vegetables businesses system*, The Office of Knowledge Management and Development (Public Organization). 2008.

35   Ibid.

36   "Executive Summary" in *Report on the Impacts of FTA on Agricultural Sector*.

37   See *Fortune*, July 21, 2008.

38   Examples of big chain superstores and supermarkets in Britain are Tesco, Safeway, Sainsbury's, Asda, Marks and Spencer, Boots, etc.

39   George Monbiot. *Captive State: The Corporate Takeover of Britain*, (London: Pan Books, 2001). Chapter 5.

40   Ibid.

41   Kuipers, P. "Thailand after the Coup: Struggle between Modern and Traditional" in *Elsevier Food Internatonal vol.10, Number 1, February 2007*. http://www.food-international.net/articles/country-profile/589/thailand-after-the-coup-..., accessed November 25, 2008.

42   Pitsinee Jitpleecheep "Waiting for a Referee", *Bangkok Post's Economic Review Year-End 2006*, http://www.bangkokpost.com/yearend2006/page47.html accessed November 25, 2008.

43   Cited in Graune, P. "The Thai Retail Market", Ninth German Technological Symposium, Thai Chamber of Commerce-German, 2007.

44   Veerayooth Kanchoochat. "Services, Servility, and Survival: The Accommodation of Big Retail", in Pasuk Phongpaichit and Chris Baker (eds.) *Thai Capital after the 1997 Crisis* (Chiang Mai: Silkworm Books, 2009) 91-92.

45   Veerayooth Kanchoochat. "Service, Servility, and Survival", see Figure 3.

46   Ibid. 98.

47   PriceWaterhouseCoopers and ACNielsen cited in Kuipers. "Thailand after the Coup".

48   Price Waterhouse Coopers cited in Kuipers (see Figure 1).

49   By 2006 the Thai baht currency was moving around 31-35 per US$.

50   Veerayooth Kanchoochat, "Service, Servility, and Survival", pp. 99, 102.

51   Cited in Mana Nimitrmongkol. *Corporate Social Responsibility: A Case of Tesco-Lotus*, Ph.D. paper, Chandrakasem Rajabhat University. 2007.

52   Sukanya jitpleecheep "Survival of the Fittest, *Bangkok Post's Mid-Year Economic Review 2002*, http://www.bangkokpost.com/midyear2002/retailing.html, accessed November 25, 2008.

53   Cited in Taveesak Rukying. *Multinational Corporations' Hypermarkets and the National Sovereignty*, Ph.D. Paper, Chandrakasem Rajabhat University. 2007.

54   Veerayooth Kanchoochat. "Service, Servility and Survival," pp. 99-101.

55   Ibid. 91.

56   Kuipers. "Thailand after the Coup".

57   Veerayooth Kanchoochat. "Service, Servility, and Survival", p. 101

Chapter 10

1   Roger Owen and Sevket Pamuk, *A History of the Middle East in the Twentieth Century*, (I.B. Tauris, 1998), pp. 131-132.

2 Marsha P. Posusney, "Irrational Workers: The Moral Economy of Labor Protest in Egypt," *World Politics*, 46, 1. (Oct., 1993), p.90.

3 Saad Eddin Ibrahim, "Egypt's Landed Bourgeoisie," in Ayse Öncü, Çaglar Keyder and Saad Eddin Ibrahim (eds.), *Developmentalism and Beyond: Society and Politics in Egypt and Turkey,* (Cairo: The American University of Cairo Press, 1994), p. 31.

4 Yahya M. Sadowski, Political Vegetables? Businessmen and Bureaucrats in the Development of Egyptian Agriculture, (The Brookings Institute, Washington D.C., 1991).

5 Syed Aziz-al Ahsan, " Economic Policy and class structure in Syria: 1958-1980," *International Journal of Middle East Studies*,16 (1984), p. 306. Tabitha Petran, *Syria*, (New York: Praeger, 1972), p. 183.

6 Moshe Ma'oz, "The Emergence of Modern Syria," in Moshe Ma'oz and Avner Yaniv (eds.) *Syria Under Assad: Domestic Constraints and Regional Risks*, (1986) pp. 19-20.

7 Ahsan, "Economic Policy and Class Structure", p. 307.

8 Sadowski, *Political Vegetables?*, pp. 66-67; Denis J. Sullivan, "The Political Economy of Reform in Egypt," *International Journal of Middle East Studies*, 22, 3 (Aug., 1990), p.330. Alan Richards, *The Political Economy of Economic Reform in the Middle East: The Challenge to Governance*, (RAND project, 2001). Robert Bianchi, "Businessmen's Associations in Egypt and Turkey," *ANNALS. AAPSS*, 482 (November, 1985). Ibrahim, "Egypt's Landed Bourgeoisie," p.28.

9 Khalid Ikram, *The Egyptian Economy, 1952-2000:Performance, Policies and Issues*, (London: Routledge, 2006), p. 13. John Waterbury, "The 'Soft State' and the Open Door: Egypt's Experience with Economic Liberalization, 1974-1984," *Comparative Politics*, (Oct, 1985), pp. 70-80.

10 Ikram, *The Egyptian Economy*, p.13.

11 Albert Hourani, *A History of the Arab Peoples*, (Cambridge, MA: Belknap Press, 1991), p. 436.

12 Ikram, *The Egyptian Economy*, pp. 20-1.

13 Waterbury, "The 'Soft State'," p. 69. Sadowski, *Political Vegetables*, p. 224.

14 Hourani, *A History of the Arab Peoples*, p. 450.

15 Nazih Ayubi, "A Comparative Perspective on Privatisation Programmes in the Arab World," 23rd International Congress of Administrative Sciences, (Dubai-Riyadh, 1995), p. 344. Bianchi, "Businessmen's Associations," p.149.

16 Waterbury, "The 'Soft State'," pp. 72-4.

17 Kais Firro, "The Syrian Economy Under The Assad Regime," in Moshe Mo'az (ed.) *Syria Under Assad*, (1986), p. 44.

18 Ahsan, "Economic Policy and Class Structure, " p. 317.

19 Petran, *Syria*, p. 216.

20 Ahsan, "Economic Policy and Class Structure," p. 320.

21 Petran, *Syria*, p. 210. Volker Perthes, "Stages of Economic and Political Liberalization," In Eberhard Kienle (ed.), *Contemporary Syria: Liberalization between Cold War and Cold Peace*, (London: British Academic Press: 1993), p. 45.

22 Ibid, p.57.

23 Petran, *Syria*, p. 252.

24 Fred Lawson, "History of Liberalization in Syria," In Berch Berberoglu (ed.), *Power and Stability in the Middle East*, (London: Zed Books, 1989), p. 26 ; Perthes, "Stages of Economic," p.46. Neil Quilliam, *Syria and the New World Order*, (UK: Ithaca.1999), p. 69.

25 Firro, "The Syrian Economy," p. 58; Ahsan, "Economic Policy and Class Structure," p. 319.

26 Lawson, "History of Liberalization in Syria," p. 27.

27 Perthes, "Stages of Economic," p. 54.

28 Ahsan, "Economic Policy and Class Structure," p. 318. Lawson, "History of Liberalization in Syria," p. 27.

29 Richards, *The Political Economy*, p. 19.

30 Ikram, *The Egyptian Economy*, p. 56.

31 Tarik M. Yousef, 'Development, Growth and Policy Reform in the Middle East and

North Africa since 1950s,' *The Journal of Economic Perspectives*, Vol. 18, No. 3, (Summer, 2004), p. 99. Paul Sullivan, "Oil: Challenges and Prospects," in Donald Heisel (ed.) *The Middle East and Development in a Changing World*. Monograph, *Cairo Papers in Social Science*. Vol. 20, 2 (Summer 1997), p. 83.

32   Sadowski, *Political Vegetables*, pp. 136-7.

33   Ayubi points out that despite supporting most of the redistributive policies of the state between 1975 and 1985, the public sector continued to perform well. Although the state reduced the share of public sector investment, the sector did not collapse. See Ayubi, "A Comparative Perspective," p. 343.

34   Sami Zubaida, "The Politics of the Islamic Investment Companies in Egypt," *Bulletin, British Society for Middle Eastern Studies*, 17, 2 (1990), pp. 152-161. Sadowski, *Political Vegetables*, p. 138; Mitchell, Timothy Mitchell, *Rule of Experts:Egypt, Technopolitics, Modernity* (Berkeley: University of California Press, 2000), p. 278-279.

35   Perthes, "Stages of Economic," p. 70.

36   Ahsan, "Economic Policy and Class Structure," p. 312.

37   Hoda Hawwa, "Linkages and Constraints of the Syrian Economy," in Youssef M. Choueiri (ed.) *State and Society in Syria and Lebanon*, (University of Exeter Press, 1993), pp. 84-86.

38   Ibid., pp. 86-87; Firro, "The Syrian Economy," p.54.

39   Richards, *The Political Economy*, p. 47.

40   Raymond Hinnebusch, "Liberalization in Syria: The Struggle of Economic and Political Rationality," in Eberhard Kienle (ed.), *Contemporary Syria*, p.101.

41   Hans Hopfinger and Marc Boeckler, "Step By Step To An Open Economic System: Syria Sets Course For Liberalization," *British Journal of Middle East Studies*, 23, 2 (1996), p. 201.

42   Perthes, "Stages of Economic," p. 55

43   Hawwa, "Linkages and Constraints," pp. 89-90.

44   Ibid., pp. 91-93.

45   Perthes, "Stages of Economic," p. 59.

46   Ibid., pp. 56-59.

47   Quilliam, *Syria and the New World Order*, pp. 91-92.

48   Sullivan, "The Political Economy of Reform," p. 320. Richards, *The Political Economy of Economic Reform*, p. 2; Ikram, *The Egyptian Economy*, pp. 60-61.

49   Marcelo M. Guigale, "The Rationale for Structural Adjustment," *Cairo Papers in Social Science*, 16, 3 (Fall, 1993), pp. 39-41.

50   Bessma Momani, "IMF-Egyptian Debt Negotiations," *Cairo Papers in Social Sciences*, 26, 3 (2005). Gouda Abdel Khalek, Stabilization and Adjustment in Egypt: Reform or de-industrialization, (Massachusetts: Edward Elgar Publishing, Inc., 2001).

51   Ikram, *The Egyptian Economy*, p. 61. Ayubi, "A Comparative Perspective," p. 346. Richards, *The Political Economy of Economic Reform*, p. 19-21.

52   Ibid., p. 20. Momani, "IMF-Egyptian Debt Negotiations."

53   Roger Owen, *State, Power and Politics in the Making of the Modern Middle East*, (New York: Routledge, 2000), p. 129. Sabry Algan, "Industrial Development: Progress and challenges in the future," in El-Ghonemy, M. Riad (ed.) *Egypt in the Twenty-First Century: Challenges for development*, (London: Routledge, 2003), p. 173. Momani, "IMF-Egyptian Debt Negotiations," p. 71.

54   Trevor Parfitt, The Politics of Adjustment in Africa with Special reference to Egypt, Monograph, Cairo Papers in Social Science. 16, 3(Fall, 1993), p. 14.

55   Ikram, *The Egyptian Economy*, p. 74, p. 82; Mitchell, *Rule of Experts*, p. 277.

56   Sylvia Polling, "Investment Law No. 10: Which Future For The Private Sector?" In Eberhard Kienle (ed.), *Contemporary Syria*, p. 19. Sukkar, "The Crisis of 1986," p. 31.

57   Kienle, 1993:p. 1; Hopfinger and Boekler, "Step by Step," p. 189, p. 194. Hawwa, "Linkages and Constraints," p. 95

58   Ibid., p. 94. Richards, *The Political Economy,"* p. 49; Sukkar, "The Crisis of 1986," p. 35 Perthes, "Stages of Economic," p. 60.

59   Hinnebusch, "Liberalization in Syria," p. 106. Perthes, "Stages of Economic," p. 60;

60   Ibid., p. 61.
61   United Nations Arab Human Development Report, 2005.
62   Perthes, "Stages of Economic," p. 63.
63   Richards, *The Political Economy*, p. 46.
64   Hinnebusch, "Liberalization in Syria," pp. 101-102.
65   The Economist Intelligence Unit, "Syria," (2008).
66   Richards, *The Political Economy*, p. 46.
67   Ikram, *The Egyptian Economy*, p. 40.
68   M. Khattab, "Constraints to Privatization: The Egyptian Experience," *Egyptian Center for Economic Studies*, Working Paper No. 38 (Cairo, 1999).
69   IMF, p.23.
70   On various sectors of the Syrian economy see, International Monetary Fund. *Syrian Arab Republic*, Article IV Consultation-Staff Report; and Public Information Notice on the Executive Board Discussion. IMF Country Report No. 05/356, October (2005). United Nations Human Development Report, *Syria* (UN, 2005).
71   For a discussion of various groups that have been formed in the course of the 1980s and 1990s in Syria See, Joya, Angela, "Syria's Transition, 1970-2005: From Centralization of the State to Market Economy," *Research in Political Economy*, Vol. 24 (Summer 2007). Also see Quilliam, *Syria and the New World Order*, pp. 87-8). Joseph Bahout, "The Syrian Business Community, its Politics and Prospects," In Eberhard Kienle (ed.) *Contemporary Syria*, pp. 73-75.
72   Quilliam, *Syria and the New World Order*, p. 81.
73   Richards, *The Political Economy*, p. 49.
74   Melhem, Hisham Melhem, "Syria between Two Transitions," *Middle East Report*, No. 203, *Lebanon and Syria: The Geopolitics of Change*. (Spring, 1997), p. 4.
75   IMF, p. 25.
76   M. RIAD El-Ghonemy (ed.), *Egypt in the Twenty-First Century: Challenges for development*, (London: Routledge, 2003), pp. 81-83. Gamal Nkrumah, 'Don't' Spoil it,' *Al-Ahram Weekly on-line*, 28February-5March, 2008, Issue No. 886.
77   Ikram, *The Egyptian Economy*, p.81; Mitchell, *Rule of Experts*, pp.279-281. Richards, *The Political Economy*, pp. 24-5) and Sadwoski, *Political Vegetables*, p.250.
78   United Nations Arab Human Development Report 2005. *Syria*. United Nations.
79   Arab World Competitiveness Report, 2005,
80   Quilliam, *Syria and the New World Order*, pp. 94-95.
81   Sami Moubayed, "Soft De-Ba'athification in Syria," (*Al-Ahram Weekly*, 2006), Available: http://weekly.ahram.org.eg/2006/788/re6.htm
82   Omayma Abdel Latif, 'What now for Syria?', (*Al Ahram Weekly*, 2006), Available: <http://weekly.ahram.org.eg/2006/783/re202.htm
83   Rime Allaf, "Open for Business: Syria's Quest for a Political Deal", *Middle East Programme Briefing Paper*, Chatham House, (MEP BP 07/03, July 2007), p. 10.
84   See Angela Joya, "Egyptian Protests: Falling wages, High Prices and the Failure of an Export-Oriented Economy," The Bullet, *Relay*, No. 111, (June 2, 2008), Toronto, Canada.

Chapter 11

1   I use the term "fix" here in the sense developed by David Harvey, *The New Imperialism* (Oxford University Press, 2003), pp. 115ff.
2   For a critique of neoliberal ideology cf. Cliff DuRand, "Neoliberalism and Globalization" http://www.globaljusticecenter.org/papers/durand2.htm
3   Cited by David Harvey, "Neoliberalism as Creative Destruction", *The ANNALS of the American Academy of Political and Social Science*, 610 (March 2007), p. 33.
4   Growth averaged 6.1 percent if we also include the years back to 1935. In spite of a sharp rise in the population, GDP per capita increased an impressive 348 percent from 1835 to 1982.
5   David Barkin, *Distorted Development: Mexico in the World Economy*. (Boulder, CO: Westview Press, 1989).
6   Maria Teresa Vazquez Castillo, *Land Privatization in Mexico: Urbanization, Formation of Regions, and Globalization in* **Ejidos** (London: Routledge, 2004).

7   Laura Carlsen, "NAFTA Free Trade Myths Lead to Farm Failure in Mexico" Americas Program, Center for International Policy, December 5, 2007 http://americas.irc-online:80/am/4794

8   At first NAFTA brought a significant movement of capital from the U.S. to Mexico where wages were 11 percent of the U.S. level. But then when China entered the WTO, hypermobile capital jumped across the Pacific to where wages are only 3 to 4 percent of the U.S. level, resulting in a decline in Mexico's maquiladoras.

9   Until Carlos Salinas became president in 1988, maquiladora "exports" were not counted in official trade figures. But then Salinas bundled them in with the rest and with a statistical sleight of hand that in fact was being utilized around the world through the shift in national accounting techniques from the Gross National Product measure to GDP, it appeared there was a great boom in Mexico's exports. This shift in national accounting techniques disguised the penetration of third world countries by global transnationals by assigning credit for production to the country where products are manufactured rather than to the country of its actual owners, giving rise to a public misperception of the emergence of self-owned and managed development in the third world.

10   Lyuba Zarsky and Kevin P. Gallagher, "NAFTA, Foreign Direct Investment, and Sustainable Industrial Development in Mexico" Americas Program, Center for International Policy, January 28, 2004. http://americas.irc-online.org

11   Juan Jose Sosa Arreola quoted in *The News* (Mexico City), June 5, 2008.

12   Andre Gunder Frank, *Latin America: Underdevelopment or Revolution.* (London: Monthly Review Press, 1969). This work gave rise to Dependency Theory, a radical alternative to the dominant Liberal Theory of Development represented by W.W. Rostow, *The Stages of Economic Growth: A Non-Communist Manifesto.* (Cambridge, MA: Cambridge University Press, 1969).

13   Cliff DuRand, "State Against Nation" http://www.globaljusticecenter.org/papers2006/durandENG.htm

14   Cliff DuRand, "Reflections on the Financial Crisis and Overaccumulation" http://www.globaljusticecenter.org/articles/financialcrisis.html

NAME INDEX

SUBJECT INDEX